What in the World?

Political Travels in Asia, Africa and the Americas

Peadar King

The Liffey Press

A catalogue record of this book is
available from the British Library.

ISBN 978-1-908308-41-2

Front cover photo: Peadar King with Mandiaye Diop in Senegal
Back cover photo: Mick O'Rourke filming in Mongolia

Printed in Spain by GraphyCems

Contents

Asia

Hope, Beauty and Redemption   241

Acknowledgements

Over a cup of coffee during a break from editing, former RTÉ commissioning editor John MacMahon suggested that I ought to consider writing a book on the experience of making the *What in the World?* television series. This book is a product of that suggestion. For almost a decade, John was a strong advocate of the series as an important contribution to RTÉ's public service broadcasting remit and I would very much like to acknowledge that.

The series itself would never have been possible without the patient, diligent and meticulous application of my partner in KMF Productions, Mick Molloy. His name hardly appears in this book, yet in many respects his imprint is on every page. Each journey is carefully choreographed by him and his is the unenviable task of dealing with bureaucracies and negotiating permits, visas, carnets and the myriad other details that this enterprise demands.

It is equally true that this series would never have seen the light of day only for the encouragement of and belief in its possibilities by the now sadly deceased Mick Melvin SVD and Mary Sheehan of KAIROS Communications. Mick's quiet and irrepressible optimism and belief in this project will always remain with me. *Ar dheis Dé go raibh a nanamacha dílse.*

Particular thanks are also owed to Séamus Callagy who in 1999 was a young editor with KAIROS Communications. Séamus generously gave extraordinarily long hours to working on *Breaking the Chains* and on the first two series of *What in the World?*

Rónán Ó Muirgheasa also worked as editor on *What in the World?*. Rónán has an instinctive and real understanding of what we were trying to achieve in the series.

What in the World? was funded by a very broad coalition of cross-denominational religious congregations, non-governmental organisations, trade unions and Irish Aid: people who are united in their concern with and advocacy for the poor, disfavoured and oppressed people of the world. Without their generous words of encouragement and year-on-year commitment that continues unabated even in these straitened times, Mick Molloy and I would never have been able to undertake this work.

In the course of making this series, I have worked with some really wonderful colleagues. We are good for each other and we are good to each other. We look out for each other. They do this work because they too have a commitment to people whose lives are blighted by unremitting poverty and human rights violations.

We have heard some extraordinary stories and met courageous, defiant people who simply refuse to be cowed by the oppressive forces that press down on them. We have also met with people who have experienced terrible loss and who carry great pain, a pain that is seldom if ever acknowledged by the world's media, which is yet another inequity in this wholly iniquitous world. As is the way of the world, the grief of the privileged few is preferred over the grief of the many. To all of those who trusted us with their stories, we are deeply grateful.

I am grateful to President Michael D. Higgins with whom on a cold February day in 2012 I discussed a range of political, and human rights issues, particularly though not exclusively with regard to the changed political landscape in Latin America from the 1980s onwards. His thoughts on that day influenced my thoughts on subsequent days.

Two people deserve particular mention. Liam Ashe whose infectious enthusiasm and ever helpful comments always ended with the upbeat 'Great, just keep going. Keep at it'. Gerard Horgan whose insatiable knowledge of international issues and whose line-by-line scrutiny of earlier drafts were invaluable.

Others read particular sections: Gerrie Lubbe, read the section on South Africa; Pien Metaal on Peru; Tomás Bril Mascarenhas on Argentina; and Molly O'Duffy on Nicaragua. But in time-honoured fashion, the final decisions, for better or for worse, on the content of the book are mine.

All the photographs were taken by colleagues who travelled with me: Ruth Meehan, Mick Cassidy, Michael O'Rourke, Ken O'Mahony, Stephen O'Connell, Gerry Nelson, Kevin O'Sullivan, Bob O'Brien and Liz Gill. The photograph of Bryan Stevenson and Walter McMillian is courtesy of the Equal Justice Initiative, Alabama, and the photographs of Robert Tarver are courtesy of Ethel Ponder.

Finally, I wish to thank David Givens of The Liffey Press for his unfailing courtesy and attention to detail in bringing this book to publication.

Dedication

For Órla, Sadhbh and Ríon

There are illuminating moments which change
you as the person who is giving witness.

Michael D. Higgins

INTRODUCTION

The caged bird sings
with a fearful trill
of things unknown
but longed for still
and his tune is heard
on the distant hill
for the caged bird
sings of freedom.
Maya Angelou – 'I know why the caged bird sings'[1]

This book is framed by the television series *What in the World?*, which was broadcast on Irish television over a five-year period between 2004 and 2012. This book deals with the years 2004–2009. It was preceded by the documentary film *Breaking the Chains* which was broadcast just prior to the Jubilee 2000 year. That year marked the culmination of a campaign that was predicated on the belief that social and economic transformation was possible if the unjust and unsustainable debt of poor countries could be cancelled.

This is a story of my encounters with people living in what is commonly known as the 'Third World' or 'Developing World', flawed concepts that fail to encapsulate the scale of the oppression hundreds of millions of people have to confront each waking moment. Of the two, I use the former as its currency as a popular descriptor still has resonance for many people. To borrow from Winston Churchill's comment on democracy, 'it is the worst form of Government except all those other forms that have been tried from time to time'.² The 'Third World' is the worst term apart from all the others.

Set in Africa, Asia and the Americas, this is a book of sel-dom-heard human stories, stories of intense pain and suffering, of small triumphs and occasional advances, of betrayal and com-plicity, of utter resilience and stout defiance. This book attempts to put in context the heart-rending stories of the poor and dis-placed people in some of the poorest parts of the planet. Their lives have been blighted by poverty spawned by neoliberal eco-nomics, social and cultural imperialism and ideologically-driven class warfare. This is the story of the human cost of flawed ide-ologies and distorted priorities.

In highlighting the corrosiveness of poverty and the violation of human rights at individual, familial and community levels, this story clearly establishes the complicity of individual poli-ticians, national and Western governments and powerful eco-nomic institutions in perpetuating the oppression of the world's poor. But equally, it seeks to challenge the sense of fatalism and inevitability that pervades much of the current thinking about global inequality. This is a story of stubborn witness and resis-tance by those who are at the bottom of what French film di-rector Costa-Gavras calls 'the pyramid of power'.³ Many of these stories are marked by deep anger and a sense of bewilderment at how the rest of us, particularly those of us in the Western world, can be so callous and indifferent to the pain of others.

While I am the principal narrator of this story, it is very much a shared encounter. Working on a television series is a collec-tive engagement and many of the observations and insights in this book are the product of long conversations with colleagues about 'the why and the what' of what we were doing. Many of the contributors to these conversations are mentioned in the text, others in the Acknowledgements. Conversations were also in-formed by people who have spent significant portions of their lives thinking and writing about our global interconnectedness.

In attempting to address these issues, this book explores the causalities of development and underdevelopment, which are often premised on the belief that the wealth of the world is created at the expense of the poor. In a 2008 interview, Bolivian President Evo Morales told us that the current economic model creates hunger and misery. This book is an illustration of that. But it is more. It is, to quote Morales again, 'a reminder of why we need to change those rules so that there is equality and justice for all'.

For that to happen it is, I believe, critically important that stories about global poverty and human rights violations continue to be aired, that the telling can make a difference, that the conversation is broadened beyond our own narrow self-interest, that we hear and are challenged by very different perspectives, that we see close-up the extraordinarily harsh and sometimes hopeless lives of others, particularly those in Africa, Asia and South America.

Paradoxically, that is also the hope of this book, that no matter how difficult the circumstances, how daunting the challenges, how repressive the regimes, how impoverished the people, how utterly desperate their plight, there is something about the human spirit that can transcend the quagmire in which it is enmeshed. In spite of that world, there is a conviviality and a sociability that often challenges our notions of other people's lives. Yes, poor and dispossessed African, Asian and Latin American people smile but often in spite of, not because of, the circumstances in which they find themselves. But it is also true that those smiles have drained from the faces of many, replaced by a hopeless stoicism, or just plain hopelessness.

Those of us living in the Western World need to understand why. People of the Third World are not a world apart from us. Now more than ever global interconnectedness binds us together. Every day of our lives we live on and off the poor of the world, but it is a world about which we hear very little. The world that is mediated to us by the mainstream media is deeply skewed in favour of the rich and the powerful. We indulge the foibles and idiosyncrasies of the few while steadfastly ignoring the desperate needs of the many. We live in a sports-obsessed, cocooned world where we probably spend more time and money reporting on greyhounds and horses than on the disfavoured peoples of the world. We certainly spend more time and energy speculating on the so-called trials and tribulations of a tiny multi-million-aire football and golfing elite. To recycle and bring up to date a phrase from Joe Dunne, the founder of the *Radharc* television series, most know that there is a Tiger in the United States, but how many know that there are no tigers in Africa?[4]

There is a view that journalists are too close to the local to be in a position to comprehend the global,[5] that our faces are pressed too close to the window, that it takes someone with more distance, more perspective, even more objectivity to capture the totality of events, that being too close to events and oppressed peoples results in work that lacks nuance, lacks subtlety. Perhaps so. There is even a view that having come close to the personal, the specific, that we all too readily go for the general, and that the results are at best mere descriptions, or at worst thought-less generalisations. There is even a view that first-hand accounts not mediated through the prism of well-established theoretical models offer little in terms of the knowledge of how the world operates. Maybe so. That is for the reader to decide.

All I know is that this book, to paraphrase Patrick Chabal from his superb 2009 book *Africa: The Politics of Suffering and Smiling*,[6] is about what happens when the camera is fixed at eye-level while engaging with politics as it is played out amongst some of the poorest communities across the globe. This is my experience of that story.

Endnotes

[1] Angelou, M (1969). *I Know Why the Caged Bird Sings*. Virago. London.

[2] This phrase is attributed to Winston Churchill. The full quote from a speech he delivered in the House of Commons on 11 November 1947 is as follows: 'No one pretends that democracy is perfect or all-wise. Indeed, it has been said that democracy is the worst form of Government except all those other forms that have been tried from time to time.' The full speech can be accessed as follows and the quote can be located at 207: http://hansard.millbanksystems.com/commons/1947/nov/11/parliament-bill#S5CV0444P0_19471111_HOC_292

[3] In an interview prior to the Berlin Film Festival, 7–17 February 2008 http://www.dw-world.de/dw/article/0,,3099374,00.html

[4] Dunn. J. (1986). *No Tigers in Africa! Recollections & Reflections on 25 Years of Radharc*. The Columba Press. Dublin.

[5] Kirby, P. (2003). *Introduction to Latin America: Twenty-first Century Challenges*. Sage Publications. London.

[6] Chabal, P. (2009). *The Politics of Suffering and Smiling,* London and New York: Zed Books.

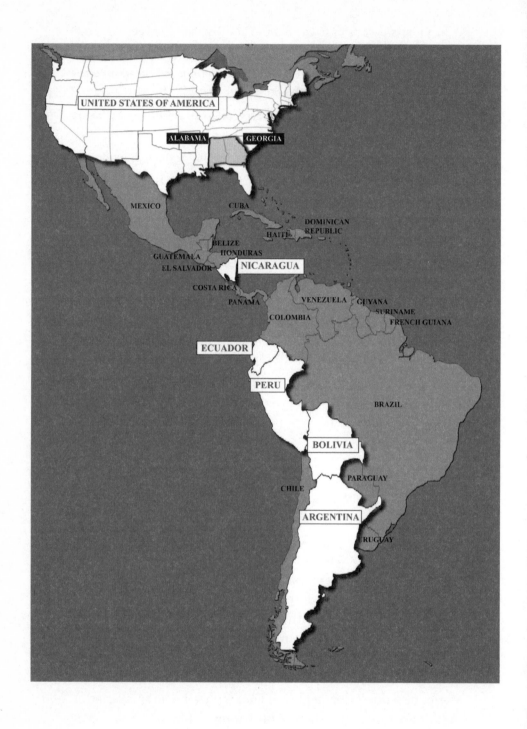

Section One

THE AMERICAS

Come and see the blood in the streets.
Come and see
the blood in the streets.
Come and see the blood
in the streets!
– *Pablo Neruda*[1]

Introduction

'So I'll see you in Managua then,' was Molly O'Duffy's part-ing shot to me when we met in the spring of 1999. Someone correctly told me that 'nobody in Ireland knows Nicaragua like Molly does'. Now it has become a good omen for me. When fi-nalising travel schedules with fixers from Bolivia to Burma and from Mongolia to Malawi my signing off comments are always, 'Yea, great, I think we're sorted. I'll see you in La Paz/Mae Sot/ Ulaanbaatar/Lilongwe.' But that was later.

Molly's engagement with Nicaragua is both personal and po-litical. Ours was a rollercoaster conversation that day in Dublin ranging from the history of the Sandinistas to the role of the United States government in funding the Contras to individual stories of sadness, loss and resilience – plus the no small matter of how we were to translate all of that into a film.

1

Latin America was the starting point of my filming and it was also the starting point of my political engagement with human rights and international politics. The visit of President Ronald Reagan to Ireland in 1984, and the protests at the bludgeoning of hundreds of thousands of Latin American people that brought thousands of Irish people on to the streets, was the catalyst of that involvement. More specifically, a talk I attended given by an Irish religious Sister on the blood-soaked carnage in Guatemala was sufficient for me to join the growing numbers who were prepared to take to the streets in protest against Reagan's visit. It was, to borrow a phrase from Michael D. Higgins, an illuminating moment. Whether it changed me or not, it is difficult to say. It certainly changed what it is I do. And certainly the *What in the World?* television series and this book are rooted in that illuminating moment.

Not that carnage was new to Latin America. Its history is steeped in blood. In his book, *Open Veins of Latin America,* a breathtakingly searing indictment of the colonial era, Eduardo Galeano characterised the Spanish invasion as 'a tide of avarice, terror and ferocity' that resulted in the genocide of a people.[2] 'The Indians of the Americas totaled no less than 70 million people when the foreign conquerors appeared on the horizon,' he claims, 'and a century and a half later they had been reduced to 3.5 million' (p. 5).

Despotism and dictatorship followed throughout Latin America. In Guatemala, a string of genocidal dictators began with the US-led Cold War coup that overthrew democratically elected Jacobo Arbenz in 1954. A thirty-six year civil war was unleashed – the longest in Latin American history. Established in 1994, the UN *Report of the Commission for Clarification*[3] concluded that over 200,000 people were killed during the conflict.

The eleventh day of September 1973 was a day of terror and bloodshed in Chile. Ushering in a seventeen-year military dictatorship, troops stormed the presidential palace and in the process destroyed the democratically elected government of President Salvador Allende and the hopes of the poor who supported him. During the Pinochet dictatorship that followed, an estimated 3,000 people were killed in Chile itself, thousands more were subjected to torture and many thousands were forced to flee the country, some of whom ended up in Dublin, Waterford, Galway and County Clare. During my time as a teacher in St. Patrick's Comprehensive School, Shannon, I taught some of the younger children of these exiles – the first time I came face-to-face with displaced people.

El Salvador too. In his 1993 book *What Uncle Sam Really Wants*, Noam Chomsky chronicles the perverse, chilling and macabre violations of human rights that took place during this period and US complicity in those killings.[4] One of the most outspoken critics of the dictatorships, and of US foreign policy that underpinned them, was Catholic Archbishop Óscar Romero. In February 1980, Romero sent a letter to US President Jimmy Carter pleading with him not to send military aid to the junta that ran the country. He said such aid would be used to 'sharpen injustice and repression against the people's organizations'[5] which were struggling 'for respect for their most basic human rights'. A few weeks later, on 24 March 1980, Archbishop Romero was dead – assassinated while saying mass at the chapel in the Hospital de la Divina Providencia.

Nine years later and the killing spree was still rampant. On 16 November 1989, six Jesuit priests, Ignacio Ellacuría, a widely respected leftist intellectual, along with Ignacio Martín-Baró, Segundo Montes, Amando López, Arnando Lopez, Joaquín López y López, and Juan Ramón Moreno, and their cook, Elba Julia Ramos, and her fifteen year-old daughter, Celina Ramosand, were murdered by the El Salvadorian army. That same week, at least twenty-eight other Salvadoran civilians were murdered, including the head of a major union, the leader of the organisation of university women, nine members of an Indian farming cooperative and ten university students.

In mid-December 1981, the army executed an utterly shocking massacre in the village El Mozote and surrounding areas. That massacre stands out from the catalogue of carnage that marked the decade of brutal bloodletting in El Salvador. On 1 December, soldiers entered the village. Their first target was the men. Beaten and blindfolded, they were locked in the church where they were systematically beheaded by machetes. Those who tried to escape were gunned down. The women, separated from the children they were trying to protect, were raped and killed. Then they turned their attention to the 131 children, three of whom were under three months of age. They were stabbed and shot to death. In total, 794 people were killed. The killing continued in neighbouring villages over the next few days culminating in over 900 murders.

In July 1979, the forty-three year-long Somoza dictatorship came crashing down. The Sandinistas took control of Managua and Somoza fled. An estimated 34,000 people (two per cent of the population) were killed in the civil war, 120,000 exiled and 600,000 rendered homeless. The economy was in ruins and the country's debt was in the region of $1.6 billion. On 17 June, Somoza fled to his million dollar home in Miami, allegedly with $3 million in his pockets to ease his transition. Embarrassed by his presence in the United States, Jimmy Carter threatened extradition. Somoza fled to Paraguay where he was assassinated at the age of fifty-four by a group of Argentinean radicals led by Enrique Haroldo Gorriarán Merlo.

It was the subsequent fate of Nicaragua that brought us to Latin America for the very first time.

Nicaragua

When we arrived in Nicaragua in 1999, the country was in a pitiful state. The hated (and in the end not just by the poor) Somoza dynasty that cannibalised the country, ferreting its meagre wealth out of the reach of the people but ever mindful of its subservient position to US hegemony in the region, was no more, but the Sandinista-inspired optimism that swept the country following the victory of the popular revolution in 1979 had long since dissipated. The dream had become a nightmare. The country was broke and broken.

In her distinctive Tyrone accent, Trócaire field director Sally O'Neill proved to be no slouch in naming the excesses of the Somoza dynasty. In vernacular detail, she spelled out how like father like son, they had made the State's interests subservient to their own. 'I came here to Nicaragua in 1971 during the Somoza regime,' she told us. She had seen the devastation of the earthquake that rocked the capital city Managua the following year. But like many ex-pats she could easily navigate between the two disparate worlds of Nicaragua. Shortly after the earthquake a friend invited her to visit one of Somoza's many farms.

> It was extraordinary, having watched people lying in the mud after the earthquake to see how Somoza's cows were being treated. He had them in beautiful surroundings and brought in music, classical music to relax them.

This type of excess typified the huge problem for O'Neill.

> I think that symbolizes a lot of what is wrong, not just with Nicaragua, but with Latin America. The fact that people like Somoza could build up enormous wealth, most of it on borrowed money that years later others have to pay back.

In 1999, Nicaragua topped the world league of the ratio of debt to national income. Every woman, man and child owed $1,500 to international bankers. The total debt was $6.3 billion. Sandinista leader Daniel Ortega was in opposition and discredited as a result of a sex scandal and what were regarded internally and internationally as sell-out compromises with the Right. For now, the United States policy of reinstating a more malleable government had succeeded and there seemed no immediate prospect of change.

Arnoldo Alemán was President, and as incorrigibly corrupt figures go he was a major league player. *The Economist* estimated that he and one other person siphoned off as much as $100 million in public funds.[6] Even his United States mentors soon tired of him. His highly personalised and corrupt presidency resulted in the literacy and health gains that had been the hallmark of the Sandinista short-lived era quickly unravelling as the country spiralled into desperate poverty. A former leader of the Somoza youth organisation, Alemán was a throw-back to the ancient regime of the pre-Sandinista era.

That was the political backdrop to our arrival in Managua in June 1999. The city has the unique and strangest feature of any capital city I have ever visited. It has no street names. The first place Molly brought us to in Managua was Revolutionary Square, but in 1999, Revolutionary Square was virtually sealed off at the behest of the administration of Alemán, fearful of its potent symbolism for those opposed to his government. Following the march of the Sandinistas into Managua on 19 July 1979, the square has come to represent the end of the old Somoza regime and the triumph of the Sandinista revolution. Off the square stands the shadow of the devastated sixteenth-century Spanish cathedral that was rocked to its foundations by the 1972 earthquake. Only a shell of the building is in place. Now it is home to squatters, drug addicts, sex workers, people who have fallen through the ever widening cracks in the social fabric of the country, and even Molly declared that it was not safe to visit.

That earthquake was the precursor of and contributed to the political earthquake that took place seven years later. Molly's longtime friend Cristina Rodriguez described for us how that torturous and painful journey unfolded.

Cristina Rodriguez

A descendent of the indigenous people of Subtiava and a life-long activist for workers' and women's rights, Cristina was born on 8 April 1940. In total, Cristina had fourteen children, four of whom died young. All her life, Cristina dedicated herself to various human rights struggles, from challenging the jack-boot despotism of the Somoza dictatorship to the authoritarianism of Nicaragua's macho culture. Cristina's life was characterised by lifelong defiance. Her interests were her struggles and her struggles were many, and all that time she worked hard to keep rice on the table and her family fed. A literacy teacher and a catechist, a coffee and cotton picker, a Sandinista and a trade unionist, her vicissitudes were many and varied. For Cristina the personal was political and the political was personal. Two years before the triumph of the revolution in 1979, she was a key player in a women's association that supported the Sandinista rebels. All of these activities meshed together in her world. She successfully combined her women's activism with her Catholicism, her support for what was a male-dominated Sandinista leadership with her feminism, and her support for the violent overthrow of the detested Somoza regime with her religious beliefs.

We first met Cristina in her home located beside a small primary school where she filled us in on aspects of her story. Even in translation she could draw us in, such was the power of her testimony. There was a stillness about her, a centre of gravity that pulled people in. Instinctively I could see why Molly had spoken so affectionately about her. Details of her early life I was to glean from her autobiography, *Cristina Rodriguez: A Nicaraguan Story*.[7]

At the age of eleven Cristina's family moved to Nicaragua's second city, Leon, and three years later she moved in with Luis Núñez and his family, where at the age of fourteen she had her first daughter. On this family farm, she did back-breaking work both in the home and in the fields under the hot tropical sun. The father of her child, who was ten years her senior, was abusive and exploitative. She left him shortly after the birth of their daughter. Cristina's second partner, with whom she had thirteen children, was equally feckless. Living in poverty, bearing child after child with a partner who refused to take any responsibility, Cristina's life was not unlike the hand dealt to many women in Nicaragua. Machismo remains a heavy burden for Nicaraguan women to carry. Marriage third time round did not prove any luckier but fourth time did. Cristina eventually found happiness with Adolfo Lainez Fuentes.

Despite the personal trauma and poverty experienced by Cristina, she joined the resistance against the Somoza regime in 1978. That September, Cristina and her family had their first taste of war. The Sandinistas had taken control of Chinandega. Two days later Somoza's National Guard attacked the town in retaliation. Her pregnant daughter Isobel was killed in what the National Guards called Operation Clean-up. Not surprisingly, Cristina remembers it not just as a terrible time for her, but for all families.

> *What hurts most is that on that day, the 17 September, I had seen them ransacking the houses, and dragging out the corpses, not knowing that my own daughter was lying dead amongst them. At the park, they were burning five corpses. Right on the corner there was another dead body that they hauled down and set fire to . . . even now in my sleep I have a feeling like a dagger through my heart and sometimes I scream and leap out of the bed like a madwoman.*

Rather than becoming engulfed in her own personal sorrow, Cristina was galvanised into action by the death of her daughter.

> *If my daughter, a pregnant woman, had been murdered for nothing more than making tortillas for the rebel command near her house, why not get more involved in the struggle and die for something more than a few tortillas.*

When it came, the revolution brought not only great joy but great opportunities. Cristina described the revolutionary period as the honeymoon she never had.

> There is no doubt the revolution did great things, things I had never seen as a worker, things we had never dreamed of during the forty-five years of the Somoza dictatorship. We had equal pay and we had subsidised state shops so that our wages went further. We had health care in our health centres; we had pre-and post-natal care. We had education for our children.

Cristina says she experienced a kind of euphoria after the coming to power of the Sandinistas, and then it all fell apart. 'I wept bitterly,' Cristina said on hearing that the Sandinistas lost the election in 1990.

> So many thousands of people had died for us to live in a better world and learn self-respect and dignity. The loss of the election was a disaster for us rural women.

But before the end of the decade Cristina had an altogether different trauma. Hurricane Mitch hit.

Nature is restless and often hostile in the tropics, and Hurricane Mitch, which struck Central America in October 1998 at a speed of 180 miles-per-hour, proved the point. The area around Posoltega is stunningly beautiful, surrounded by a necklace of smouldering, steaming volcanoes. While there, we drove to the top of one of them, San Cristobel. It was a sobering experience peering over the rim of a smouldering volcano that one year previously had caused such havoc. It was the thirteenth tropical storm and third major hurricane of that year. An unprecedented seventy-five inches of rain fell between 29 October and 3 November. The rain filled up one of the volcanic funnels that bookended the western coast of the country. Some were unable to hold that volume of rainfall and the volcanoes burst open releasing a torrent of water, rock and sludge that swept everything before it. Between Honduras and Nicaragua nearly 11,000 people were killed and 8,000 were missing in what was the second deadliest hurricane in history. It caused an estimated $5 billion in damages.

In one tumultuous day Cristina Rodriguez lost forty members of her family. Her testimony was powerful, poignant, dignified and deeply moving.

We decided to do Cristina's interview in three locations: in her home, by the sea and at the site of Hurricane Mitch's devastation. Gerry Gregg, the director, suggested that we go to the sea to give Cristina more personal space to tell the second part of her story. It was an inspired choice for two reasons. We travelled for about forty minutes to a deserted beach on the Pacific. This was the very beach that the waters from the burst volcano of San Cristobel had washed into the sea. Human and animal remains, along with trees, shrubs, crops, boulders and bits of houses, had all been washed into the sea at the spot where we were to interview Cristina. Hence it was almost deserted. Nobody would build along this coast now.

It was also spectacularly beautiful, with sparkling, swivelling waters and miles of beach. This was a tropical paradise with an occasional abandoned boat casually strewn on the beach, and in the foreground three fishermen riding the waves in their wooden green and red boat. At the far end of the beach, a fire smouldered in front of a reed-covered hut. It was as if an art director had dressed the set for us. And the water – inviting but threatening.

After lunch we travelled with Cristina to Postolega where the hurricane in Nicaragua had hit hardest. On the side of the mountain beside the track that swept 3,000 people to their deaths, Cristina took us through that fateful day. She had travelled to Managua earlier that day so she missed its immediate and terrible impact. On her way home, she listened to accounts on the radio of the hurricane's increasing intensity. Initially it was heading for Honduras. Nicaragua was next. Composed but tearful, Cristina vividly described its full horror.

> *It was a disaster like we had never seen before. We used to be so proud of our range of volcanoes but now it's different because they have destroyed us. The water and the rocks*

came out hot and poured out over the rim of the volcano. It was as if the volcano could not hold all the rain and as the rim tore open, the mountain groaned and an enormous landslide was let loose. It cut an enormous cleft. You can still see the huge scar where the landslide ripped up houses, coffee trees and everything else that came in its way.

It was like a surgeon's incision. The scar measured about four feet deep and was about fifteen feet wide. It was remarkably even. Then it divided like two tributaries of a river just before Posoltega where it swept everything in its path into the Pacific Ocean at the very point where we had just interviewed Cristina. Even a year later, there were remnants of the flood – a faded teddy bear on a tree stump, bits of cloth lying randomly on the ground and upended trees with their roots facing the sky. As we looked over the stricken landscape, Cristina told us of her own loss.

I lost forty members of my family that day – brothers, sisters, cousins, nieces and nephews of my mother. My mother's family was almost completely wiped out. Even to this day, I don't know where they are buried.

Hearing the children was the worst. Some were left on the banks over there by the Tollar River. They were stuck in the cane fields. They were dumped like debris by the flood. But no-one could get to them because the earth was too soft. They were left there. Some died straight away. Others were stuck in the mud, hurt, crying and trying to free themselves. But they couldn't. In other places children died falling out of trees they had climbed. Weak from the hunger after all the rain they just fell into the flood and nothing could be done to save them.

Cristina stopped her pained recollection and looked away. Conscious of the moment, we waited; there was no rush. Then she said in a half-whisper, 'it hurts to remember. to have lost family and not to have been able to bury them properly'. Very poignantly, she then said:

The truth is we always suffer. Those at the bottom always suffer. Everything falls harder on us.

Defiantly, Cristiana concluded:

But we always have to be strong to resist the next blow life deals us.

We backed off and Gerry Gregg asked Molly to go to Cristina. It was an important gesture, not just from Gerry. There are times when you need to turn off the camera and let people be and I suspect that Gerry knew that. But it was also a tribute to the skill and sensitivity of Ronan Fox and Mick Cassidy who could hold the camera and microphone in a way that allowed Cristina to tell her story at her own pace and in her own time. We also knew, and this can be the crass element of filming, that we had the story.

Mother of five Doris Cano worked as a teacher in an Irish Aid-funded school. Despite what might seem a plumb job, she lived in a one-room house with her children. Only a small wardrobe partially separated the bedroom from the rest of the kitchen. Her house was practically bare – just the minimum of cooking utensils – and how could such a small wardrobe hold all the clothes for six people? Laundry, I remember thinking, is a rich person's problem, a concern of the privileged. Her precarious existence was very evident.

Most of us primary school teachers have the same problems; the salaries they pay us are so low. The price of food is very high, and my salary doesn't cover the cost. We don't buy it in bulk; we buy it every day, because we can't afford to buy everything in bulk. And detergent and soap the same, I get a shock every day when I go to the corner shop and they tell me, no soap isn't the same price any more, it's gone up a little. And as for clothes, don't talk! And if you think about it, with five children, if I buy something for her I can't buy anything for the others. So you see the difficulties we face, but we look for ways to get around the problems and we keep going.

Then there was the plight of sixteen-year-old Irma Sanchez, disabled by meningitis. Unable to walk or talk, she had to be carried by her mother who could not afford a wheelchair for her. Nor could her mother work outside the home. The cost of child care was beyond her. She opened a small shop in her dusty barrio that appeared to sell little else other than blackened bananas.

What I'd like is a wheelchair for her, so that I could take her out, take her out for a walk, otherwise I have to leave her here, or in a hammock or leave her in bed here. But most of the time I have to dedicate to her . . . I have to wash her, I feed her, and for that reason I can't get a job, because who's going to look after her if I don't? She can't talk, she can't walk. Sometimes she gets sick and I need to buy medicines for her, and medicines are very expensive. As you know well . . .

There was also Maria Elsa Amador Osejo, or simply Elsa Amador as she was known, Molly O'Duffy's great friend who cooked the most wonderful tortillas I have ever eaten. She told us her story of her descent into poverty. She had been president of a fourteen-family cooperative established during the Sandinista regime. But the supports that provided her family and the cooperative were gradually eaten away. Electricity was privatised, dramatically increasing their overhead costs. Seeds and fertilizer became more expensive. Then they were told that they should gear themselves for the export market. This was the new post-Sandinista orthodoxy. So they did. They invested in onions but others had received the same advice so there was a huge glut of onions. The business collapsed and they were left in debt. They were then advised to stay with the onions as the market would pick up the following year, but it didn't – they were now deeper in debt. 'Don't talk to me about the onions,' was her plaintive cry. She too was a victim of Hurricane Mitch.

We've really had it with the onions. All they did was get us further into debt. We sowed them with the intention of making a bit of money. The prices were supposed to be good. Bur we just lost money on them. It was a huge amount of work. We couldn't sleep for worrying about them. We had so many worries during the planting season. In the end we didn't even cover our planting costs. All our current debt is from growing onions for export to the United States.

They restructured our debt and we began again. Then Mitch hit. First Hurricane Mitch wiped out the crop. It washed away one section we had transplanted and it washed away the topsoil. We lost everything.

Hopes, dreams and livelihoods were washed away that night. Eventually the cooperative went under despite significant subsidies from friends in Ireland. Devoid of her income, one of Elsa's daughters subsequently died as in the new dispensation in the country, everything had to be paid for and she could not afford the medicines for her sick child. Prior to that she lost her son, Alfonso, killed in a pub brawl over a perceived gay slur in what was still a quintessentially macho culture with correspondingly high levels of homophobia. Four years later, I was back in Nicaragua where I briefly met Elsa, saddened beyond recognition, her heart broken by the world.

After Cristina's final interview we returned to Leon, which was our base for most of the film shoot. It is as stunningly beautiful as Managua is not. Founded in 1524 by Francisco Hernández de Córdoba, it is a classical South American Spanish city. Its central square is dominated by the largest cathedral in Central America, the Basilica de la Asunción, and is a stunning piece of architecture. Sitting in the square in Leon, which was dominated by the cathedral and statues of lions in the foreground, I was torn between admiration of its beauty and its symbolism of Spanish colonialism. This is the paradox. Spanish colonialism was an unmitigated disaster for indigenous peoples and its legacy of oppression is still very much in evidence today. Its architecture is testimony to the vanished and the vanquished of a whole subcontinent. But without that we would not feel the cool red and white marble under our feet or enjoy the many other examples of its colonial heritage.

But there was another side to Leon that rattled us all. Poverty, especially child poverty, is ubiquitous in the city. One night we were having dinner in one of the few restaurants just off the square. Our plates were overflowing, more food than we could eat in any one meal. Sitting on the side of the street just in front of the restaurant, we could not help but notice that we were under surveillance – from the street children. Gradually their confidence increased and they slowly but steadily began to move in our direction until eventually they were by our side. One thin girl in a loose fitting cotton dress was the boldest of the group and she eventually stood right by our side eyeing us and the food. Without a word she began to eat off our unfinished plates and soon was joined by about three or four others. The restaurant owner tried to intervene but we declined his intervention. They simply wolfed down our leftovers. Crumbs from the rich man's table. Later we saw the same young girl vomiting – the food was too rich for her to digest. That is one lingering memory that remains fresh over a decade later.

Another and altogether more uplifting image is of Cristina Rodriguez sitting in one of those distinctively Nicaraguan rocking chairs, looking out pensively at her grandchildren playing in a dusty yard. This was the only time in the days we spent with her that Cristina admitted to being tired, 'worn out by life'. But defeatism was not her style. She was too much of an activist to give in to that.

> *I don't want to die just yet. I want to keep on struggling. I think it's my Indian blood that rebels because I have suffered some very hard blows. But I always rise above them.*

Cristina Rodriguez died in 2006, six years after uttering those defiant words.

Ecuador

It was without doubt the most tense forty-five minute meeting in our entire experience of filming the *What in the World?* series. We had come a long way. From Ireland, we flew to the transatlantic hub in Atlanta and from there to Managua. From Managua, we flew to Quito, Ecuador's capital, followed by an internal flight to Macas. We still were not at or near our final destination.

Molly O'Duffy and I sat opposite Milton Callera, President of the Achuar Federation, in his bare Macas office in the southeastern part of Ecuador. He was utterly impassive, hands joined on a simple wooden table that divided us. We explained our intention to film the Achuar people deep in the Amazonian jungle who were resisting the incursion of multinational oil companies into what they regarded as their autonomous territory. What I had initially regarded as a courtesy chat was now turning into a critical decision-making meeting. The outcome would determine whether we would have to go home empty-handed or could proceed with our film-making plans. The prospect of going home empty-handed filled me with an enormous dread. We had invested heavily in getting here, had a broadcasting contract to honour, which included getting this story, and now this unexpected development.

Earlier in the year, when I wasn't even sure if I had any money for this project, I travelled to Rome to meet with Italian teachers who were working with the Achuar. They gave me a long to-do list, people to contact, approvals and clearances. I had done them all. Gone through all the hoops. Ticked all the boxes. I even had a letter of introduction and clearance from the Vice-President of the Achuar Federation, but now I discovered that the Vice-

President's letter had very little currency. It was the President's call and he was giving nothing away, making us work hard.

This was also the first face-to-face with an 'Indian'. My childhood might have been filled with heroic cowboys and feckless Indians, but this was far from the fictional worlds of my childhood. In this setting, he held all the aces. That easy and all too prevalent stereotype he was not. Cautious, astute, he let us make our case, and then there was a long pause, a long impenetrable pause. Or so it seemed to me. I shifted uncomfortably on my chair thrust forward, not daring to look at Molly who was sitting beside me if not behind me at that stage. Then he simply said, 'that's fine, you have my permission'. I sat back and exhaled slowly. I could now look Molly in the eye. I think the significance of what he had just said, or rather the consequences of a different response, were just beginning to sink in. One man's word. Such is the fickleness of life. My instinct was to throw my arms around him and thank him effusively. Fortunately, I restrained myself, thanked him politely, invited him for a drink which he declined and left. As we were leaving, he said that he would meet us after dinner in our hotel to finalise arrangements. When he met us he had the all-important document. Hard-earned as it was, I've kept the original. It reads:

> *Tienen el espíritu de promover a nivel Internacional la defense de territorio del pueblo Achuar, son legalmente autorizado por esta autoridad para que realicen actividades ya mencionadas.*
>
> *[signed] Milton Callera, President FINAE*

While no clear definition of what it is to be indigenous has been agreed, attachment to land and ancestors who have for centuries lived on that land are critical to indigenous identity. According to the United Nations, there are about 370 million indigenous people (5.4 per cent) in the world. The Ecuadorian 2001 census reported that 9.2 per cent of the population belonged to a household in which either at least one member of the family self-identified as indigenous or spoke an indigenous language.

In total there are thirteen clearly defined indigenous groups and we divided our time between two – the Achuar and the Cófan. There are no more than 3,500 Achuar occupying half-a-million acres of unspoiled tropical rain forest in the Amazon basin, their ways almost untouched by, but not unaware of, the outside world they first came into contact with fifty years previously. Approximately another 3,000 Achuar live in neighboring Peru, the great Achuar nation transcending the colonialists' borders. Now that we had secured permission from Milton we could visit one of those communities.

Over several cold beers we celebrated our fraught success and I savoured the moment. As a party location, Macas, this gateway to the Amazon located east of the Andes in the lovely Upano Valley, is one beautiful place. With a population of 30,000 people, its gridded lay-out and wide streets give it an open, accessible and busy feel. The town itself is dominated by the typically colourful Spanish colonial Catholic church of the Virgin Purísima, with its tiered, stepped entrance and the life-size mural of Mary dominating its exterior. Inside it is brilliantly lit with stunning views of the river valley from the back of the church.

Attractive as it is, sitting around in bars doesn't get a documentary made. We had hired two four-seater airplanes to fly us into the jungle. There we were met by Argentinean missionaries from the Roman Catholic Salesian congregation, who provided us with three wooden huts for the duration of our four-day stay. But we had to bring absolutely everything we needed – food (and beer), water, candles and gas for the two-ringed cooker that would cook all our meals over the following days. Even mattresses for the beds. As we loaded our planes in Macas with all our goods, there was a tangible sense of anticipation.

The Achuar

For all our anticipation and undisguised excitement, flying over the Amazon through wisps of cloud was somewhat discordantly an underwhelming experience. We were like a moth flying just above bunches of tightly compacted broccoli. Any break in the density revealed brown, sludge-like, slowly meandering rivers, and that was it, mile after mile in one of the world's most biologically diverse regions. It seemed just too cavalier to be unmoved by the experience. What I had been expecting I'm not too sure. Perhaps squawking, soaring, colourful birds. Silver fast-flowing streams. Tightly-fisted monkeys sitting in tree-tops clenching their fists at our aural intrusion. Clusters of villages. But nothing more than a dense green carpet was visible below and the only sound track was the drone of our plane.

On a brown earthen airstrip where we touched down, we were greeted by wellington-wearing and face-painted members of the Achuar. From the airstrip, we had to carry our belongings about a kilometre through the jungle to our temporary homes. It was hot and the heavy cloying mud clung to our boots, weighing us down. That and the humidity made the going tough. But what a sight – four small wooden huts close to but not in sight of the missionary school.

Tea in the missionary house followed our settling in. Argentinean-born Father Francesco was our most genial host. Gorgeously soft spoken and welcoming, he gave us a good steer on the cultural norms of the Achuar as well as their struggle with the oil companies. Clearly he was on the side of the Achuar in this David and Goliath contest. Fortified by his insights, we set out for our first three kilometre trek through the jungle, one that we would repeat every day for the next four days. If the birds' eye view of the Amazonian jungle was somewhat underwhelming, this trek made up for it. Guided by Luis Freire, a member of the Achuar, we slowly made our way through the soft, muddied tracks under the most awe-inspiring canopies penetrated by shimmering light. We walked through a narrow, cloister-like pathway surrounded on either side by tree-pillars in this most sacred of secular cathedrals.

Underneath, what appeared to our untrained eyes to be large ferns competed with each other for shafts of light. But it was the trees towering above us for countless metres that had our heads tilted upwards, our necks straining to the sky. What struck us most was the silence. Not a sound in nature's cathedral. The only break in the ever changing sea of green were colonies of pristine white butterflies. *The Rough Guide to Ecuador* tells us that this 'tiny nation is one of the most species-rich countries on the planet. Ecologists have labelled Ecuador one of the world's "megadiversity hotspots".[8] *The Rough Guide* lists 1,600 species of birds, 230 different mammals, 680 amphibians and reptiles, 20,000 different flowering plants and more than a million insects.[9] If that is so, we did not see them or at least very few of them. Later, we learned that conscious of human presence, wildlife takes refuge in more private, hard-to-reach parts of the forest.

Even these wonderful canopies could not protect us from the searing heat and humidity. Sweat-soaked, with mud-caked boots that deadened our legs, we were simply no match for our sure-footed guide. But worse was to come when we had to cross over streams using the most slender of felled trees. This was no place for the self-conscious. Luis simply skipped across one of the trunks that naturally bridged the river. Clumsily, we tried to do the same but to no avail. Nothing for it but to take his hand and clam-like cling on to him in the hope that we would not drag him down in to the swirling waters below. No fear, even we couldn't upend him.

The bucket-loads of sweat that seemed to be pouring off us did not even dampen our spirits. This was some journey and we knew it. We were like young calves in spring grass such was our enthusiasm for our new surroundings. And then one of the most truly amazing experiences of my life. We walked up a hill, rounded a corner of forest and came to an opening that revealed a clearing that held a fully functioning, elaborately planned Achuar village. We stopped at the opening, partly to catch our breath, partly at the wonder of it all. Stretching out in front of us was an extraordinarily well-planned village with individual houses radiating out from a central building that we later learned was the meeting house. It was also remarkably quiet. People were busy working their plots or doing the normal chores that mark all our days. We had made it. From Cork to here via Dublin, Atlanta, Managua, Quito, Macas and now this.

However, as often happens in places where communication systems are haphazard, they were as surprised to see us as we were delighted to see them. Word had not yet reached them of our imminent arrival and they were none too pleased at this sudden and unwelcome intrusion on their daily life. People stopped their midday chores. Children fled. Elders gathered. We were invited to one of the houses. Women hurriedly swept the earthen floors. Conference time.

For the second time since my arrival in Ecuador, I was gripped by panic. What if they now decided not to cooperate? What if they sent us packing? They weren't exactly fulsome in their welcome. The elders gathered, all men. The women stayed in the background. We were invited to state our case. I told them of our journey, across seas, over land, days and night spent travelling. I said that we had come in friendship and solidarity, that we had nothing to do with the oil companies, that our sympathies were with them in their struggle. I told them of our meeting with Milton in Macas and that he had approved our visit. Gradually, the mood lightened. Invited to partake in the communal drink, *chichi*, we felt this was the first breakthrough. We whispered our anxieties to each other as they consulted. All was fine. 'Come back the next day,' their spokesperson said. 'Yes they would talk to us and yes we could film here.' Relief, nothing more, just pure relief.

This time there was no beer to celebrate. We made our way home, unpacked our provisions, unwrapped our mattresses, and prepared our first meal in this once-in-a-lifetime setting. Then Ken O'Mahony noticed we had no beer. We had eggs, lots of eggs, and rice but no beer. Apparently the plane that carried us was also doing a food drop to a priest who was working in another part of the jungle. Some of the boxes got mixed up. He now had our beer but we had his food. Eggs and lots of them. We hoped that the beer would provide some consolation for him. Ken wasn't so easily placated. More than likely the priest wasn't either.

The following morning we made French toast. Luis was having none of it. French toast and coffee in the Amazonian jungle. Sometimes you have to remind yourself that things may not get better than this, but not for Luis. Breakfast was only breakfast if it included rice, though on day one he was too polite to say so. Not so on day two. Fortified by the priest's eggs we began our hour-long trek. This time though we were loaded with gear – camera, tripod, lens bag, as well as all of Mick Cassidy's sound equipment, plus water, lots of water. Fording the river now would be even more challenging, but we managed. 'Better this than the traffic chaos of Dublin's Red Cow roundabout,' quipped Mick as we headed off.

As we arrived, the early morning traditional call from Wampush Muquink, the chief, the Sindico, blowing into a bull-horn summoned the community to the meeting house to plan and allocate the work for the day as their ancestors had done before them. We sat and drank *chichi,* a yellowish, slightly lemon-flavoured but to our palates at least somewhat sour drink. The Achuar believe that *chichi* is a source of strength for their work and drinking *chichi* is a ritual repeated several times a day. The women serve this drink in brittle-brown, ornate, hand-made glazed bowls, the size of an average western cereal bowl, and the men then pass them around. As a sign that we were accepted guests, we too were invited to drink. Later in the day we would film the women making the *chichi*. The yucca plant is boiled for hours in large vats, the women constantly stirring with large wooden spoons while they sit on their hunkers. The women chew and swallow the boiled yucca, which they then regurgitate back into the vat. Later, the drink will be strained and served in bowls. The women's saliva speeds the fermentation process to make it mildly alcoholic. The yucca is the heart of the Achuar diet, the staple, and when not being drunk is peeled, boiled and served like mashed potatoes. The yucca and the other staples of the jungle, mainly wild turkey and boar, allow this self-sufficient community to live life on their terms.

The discussion on what we could film was led by Wampush. Dressed in sports shorts and football jersey, and wearing his bright red headdress made from toucan feathers, his face streaked with red paint, he cut an impressive figure. Like their President, he and the other members of the community were absolutely clear about the boundaries within which they would allow us operate. We could film in the meeting house, the exterior of the twenty-six houses in the village and the interior of one designated house. We could film all the village activities but only after we had established their prior consent.

That day they were building a house and that's where we could start. From where we were sitting, we could see that one oval-shaped house was under construction. Known as the jewels of the jungle, these elaborately constructed timber and thatch houses can last up to fifty years. Twelve posts are put into the ground for each house and a bamboo roof is carefully webbed together from the top down leaving only the bottom three feet uncovered. The houses are about thirty feet in height, though the size depends on the status of the family. Within each house there are separate quarters and separate entrances for women and men. The women cannot enter the men's quarters except to serve the food. Apart from ever so comfortable open bamboo beds built on stilts, which are used for dining and sleeping, the houses were sparsely furnished. While they worked, they told us about their lives.

'Achuar men mainly do the heavy work,' Wampush told us, 'digging the fields and hunting.'

> But as well as that we also make crafts . . . like baskets or weaving. The women do very much the same. But they also tend to the crops . . . and tend to the vegetable gardens. The women also make our pottery vessels, called 'pinnace' and 'teaches'. All these things they do, but in a much planned way. We always agree who will do what, before we start . . . we learned this from our ancestors, they planned everything together. We are proud to still live this way.

We asked Yoanas Pujjciapat, Wampush's wife, about women's role in the community. 'We women help our men to build these houses,' she told us.

> We still use wood and leaves like our ancestors . . . that is why conserving the jungle has always been our way . . . because the jungle gives us our home. To build a house we work in a group, so we can build it quickly. It would take one person a year to build a big house so we always lend a hand, to get it built faster.

Under Threat

The ancient, community-based lifestyle where the Achuar have lived undisturbed lives for thousands of years is under threat, for they sit on that most valuable commodity – oil. Essential to our world, it could spell the end of theirs. In 1998, six years before our arrival on Achuar land, the Ecuadorian government gave US-based multinational ARCO a license to explore for oil in what has become known as Block 24.[10] The following year Burlington Oil purchased the drilling rights from ARCO. At the time, Burlington very publically claimed on their official website that 95 per cent of the Achuar supported them.[11] We did not find those supporters. In fact, what we did find was an extraordinarily acrimonious relationship.

In 2000, in violation of Ecuadorian and international law, Burlington Oil repeatedly entered indigenous ancestral lands without prior consultation with recognised tribal authorities, while simultaneously pursuing well-established divide and rule tactics. Convention 169 of the International Labour Organization[12] clearly states that ancestral owners have rights to the land where they have lived for thousands of years, and that governments have to protect that land and the indigenous people. Furthermore, it stipulates that in any exploitation of non-renewable natural resources, there has to be consultation with the indigenous people, and those rights are also protected in the country's own constitution. Article 84 states that the indigenous peoples have the right to plan their own development, and it also guarantees their right to live in a healthy environment. But that did not happen in Ecuador.

The Ecuadorian government claimed an opt-out clause. While certainly the indigenous people had rights to the land they did not have rights to what lay below the land, and given that the oil was below the land the government could have access to it. The sub-soil was excluded so the government and anybody they nominated could exploit the non-renewable resources beneath the soil. The Achuar and others were outraged by what they perceived as this betrayal.

Quite apart from the impact on the Achuar people, the deal with Burlington Oil was never in the interests of the Ecuadorian people. Only 12.5 per cent of the profits were to go to the people of Ecuador, while Burlington would retain 87.5 per cent, a hugely unequal division of the spoils by any yardstick.

Elected by the urban poor, small farmers and the Federation of Indigenous People, but interestingly not members of the Achuar, the government of then President Lucio Gutierrez backed the oil company and even sent in the military in November 2003. Violence flared. Death threats. Intimidation. Torture. Dozens were detained by force. Many fled into the forests. The Achuar, now allied to ancient rivals the Shuar, and the Guarani responded in kind with equally well-established tactics of their own, as Luis Freire told us.

> We detained some officials from the oil company . . . we held eight of their people. We did not treat them badly. Our aim was to negotiate. The company had been doing exploratory drilling, but they stopped. Then we sent back the people we were holding in our community.

Should the oil company return, Luis warned that they would apply the ancestral punishment to any workers caught infringing their territorial space.

> We know that if the oil company comes it will lay waste to the rain forest, and to everything. So the companies or the people who try to come in, if they come up to a certain point we will show them respect. But if they don't respect us, and if they come to destroy everything we have we will do everything to prevent that. And if we have to punish them, we will apply the ancestral punishment, which is to put chili in their eyes. That is a punishment that in ancient times our mothers used if one of the sons or daughters was contrary and would not do what it was told.

> We would also carry them off, us together with our men, so that they would have to spend five days fasting, and we would make them take guantu or maichua. We would use these kinds of punishments, but we wouldn't treat them

*badly or hit them, we would just apply the punishment
they would deserve if they came without respecting us.*

While there are probably worse things than having chili
rubbed in one's eyes, we were nonetheless glad that we were
never mistaken for oil workers. We never found out what *gauntu*
or *maichua* was, but we felt none the poorer for that. But while
the Achuar might have adopted guerilla hit and run tactics, they
were clear that they did not regard themselves as terrorists. That
all too easy accusation simply did not wash with them.

All this time the Burlington Oil Company claimed that it
has the support of the Achuar people. In a press release dated 14
January 2004 it stated as follows.[13]

> *As corporate citizens, we are committed to managing our
> operations in Ecuador and elsewhere around the world in
> a socially responsible manner. This has led us to under-
> stand and address the unique needs of the indigenous peo-
> ples in Blocks 23 and 24. We have worked through the vari-
> ous Federations and have provided much-needed medical
> aid to several local communities. Also, as required under
> Ecuadorian law, we have worked with leaders and repre-
> sentatives of approximately 55 local communities. These
> efforts have been conducted in an open and honest man-
> ner. We believe that through their official representatives
> more than 95 per cent of the indigenous peoples within the
> blocks are receptive to petroleum activities.*

Nothing that we heard would support that claim. Nothing.
The Achuar's sense of their own history and confidence in their
own skin was clear. These were a defiant people that would never
simply roll over. Their foremothers and forefathers in other parts
of the vast continent of the Americas might have been bought
off with simple worthless inducements, but those days were long
gone. 'We have never been colonized,' Luis Freire tells us.

> *We never fell to the Spanish. So we don't want the govern-
> ment . . . to sell us off just for money. We Achuar don't feel
> weak, on the contrary . . . we feel strong. Because we are
> in our home. We are in our jungle . . . we have lived here*

for many many years. So that makes us feel proud and we
will fight.

Fight they did and they won, or at least the other side didn't win. Stalemate. Burlington Oil is no more. Now owned by ConocoPhillips, not a drop of oil has been drilled from Block 24 or from neighbouring Block 23. According to the ConocoPhillips official website: 'Blocks 23 and 24 are explorations blocks that have been under force majeure for the past seven years. No activity is planned for 2007.'[14] No update since then is recorded. Sometimes, to quote from the Book of Ecclesiastes, 'the race is neither to the swift nor the battle to the strong'.

There are however exceptions to that saying. The Achuar play what is to us an unusual version of volleyball in which they use their feet to kick the ball as well as their hands. As the days progressed, we began to relax in each others' company and the strictures that were in place at the beginning began to dissipate. And each day brought new wonders. We all ate together in the middle of the day, meat and rice served on palm leaves. They even managed to locate some forks having watched our clumsy efforts to eat with our hands. There were times when they became the film-makers, laughing at each other as they looked through the lens of Ken's camera and listened to the sounds through Mick's speakers. In turn, we became the subjects of their film-making.

Carried away with our new-found ease, one of us had the temerity to say that we would take them on in their version of volleyball. This was midday in the tropical sun. Now as a crew, stamina we might have, but volleyball or any other footballing skills we do not. Molly agreed to play umpire and score-keeper reminding us, not for the first time, that while linguistically confident she is severely numerically challenged. So wrapping the green flag round us, at least figuratively speaking, Ken, Mick and I representing Ireland took on the Achuar nation. We were awful, deplorable, worse than terrible. We did not score a single point. Not once did we get the ball over the line that they could not respond with force. Time and again we were caught flat-footed. Had Eamon Dunphy been watching us, he would have been unforgiving. The Achuar were delighted and merciless. Molly lost count of the score. On that occasion the race was to the swift.

Sunday was our final day with the Achuar, also their day of rest. As we were about to leave, we asked them if they had any musical instruments and if they would play for us. Wampush produced a home-made flute and played the most beautiful slow air, haunting and melodic. Then the women danced. But they didn't want us to film their dance. This was a present from them to us alone. It was quite a moment. In return one of us sang the traditional Irish song *Téir Abhaile Riu,* if for no other reason than the desire to reciprocate. So we left the Achuar people with a tremendous sense of warmth and a deep sense of privilege. For days, we felt part of their world, not an exotic world, not an altogether different world, a world that more than likely has its own tensions, cracks and fissures, but a wonderfully welcoming world notwithstanding our understandably cautious initial meeting.

But we were not yet finished with the story of oil in Ecuador. In all our conversations, the Achuar kept repeating that they did not want what happened to the Cofán people to befall them. What they described amounted to a post-apocalyptic world. Whatever had happened, we needed to see it for ourselves.

Flying back to Macas brought more drama. I was on the second flight out on our charted four-seater planes so I didn't see or experience the full impact. As our first plane was circling the airstrip in Macas a sudden plume of smoke spiraled into the sky. The four-seater that preceded us had crash-landed killing the pilot and one passenger. We were to fly out from this airstrip the following day. Sobering. The following morning we flew to Lago Agrio, incident-free.

Lago Agrio's Oil Wars

Situated in the north east of the country, close to the Colombian border, Lago Agrio is a typical oil town carved out of the forest. Forty years earlier there was not a stone in this place. Now it was a bustling, thriving frontier town of 40,000 people. But we were amply warned that this was one rough town. We were not to venture out after dark, were not to go to bars other than the hotel we were staying in, but such warnings are hard to heed. We found a bar close to the hotel. Quickly, it seemed the word got out. The Irish were in town. Not that we were conscious of that until, that is, someone approached us and asked if we were part of the IRA. Apparently, the FARC (Fuerzas Armadas Revolucionarias de Colombia – Ejército del Pueblo) regularly come over the border for some rest and relaxation. Whether any IRA people had been there before us we could not, or did not want to, establish.

Perhaps not untypically of a frontier town, there was a big prostitution business in Lago Agrio along the oil road of Orellana, and one by all accounts that involved children and bonded sex-workers. As well as having huge numbers of oil workers, this is also a very heavily militarised area, and prostitution is part and parcel of both worlds. But what struck us most, apart from the usual garish colours and come-ons, was the superimposed image of Che Guevara on the brothels. How Che Guevara would have felt about it, or the broader way in which his image has been commodified, we can only surmise.

Texaco first began prospecting for oil here in 1964. In Lago Agrio the locals, namely the Cofán, vehemently opposed the drilling from the beginning, but to no avail. Powerless, they watched helplessly from the sidelines as their world was transformed. Unconcerned with local reaction, Texaco operated a five million acre concession (about a quarter the size of Ireland).

Texaco began drilling in 1972, but, as in all of these transnational multimillion investments, the who, why, where, when and what becomes somewhat clouded. At its simplest, the operational extraction developed as follows: In 1974, Petroecuador's predecessor company, CEPE, bought a 25 per cent share in the Texaco concession. In 1977, CEPE became a majority (62.5 per cent) financial partner. In 1989, Texaco transferred operational responsibilities for the TransEcuadorian pipeline (but not the wells, waste sites or stations) to a subsidiary of Petroecuador. In 1992, Texaco's contract in Ecuador expired. So Texaco operations in the country spanned twenty years from 1972 to 1992. In that time it extracted 1.5 billion barrels of oil, and during that period there emerged one of the most strongly contested international law suits in oil exploration history, one that centred on an allegation that Texaco, in order to save an estimated $3.00 per barrel, simply dumped the toxic waste from its operations into the pristine rivers, forest streams and wetlands, contrary to internationally-recognized industrial standards.

In those twenty years, the Cofán and other indigenous peoples claim that Texaco dumped eighteen billion gallons of oil-laden water, poisoned with mercury and cadmium, letting toxins seep into the soil, damaging crops, killing farm animals, and causing cancer among the population. Rather than pour the toxic waste back into well cavities, the standard operating procedure, it was dumped into hundreds of unlined pits, which then leeched into streams, rivers and marshes that feed the Amazon River. Environmentalists have called it the worst disaster since Chernobyl. It is difficult to overstate the scale of the destruction. What we saw was only a small fraction of it.

Still in his early twenties, the slightly built and highly eloquent Fidel Aquinda Mastracón, leader of the Cofán people of Lagro Agrio, vividly described the damage as we made our way out of the town to a well-known landmark that signaled the precise location of the equator. It was also the one of the most environmentally damaged sites in the area.

> When the oil companies came, like Texaco for example . . . many illnesses started in our communities . . . things we had never known. For example cancer. We Cofán did not know what cancer was. When the oil companies came, they took a huge part of our territory . . . we had to accept a new boundary to stay here as an indigenous group. The river 'Pisurie' runs through our land . . . and in the past the Cofán drank from it. Nowadays, we cannot drink from it, because it's contaminated. It is totally contaminated by the oil well . . . up at the headwater of the river. There is also a lot of air pollution now . . . from all the smoke. Another piece of environmental damage . . . is that animals come to the estuaries and rivers . . . and drink the contaminated water, and they die. The fish die too.

People in one of the most biologically diverse regions of the world were now reduced to eating canned tuna. Not only did the pollution kill the physical world, but according to Fidel it killed the spirit world.

> *Our ancestors have told us . . . that oil is the blood of the Cuancuan – Cuancuan are people who live under the ground. They are owners of the hunt, and owners of the animals. Our ancestors said, 'when there are Cuancuan the hunt is good'. We believe this, because since the oil companies came . . . the Cuancuan have been dying . . . and there is hardly any hunting left.*

Everywhere we looked, we could see the scarring of the landscape. Roadless rainforest had been transformed into highways. Huge pipelines lay above the traditional hunting ground of the Cofán. Smoke and balls of fire billowed into the air. Rivers and lakes shimmered in an unnatural kaleidoscope of rich, oil-slick colours. There were times it was hard to imagine that this place once held pristine forest. Sludge oozed up from the ground at every twist and turn. Our boots were caked in its black debris.

In 1993, a class action suit on behalf of an estimated 30,000 Amazon residents, now known as Los Afectados (the Affected Ones) was filed against Texaco (owned by Chevron since 2001) under the Alien Tort Claims Act in a federal court in New York, for polluting their environment.[15] For nine years, the case made its torturous route through the courts. Round one went to Chevron. In what many regard as an effort to get the story off the front pages of the international media, and because at the time Chevron felt that the government was sympathetic to their cause, they succeeded in having the US courts send the case to be heard in Ecuador.

When Texaco initially started prospecting for oil in Ecuador's pristine Amazonian forests in the early 1960s, a cabal of military officers controlled the country, their power base underpinned by the CIA. US interests were well protected by successive Ecuadorian governments until left-wing President Rafael Correa swept into power in 2007 on the back of the red tide that rolled across South America in the first decade of the twenty-first century. Now all had changed. Having fought long and hard to have the case heard in Ecuador, Chevron now felt it was battling not only a hostile government but a well-orchestrated international campaign as well.

Thinking it would get them out of the woods, and in a further effort to ease international pressure, Texaco paid $40 million in compensation to the Ecuadorian government in 1995. This did not go any distance in meeting the clean-up costs, and the clean-up that was done was partial and ham-fisted. It made little impact. Chevron was forced to defend themselves in the town's ramshackle courtroom. We could only film from the outside. Inside the air-conditioning only worked sporadically, we were told, and the electricity kept breaking down. Critically, though, these never stopped the story from getting out.

A slew of national and international studies support the assertions of the indigenous peoples, including ones from the Harvard School of Public Health and the London School of Hygiene and Tropical Medicine. In a 2004 article, 'Incidence of Childhood Leukemia and Oil Exploration in the Amazon Basin in Ecuador', Anna-Karin Hurtig and Miguel San Sebastián claimed that significantly elevated risks for all leukemias existed in the Lagio Agrio region.[16]

> *Crude oil is a complex mixture of many chemical compounds, mostly hydrocarbons. The petroleum hydrocarbons of most toxicologic interest are volatile organic compounds (benzene, xylene and toluene) and polynuclear aromatic hudrocarbons (PAH) Benzene is a well-known cause of leukemia and perhaps other hematologic neoplasms and disorders (p. 247).*

> *The relative risks for all leukemias indicated significantly elevated levels in the youngest age-group (0-4) for both genders and for (0-14) for females (p. 235).*

> *The reasons for higher incidence (for girls) are unclear. A possible explanation might be more exposure to contaminated water during daily activities (p. 247).*

An earlier article (2002), 'Outcomes of Pregnancy among Women Living in the Proximity of Oil Fields in the Amazon Basin of Ecuador',[17] found that pregnant women living in exposed communities were more likely to see their pregnancy end in spontaneous abortion.

> *The study revealed a risk of spontaneous abortion 2.34 times higher among women living in communities exposed to oil pollutants. No association was observed for still births (p. 316).*

As for Chevron, they relied on their political contacts to usurp the course of justice. In 2008, they sought to use the special trade preference for Ecuador as leverage to block the progress of the case. They lobbied the George W. Bush administration to put pressure on the Ecuadorian government to block the progress of the case under threat of having their trade status downgraded. It did not work.

Leading the defence for the indigenous cause was attorney Steven Donzinger, a basketball buddy of Barack Obama at Harvard Law School. Also lobbying for the indigenous people was Kerry Kennedy, President of the Robert F. Kennedy Centre for Justice and Human Rights. Kennedy has accused Chevron of cultural genocide. But Chevron was not without its fair share of high profile advocates. Republican stalwart and former Senate Majority Leader Trent Lott was backing Chevron as was Mack McLarty, Bill Clinton's former chief of staff, and Mickey Kantor, Clinton's former Secretary of Commerce. In December 2009, Chevron backers strongly lobbied Obama to drop Ecuador's preferential trade status as a punishment for allowing indigenous groups to sue them. Obama refused.

Caught in the middle as the courtroom pressure mounted and as the big stake players lined up for the final showdown was Judge Juan Núñez, an aficionado of Russian novelist Fyodor Dostoevsky and a recent convert to Islam in a country that is 95 per cent Catholic. After seventeen years of labyrinthine litigation, a decision in the decades-old dispute between the indigenous people of Northeastern Ecuador and the multi-billion dollar oil company Chevron was reached in February 2011. The 30,000 plaintiffs claimed $27.3 billion in damages. Judge Juan Núñez ruled that the oil giant Chevron pay more than $17 billion in fines – an initial $8.6 billion fine and an equal amount in punitive damages. It's the second-largest total assessed for environmental damages behind the $20 billion compensation fund for BP's Gulf Coast oil spill.

Chevron's determination runs deep and it has vowed to appeal, but it has also suggested it will not pay up under any circumstance, calling the ruling 'illegitimate and unenforceable'. Embarrassed by the outcome, some shareholders want to settle. Chevron spokesman Kent Robertson dismissed the shareholder pressure in an email, saying the company would fight the 'fraudulent' award, not settle it. In equally belligerent mood, a different company spokesman, Donald Campbell, outlined the oil giant's legal strategy in 2009: 'We're going to fight this until hell freezes over. And then we'll fight it out on the ice',[18] a phrase also attributed to CEO John Watson.

Both sides are to appeal, the plaintiffs because the damages are too low. It is expected that the saga will continue long into the future, but the first victory goes to the indigenous people of Ecuador. While this story will run and run it nonetheless represents a sweet victory for the indigenous people and their supporters. For one of the largest corporations in the world, it is an appalling vista, notwithstanding their swaggering defiance.

At the end of the day's shoot on the Equator we too had to make a run for it. At 18.10 darkness was falling and twenty minutes later there was just the smallest hints of daylight, the afterglow of the tropical sun. We were an hour and a half from Lago Agrio at this stage and just as we were about to leave the bus driver came clean: he told us we had no lights on the bus. We were facing into a journey through mud roads with no lights. Nothing. Our flight to Quito was booked for the following day. There was nothing for it but to go for it. After about half-an-hour Ken thought of his pag-light, part of his camera gear, and so the only light we had to guide us home was the equivalent of a bicycle light on our clapped-out bus. I took some consolation from the fact that our fixer, Alexandra Almeida, who was travelling with her eight-year-old daughter, was sound asleep. Clearly, she was not the least bit perturbed by this development. It was nonetheless one of the most seemingly endless journeys that we have ever undertaken, except perhaps for a journey we made in Peru.

But that's another story.

The United States

Carter Country

This was a complicated flight. Cork, Dublin, Shannon, Atlanta, Montgomery, back to Atlanta, Lima, Cusco, Tarapoto, back to Lima, Atlanta, New York, Dublin, Cork, and all in twenty days. Some explaining is needed. I travel to Dublin so that when we are putting our luggage through, we can spread the weight and keep our excess baggage down. Carrying television gear these days is an expensive undertaking. So every leg of the shoot has to be coordinated down to the smallest detail in advance. There is no flexibility. Nothing can be changed, so we need to know how long we will be in Lima, how much time we will need in Cusco, not to mention Tarapoto, and all of this long before leaving Ireland.

Days after having confirmed the flight we realised that we didn't need the Atlanta–Montgomery leg, but we had no choice. If we didn't take that leg the whole ticket was invalid. So the following day we left Montgomery early to drive back to Atlanta. There was a serious misunderstanding on my part. Just days before we left, I realised that the interview we had agreed with Ethel Ponder was to take place in Atlanta and not in Montgomery as I had thought. So we had to fly to Montgomery and drive back to Atlanta the following morning. This was an unnecessary road journey and in a packed schedule one that we could have done without.

The previous day we had driven for over four hours to Plains, Georgia where former US First Lady Rosalynn Carter lives. Plains is a quintessentially sleepy Southern town with a population of just over 600 people, the majority of whom are African-American. It is not so much a one-horse town as a one-president town because Jimmy Carter, the thirty-ninth president of the United States, was not only born there but is living out his very active retirement in his home town. The whole town is one big homage to a local boy made good. All the shops and the tourist trail are Carter-centered. We stayed in the seven-bedroom Plains Historic Inn, without doubt one of the most delightful hotels we have stayed in on all our travels. 'Jimmy and Rosalynn Carter have joined their hometown in developing a Historic Inn & Antiques Mall, on Main Street, Plains' their website proudly asserts. Well, they did a superb job.

We were to meet with Rosalynn the morning after our arrival in Plains and it did not take long to check out the town. There was one extremely wide street through which an old lumbering train rolls every day, and one typically Southern restaurant with enough food for all five of us on each individual plate. Only the banter exceeded the food for value. It was my first time in Southern USA and this was top class Southern hospitality down to the departing 'ye all boys come back soon again now, won't ye?' If we were fascinated with their Southern drawl our Irish accents held equal interest. Even the kitchen staff came out to hear us.

The following day it was down to business. We were to meet with Mrs. Carter in Miss Lillian's house, Jimmy's mother, an incorrigibly independent-minded woman who was never overwhelmed by her son's success. Neither was his wife. She never lost that independent streak. On the death penalty, Rosalynn was unequivocal. It was neither just nor effective. And this was at a time when George W. Bush was in the White House. During Bush's six-year tenure as Governor of Texas, he presided over 152 executions, more than any other governor in the recent history of the United States.[19] Thirty-three-year-old mentally retarded Terry Washington was one of the 152. He had the communication skills of a seven-year-old. Thirty-eight per cent of all executions since 1976 have taken place in Texas, although not all on George Bush's watch. In that context it was, I believe, brave of former First Lady Carter to openly declare her hand.

We weren't just interested in highlighting how blunt and unjust an instrument the death penalty was, but the way in which it targets racial minorities, the poor and people who are soft targets for the increasingly belligerent media and public who require quick fix convictions for a variety of crimes. But Carter went further. Not only did she highlight the racism that attaches itself to the death penalty but to the criminal justice system as a whole. 'Racism pervades the criminal justice system in our country,' she told us. 'The death penalty does not depend on the crime, it depends on the race, where they live and whether they have any money or not.'

To vent criticisms of the United States is to invite knee-jerk and predictable criticisms of being anti-American. Yet here was a former First Lady of the country, a woman who occasionally sat in on cabinet meetings, lambasting the US judicial system.

> *People think we are a beacon for human rights . . . we have been in the past but I don't think that is true anymore. In our country black people make up 20 per cent of the population, on Death Row they are 40 per cent. One-third killed are African Americans. Which seems to mean that we favour a white life more than the life of a black . . .*

But it wasn't just racial inequality that underpinned Rosalynn Carter's full-frontal criticisms of the US judicial system. She also believed that it radically disfavoured poor people as well. 'The inability of the poor,' she told us, 'to receive adequate legal representation has become a defining feature of America's death penalty.'

Her figures may not have been quite right but all the data support her broad assertion. The United States is a harsh society. More people are imprisoned in the United States and for longer periods than in any other democracy. The United States constitutes only five per cent of the world's population but it has twelve per cent of the world's prison population, estimated at nine million. According to US Department of Justice statistics, the country's prison population grew to 2,266,800 at the end of 2010.[20] One in every 104 people in the United States is in the custody of state or federal prisons or local jails. Astonishingly, one in every thirty-three people in the US is under the supervision by an adult correctional facility. Black men of all ages are incarcerated at more than seven times the rate of white men. One out of every three African-American men between the ages of 18 and 35 is in jail, on probation or on parole.

Prior to the interview we were told of all kinds of protocols and an obviously heavily armed woman kept a close watch on everything. But Rosalynn was utterly disarming and afterwards she invited us back to the house to meet Jimmy. We immediately stocked up on books that he had written ready for him to autograph. He entered the reception room with his trademark broad smile. Wearing only shorts and t-shirt and in bare feet, he told us he was preparing the proofs of his latest book, *Palestine: Peace Not Apartheid*,[21] which was subsequently to get him into some trouble with the Right in the States and elsewhere, and apologised for our short stay. As we were leaving he threw a bag of peanuts after us – the ultimate present from the peanut farmer turned President.

Racism, Lynching and the Death Penalty

If we were charmed by the Carters, we were bowled over by African American lawyer Bryan Stevenson. Stevenson is the Executive Director of the Equal Justice Initiative (EJI)[22] of Alabama and also a Professor of Law at the New York University School of Law. He is recognised as one of the top public interest lawyers in the US and his efforts to confront bias against the poor and people of colour in the criminal justice system have earned him dozens of accolades. EJI has been successful in overturning numerous capital murder cases and death sentences where poor, mainly black, people have been unconstitutionally convicted or sentenced.

Tall, strikingly good-looking, he remains one of the most eloquent, charming, intensely gifted people I have met on this journey. Clear, single-minded and deeply respectful of the people on whose behalf he works, he has dedicated his life to defending people on death row while campaigning for its ultimate abandonment.

William Schabas, formerly of the Irish Centre for Human Rights in NUI Galway, put me in contact with Bryan initially and described him as:

> . . . *one of the most iconic figures in the US campaign against capital punishment and one of the pre-eminent lawyers in the United States. He is also a fabulous role model for young human rights activists contemplating careers in the field. For some people, meeting Bryan Stevenson and hearing him speak will transform their lives.*

Seldom do people live up to such reputations but in this case Bryan did.

He spoke in perfect sentences and the rhythm and cadence of his speech was seductive. Listening to him I felt we should just let the camera roll and let people hear him unabridged. Yet he pulled no punches, and like Rosalynn Carter he too sees race and poverty as central to the way in which the death penalty is used against minority communities. His arguments defied rebuttal.

> *The death penalty, in my view, is the ultimate expression of hopelessness because what we're saying is that this person is beyond redemption. Their life has no meaning. Their life has no purpose. Their life has no value. And when societies become that hopeless about an individual, to get them to pay attention about their basic rights, whether they were tried fairly, whether they were actually tried properly, is very difficult.*

He claimed that most poor people, and most black people, particularly though not exclusively in the Deep South, do not get a fair hearing. He also firmly placed the death penalty in its historical context. The modern day death penalty has become state-sanctioned lynching.

Stevenson is not alone in this view. Franklin E. Zimring, in his book *The Contradictions of American Capital Punishment,*[23] which informed much of the film we made, concludes that 'the propensity to execute in the twenty-first century is a direct legacy of a history of lynching and of the vigilante tradition' (p. 89), which in turn is a direct consequence of the slave trade that resulted in:

> ... *the kidnapping of 50 million souls in Africa and their forced transportation across the Atlantic Ocean, 244 years of legalised slavery, 71 years of oppression and discrimination and for 51 years of those 71 years, one black person was lynched about every two and a half days (p. 16).*[24]

The term 'lynching' owes its origins to Charles Lynch, a Virginian planter (1736-1796) who presided over illegal executions during the revolutionary war period. Between 1882 and 1968, 4,743 people were lynched in the United States, and African Americans (74 per cent), followed by Native Americans, comprised the overwhelming majority of victims (p. 90). Most of these killings involved hanging, but shooting, beatings and stoning were also used in these extrajudicial executions.

Comparing historical incidences of lynching with current death penalty executions, Zimring found that 88 per cent of the extrajudicial lynching in the period 1889-1918 took place in the South, while 81 per cent of the judicial executions in the period 1997-2000 took place in the South. There were virtually no (0.3 per cent) lynching in the Northeast in the same period, and virtually no executions (0.05 per cent) in the 1976-2000 period (p. 95).

Eleven of the fourteen states with the lowest lynching histories have had no executions in the twenty-five years after 1976, while the fourteen states in the high lynching category together account for 85 per cent of the post-1976 executions. The evidence indicates not only that lynching history predicts current levels and patterns of executions, but that this history is heavily racially tinged. Reviewing the evidence, Zimring suggests that the lynch mob and the lethal injection are found in the same American neighbourhood (p. 118).

Since the reintroduction of the death penalty in 1976, 1,320 people have been executed in the United States and there are currently (January 2013) 3,170 people on death row. Of those ex-executed, twenty-two were under the age of eighteen, some as young as sixteen years of age. They were not the youngest to be executed in the United States. George Stinney was executed at the age of fourteen in the state of South Carolina in 1944. But in 2005, the United States Supreme Court declared the execution of juveniles unconstitutional in *Roper v. Simmons*. Writing for the majority, Justice Kennedy stated:[25]

> *When a juvenile offender commits a heinous crime, the State can exact forfeiture of some of the most basic liberties, but the State cannot extinguish his life and his potential to attain a mature understanding of his own humanity.*

Scott Allen Hain was the last person to be executed for a crime committed while he was a juvenile. He was executed in March 2003 at the age of thirty-two for a crime committed in Oklahoma at the age of seventeen. The previous year Toronto Patterson was executed at the age of twenty-seven for a crime committed in Texas when he was seventeen. Steven Roach was only twenty-three when he was executed in Virginia for a crime he committed when he was seventeen, and Sean Sellers was executed in Oklahoma at the age of twenty-nine for a crime he committed when he was only sixteen.

Bryan Stevenson has a ready array of grim statistics, which he draws on when he speaks in various public fora. At the United Nations in May 2008,[26] he itemised the harshness of the US criminal justice system and the manner in which it discriminated against people of colour.

> *Our prison population has grown from 300,000 in the early 1970s to over 2.3 million people behind bars today. One out of every 100 adults is imprisoned. Nearly six million people's lives are constrained because they are on probation or parole. One-third of black males born today will spend at least some part of their lives behind bars. Almost one out of three black males in their twenties are currently in jail, prison or parole or otherwise under criminal justice control. The annual arrest rate among African Americans is more than two-and-a-half times the white rate. Fourteen states permanently bar voting rights for some or all*

ex-felony offenders unless they are pardoned. In Alabama thirty-one per cent of the black male population has lost the right to vote as a result of criminal justice system dis-enfranchisement. For too many poor citizens and people of colour, arrest and imprisonment have become an in-evitable and seemingly unavoidable part of the American experience.

While other states have dramatically slowed their rates of death sentencing and executions in recent years as evidence about unreliable imposition of the death penalty has grown, Alabama's death sentencing rate remains the highest in the nation. Furthermore, Alabama is the only state in the US without a state-funded programme to provide legal assistance to death row prisoners. There is no state-wide public defender programme and, according to Bryan Stevenson, half of the 200 people on Alabama's death row were represented at trial by appointed lawyers whose compensation for out-of-court preparation was capped at $1,000.

Those with mental health problems are not spared. While in *Atkins v. Virginia*[27] the United States Supreme Court ruled that executing the mentally retarded violated the constitution, the Supreme Court also ruled on 8 January 2013, in *Ryan v. Gonzales,*[28] that a federal court review in death penalty cases should go forward even when the death row prisoner is mentally incompetent to understand the proceedings and assist his lawyer. While *Atkins v. Virginia* is binding on all states, the procedures and standards that define mental retardation are left to each state and vary widely. Alabama has not enacted any statute to implement the Atkins decision. Stevenson and his colleagues have had some success in shielding some death row prisoners with mental retardation. However, some people with mental retardation have been deemed not entitled to relief based on the judge and the kind of advocacy that had been made. Nor has the state of Alabama passed any law expressly banning the death penalty for juveniles, but since age is simple to prove all juveniles have been removed from death row there.

Racism runs deep in Alabama. It is the heart of the American South. The Confederacy was formed in Alabama in 1860, joined by South Carolina, Mississippi, Florida, Georgia, Louisiana and Texas. They decided to cede from the United States, mainly because the government failed to enforce the Fugitive Slave Laws and allow slavery to continue in these territories. To this day Montgomery, Alabama's capital city, proudly advertises itself as the first capital of the Confederacy. It was here that George Wallace wrapped himself in the Confederate flag and famously said on his inauguration as Governor of Alabama in 1963:

> . . . *from this cradle of the Confederacy, this very heart of the great Anglo-Saxon Southland . . . I draw the line in the dust and toss the gauntlet before the feet of tyranny . . . and I say . . . segregation today, segregation tomorrow, segregation forever.*[29]

The Confederate flag is still hoisted by many white Alabamans in defiance of the expressed wishes of the African-American community there. For the many white people who continue to embrace it, the Confederate flag remains a potent and cherished symbol of white supremacy, of deep-seated hostility to black people and a consciously proud and obdurate resistance to the rights not only of African-Americans but of Native Americans as well. It's a very public and deliberate reminder to African-American people of white hegemony, of the days of their utter subjugation – of horrific violence, lynchings, slavery and the whole edifice of apartheid that existed up to fifty years ago, as well as the social, economic and legal hold that many white people continue to exert over the African-American community. As a symbol of subordination of black people, and as a reminder of the precarious world in which they live, the Confederate flag retains its power to threaten and insult.

Flying the Confederate flag is a particularly noxious symbol of injustice. Every day black people are confronted with the legacy of slavery. The State's constitution still prohibits black and white children from going to school together, and an attempt in 2012 to change that constitutional provision failed. Not surprisingly, the professional classes in Alabama are nearly bereft of black people. In a state where twenty-eight per cent of the population is black, only 5.7 per cent of all attorneys are African-American.[30] Less than one per cent of all lawyers in the State are African-American and less than two-tenths of one per cent of all doctors are African-American. As the great civil rights leader Martin Luther King once said, 'Injustice anywhere is a threat to justice everywhere.'

It is in the area of criminal law, however, that African-Americans are most confronted with racism's insidious hand, and none more so than James Bo Cochran, Walter McMillian and Robert Lee Tarver.

James Bo Cochran and Walter McMillian

James Bo Cochran was convicted in 1982 of the murder of Stephen Ganey, an assistant manager of a grocery store. The State's case against Cochrane rested entirely on a money band found in his jacket pocket. Mr. Cochran was tried three times, each time in front of a jury that comprised of eleven whites and one African-American. Convicted and given the death penalty, he was subsequently exonerated in 2003.

On 7 June 1987, at the age of forty-four, Walter McMillian was stopped by the County Sheriff just outside Monroeville. Monroeville is the hometown of Nellie Harper Lee, acclaimed author of *To Kill a Mocking Bird*.[31] Pulitzer Prize winner (1961) Harper Lee was inspired to write *Mockingbird* by the 1930s trial of nine black men accused of raping two white women in Alabama. In Harper Lee's book, white lawyer Atticus Finch struggles to defend Tom Robinson, an innocent black man wrongly accused of raping a white woman. However, in celebrating the heroics of Finch, Tom Robinson's life is seldom brought into focus, and that too is the experience of real-life black people who are similarly accused.

Like the fictitious Tom Robinson, Mr. McMillian was also innocent but it was his affair with a white woman that found him at the centre of a capital trial. Walter McMillian's trial lasted just two days; jury selection was completed in hours. In a county with a forty per cent black population, only one African-American served on the jury. Found guilty, he was put on death row. In March 1993, after six years on death row, the state finally acknowledged Walter McMillian's innocence. The supreme irony is that while the fictional character Tom Robinson is celebrated, Mr. McMillian remains somewhat of a pariah and, not surprisingly, is bitter about his fate. He feels that while he has been fully exonerated many in the area do not accept the judgement. The trial and his subsequent jailing destroyed his family life. As he sat in his trailer park he told us his story. He still seems utterly perplexed that an innocent man could be taken off the street and put on death row. The indignation still rings high.

> *I was comin' up the road. They just blocked the whole highway, blocked the whole highway. They told me to get out so-an-so this and so-an-so that. All that ole cussin'. 'We'll knock your God-damn head off'. 'Nigger, Nigger, Nigger' was all they was sayin. He never would tell me what I have done. Pick me up. Put me in prison. And put me on death row for six years.*

> *They ain't nothin' you can do. Bring 'em in. Out to that chair. Put 'em in it. Take the juice to 'em.*

> *I don't see how the system can be that rotten. Take a man off the street. Put him on death row. And you have no evidence. No kind of evidence.*

Mr. McMillian was convicted in spite of the fact that there was no physical evidence against him. More than a dozen family members and friends testified that at the time of the murder he was helping his sister run a fish fry to raise money for their church. Walter was convicted on the perjured testimony of three witnesses. Even more shocking, Walter McMillian has one other distinction. He was the only person in US judicial history to be put on death row even before his trial began. Walter McMillian and James Cochran were two of the 'lucky' ones, however. They were exonerated and eventually freed. Not so Robert Lee Tarver.

Robert Tarver

Robert Tarver was born in 1950 in Alabama. His family were devout, church-going sharecroppers who worked in the cotton fields of Bullock and Pike counties where they picked cotton by hand in the fields of white landowners. Their payment was based on the total weight of cotton picked during the harvest season. The rate in Alabama in the 1950s was $3.00/100 lbs. This was quintessential segregated territory. White supremacy ruled over black subservence.

Ethel Ponder grew up with Robert. Ethel was Robert's aunt. They were the same age and she took us through the daily reality of life for black people in apartheid USA.

One of the awful things about growing up in such hateful conditions is that you learn to accept it: the white people of places like Bullock and Pike Counties did not feel that their black neighbors belonged in their world. As a young girl, I learned to fear violence from whites, we lived our lives in fear, fear of white people, fear of violence, fear of being raped, fear of being burned out of our homes. I re-member the terror we all felt when we got word of Emmett Till's lynching. To avoid anything like that we learned to behave respectfully to white people regardless of how they treated us: to drop our eyes . . . the reality is we lived in a constant battlefield. There were no protection from the law. In actual fact the policemen were probably the ones that was out there terrorizing the blacks.

There were no mingling – we had separate schools and our school was probably more like a two room shack. As I recall, they had a brick school but that was something that you were taught. You were taught not to talk back. You stayed within that perimeter at all times because what was given to us was the bad bit that your life can be taken. You didn't look . . . men were taught, 'You did not look at a white lady'. Period. Because many had lost their lives just from doing that. When you're a child you're curious about things. I remember asking my mom, 'Well, why do they hate us so much? What did we do?' and she didn't really have an ex-

planation. I don't think any of them did but that was how
we operated, that's how we spent our childhood. Robert, me
and all the other black kids. That's what life felt like for us
African-American children in the 1950s and 1960s.

Adult life brought its own challenges for black adults in the American South, but nothing could have prepared Robert or his family for the fall-out from the shooting of white store owner Hugh Kite in Russell County in 1984. Robert was charged with Mr. Kite's murder and on 11 January 1985 he was convicted of capital murder. The jury of eleven white and one black person returned a verdict of life imprisonment without parole. However, the trial judge overrode the jury's verdict and imposed the death penalty. Trial judges are elected by the public in the United States and, particularly coming up to re-election, there is enormous pressure to be seen to be tough on crime.

In a county that has a forty per cent black population, the state used thirteen out of sixteen peremptory strikes (the right to challenge a juror without being required to assign a reason for the challenge) to exclude qualified black people from the jury during Mr. Tarver's trial. Furthermore, the court was not told of any aspect of Mr. Tarver's reputation for hard work or any other details of his character. None of the core constitutional concerns relating to the Eight and Fourteenth Amendments that a sentence of death be imposed only after complete and full consideration of the circumstances of the offender, his character and his background were satisfied at Mr. Tarver's hearing.

The case went to the US Supreme Court. Bryan Stevenson was now Mr. Tarver's attorney. On 3 February 2000, the Court granted a stay of execution. During that hearing Assistant District Attorney for the prosecution Mark Carter admitted that 'it was our belief at the time that black people would not be favourable to the State as white jurors and consequently we excluded black prospective jurors with peremptory strikes'.[32] Alabama state law specifically prohibits discrimination in the selection of jurors.

It was, it would appear, a clear-cut case, but the process was flawed. Robert Tarver should have been exonerated, but that wasn't how it panned out. Mr. Tarver was executed in April 2000, even after the prosecutor admitted to racially biased jury selection. Bryan Stevenson believes that this was an illegal execution.

Robert Tarver asserted his innocence to the very end. Standing by his grave gave us a real sense of a life prematurely and unnecessarily ended. And there was little dignity about the way in which it ended. Her face still etched in pain, Ethel Ponder took us through his harrowing final hours.

> *I remember it was raining: it was raining cats and dogs. Once they took him off, they told us to get out. They didn't tell us what was gonna happen or afterwards what to expect – where to get the remains. Nothin'. They literally threw us out in the rain.*

But, as Ethel told us, at the very end Robert Tarver remained remarkably dignified.

> *Right before they took him away, he was smiling. He gave me a big hug, gave everyone a big hug and he says, 'this will not be the last time you'll see me. I'll be with ye all. I'll be with ye all, all the time'.*

May he rest in peace.

Peru

Navigating the War on Drugs

The music in the late-night café in Tarapoto was deafening when we first met with Nancy Obregón, illegal coca farmer, then newly elected member of the Peruvian parliament and President of a local growers' association. With a population of 56,000 people and located in the high Amazonian jungle of north-eastern Peru, Tarapoto has been the centre of drug-related conflict and civil strife for many years. It was ten o'clock at night and we were just off a flight from Cusco, the ancient seat of the Inca Empire. Shouted conversations centred on the next day's filming. We were to meet with illegal coca growers – Nancy Obregón's constituents – seventy per cent of whom live below the poverty line and whose circumstances are made worse by forced coca eradication.

But first we had to secure transport. Our scheduled Land Rovers had not materialised. It was difficult to understand why and the noise wasn't helping, nor were the three languages we were trying to bridge. What? No cars? It was now midnight and we were to leave at seven o'clock the next morning. It was my job to have that in place and I hadn't delivered. I couldn't leave the meeting so without complaint or a word of rancour, Gerry Nelson agreed to go in search of transport with a local from the café. Two hours later, he returned with three beat-up Toyota cars of indeterminate models. It was some achievement and I've never fully established how he managed to do it. Nor can I remember why we did not decide to move to a different café. Perhaps we were just too weary to do so.

By seven o'clock the following morning we were on the road. The Andean valley of Tarapoto, known locally as the land of waterfalls, quickly gives way to towering mountains that spectacularly rise to about 8,000 feet above sea-level. It is a breathtakingly beautiful place.

Seven and a half hours later, having forded four rivers and negotiated one of the most rutted, cratered roads I had, up to then, ever travelled, we arrived to a warm welcome in Nancy's village in the Alto Huallaga region. The journey wasn't meant to be like this – a four-hour journey maximum, stretched to five and then six. Then we were told it was just around the corner, but it took another hour to round that corner, and then it was just around another corner. We were in an altogether different time zone.

Gerry Nelson stopped asking me how much longer. I felt I was avoiding eye contact with him. What could I do? But without this part of the story we had no story. As it was, we only had twenty-four hours to parachute in and grab it, and now those hours were ever so slowly slipping away. As we headed up and up we felt the air getting thinner, the oxygen sucked out of our bodies. Fatigue had set in a long time ago and was made worse by the numbness of our backsides and the stickiness of too close physical contact. Whatever discomfort we experienced on the way, though, paled in comparison with the stories we were about to hear, which included threats, death squads, forced crop destruction, community upheaval and strife. This is how it all started.

The Coca Leaf

For thousands of years, pre-Incas, pre-Columbus, pre-Christianity, the coca leaf has been an integral part of the lives of the people of Peru. Rich in vitamins and nutrients, the plant's natural stimulant properties ward off fatigue and hunger, enhance endurance and give a sense of general well-being. Coca cultivation is well-suited to high altitude and a range of soil and climatic conditions. More than any other crop, it will thrive in a poor environment. Coca is also a high-yield crop, thereby suiting small or transitory landholders. Furthermore, it is rarely mono-cropped as it is produced in parallel with local food crops.

In Andean-Amazonian communities in South America, the coca leaf is considered sacred, venerated as a gift from the gods. As well as having several medical applications, it fulfils important social and spiritual functions, functions that have been recognised by such disparate world leaders as Fidel Castro, Queen Sofia of Spain and Pope John Paul II. All publicly drank coca-leaf tea, *mate de coca,* a herbal drink that can help breathing at high altitudes, on visits to South America.

For the western world, and in particular the United States, the leaf is perceived as a scourge because when chemically processed it produces cocaine, and this reality over-shadows the leaf's cultural roots, resulting in its demonisation and forced eradication.

In the mountains above the town of Quillabamba 800 miles away from Nancy's village in the Alto Huallaga region, Pien Metaal, an astute analyst of the global drug trade, without whose presence on the crew it would not have been possible to gain the confidence of the coca producing communities, introduced us to Julia Cahuana, one of Peru's legal coca growers, who chewed constantly – it's actually a misnomer to describe it as chewing although that is the term that is used, it is more of a sucking action. A 1950 United Nations report[33] of which Pien Metaal, as outlined below, is hugely critical, clarifies the act of chewing.

> The expression of chewing is not quite accurate. The Indian does not chew coca. The leaves are placed in the mouth between the inner side of the cheek and the gum of the same side until they form a bolus or quid, which varies in size. In most cases, the bolus forms a more or less noticeable protuberance on the side of the face. In Peru the Quechan expression chacchar and picchar are preferred.

Julia Cahuana explained to us the leaf's economic and cultural importance. As she did the protuberance was very evident on one cheek of her face.

> We live from this coca. No other plant can grow on these dry hillsides. Coca for us means paying honour to the sa-

cred mother earth. Coca is very beneficial as a medicine, chewing it at altitude where it is very cold. It warms our bodies. It's a sacred leaf.

Nancy Obregón also talked to us about the leaf's spiritual quality.

Coca is very important for us socially, culturally and economically because our ancestors left it to us as a heritage. We enjoy the old tradition of chewing coca. It's like a confraternity, a mystical thing, you can't explain. It's like a spiritual gathering with our ancestors. It also supports the social structure in the Amazon and the Andes that would otherwise disappear.

The War on Drugs

The war on drugs was the brainchild of Richard Nixon who was concerned about the impact drug use was having on soldiers serving in Vietnam, and not with the ghettoes of Washington or New York. He warned Congress on 17 July 1971 that drug addiction had 'assumed the dimensions of a national emergency' and that illegal drugs were 'public enemy number one'.[34]

What Nixon started, other US presidents embraced with enthusiasm. Ford, Reagan, Clinton and the two Bushes all bought into a militaristic response to the global drug trade.[35] The Obama administration continues to hold the line. No real change there. While activists across the world are calling for a response based on human rights and for the protection of the health needs of people in producing and consuming countries, that call has not resonated with US authorities. Perhaps Clinton more than others.

Plan Colombia was Clinton's, and then Colombian President Andreas Pastrana's, great panacea. The cocaine trade was to be cut off by destroying all coca plants. (The political context of Plan Colombia and the war on drugs is discussed in much greater detail in *The Politics of Drugs: From Production to Consumption*.[36]) Despite the cost, despite the terrible disruption and the brutalising effect it had on indigenous people in particular, it was a dismal failure. A 2005 report, *Plan Colombia: A Progress Report* authored by Connie Veilette,[37] concluded that 'despite increased eradication of drug crops and interdiction . . . the availability, price and purity of cocaine and heroin in the United States have remained stable' (p. 3). Overall, an estimated $7.5 billion[38] was spent on what many regard as an inefficient, ineffective and wholly inappropriate plan. Not only did it fail to dent the production of the coca leaf, but estimates suggest that coca cultivation increased by fifteen per cent during that period.

What failed in Colombia was replicated in Peru. Former President Alan Garcia, one of the few pro-US Presidents left standing in the aftermath of the so-called red tide that flowed over South America in the first decade of the new millennium, until his replacement by the left-leaning Ollanta Humala in July 2011, endorsed forced eradication with enthusiasm. As a result, the illegal coca growers of Peru were under enormous pressure. These were the people – friends and neighbours of Nancy Obregón, peasant leader and illegal coca grower – that we travelled deep into the mountainous jungle to meet.

It was not just the United States that adopted a hard line attitude, but the United Nations did as well, in a policy that predated Nixon's war on drugs. The 1950 United Nations Economic and Social Council (ECOSOC) study that, according to Pien Metaal, 'would never survive the scrutiny of modern day science and was flawed with ill-conceived and even blatant racist perceptions,' forms the basis of the coca leaf's persecution and the US war on drugs.

In 1961, the United Nations[39] agreed the Single Convention on Narcotic Drugs, which replaced all previous treaties on drug control and outlined very clearly how it perceived the threat from illicit drugs:

> . . . *recognizing that addiction to narcotic drugs constitutes a serious evil for the individual and is fraught with social and economic danger to mankind.*

It sought the eradication of the cultivation, production, manufacture, export, import, trade, use and possession of illicit drugs with special attention to the plant-based drugs of opium and the coca leaf. Article 26.2 states:

> The Parties shall so far as possible enforce the uprooting of all coca bushes which grow wild. They shall destroy the coca bushes if illegally cultivated.

The UN even set a deadline of twenty-five years for eliminating the habit of coca production. Clearly, this deadline was never reached. The highly respected Amsterdam-based research organisation, the Transnational Institute, for which Pien works, has been consistently critical of the 1961 and subsequent conventions.[40]

> The 1961 Convention was a landmark in the history of the campaign against narcotic drugs (that imposed) a fully-fledged prohibition regime for some psychoactive substances of natural origin. The Convention provided the international law basis for the 'war on drugs' that developed later against drug-related crops and farmers (p. 16).

> The Convention also forced many so-called developing countries to abolish all 'non-medical and scientific' uses of the three plants that for many centuries had been embedded in social, cultural and religious traditions (p. 17).

Two further agreements – the 1988 UN Trafficking Convention and the 1998 UN General Assembly Special Session (UN-GASS) – resulted in a commitment to plough ahead with the war on drugs. Article 19 of the UNGASS agreement, for example, called for 'eliminating or significantly reducing the illicit cultivation of the coca bush, the cannabis plant and the opium poppy by 2008'.[41] The same policies with the same failed outcome. Securing the elimination of the coca bush was never going to happen and it did not happen.

Even the British House of Commons Home Affairs Select Committee, an unlikely ally of producing countries, concluded:

> *. . . if there is any single lesson from the experience of the last thirty years, it is that policies based wholly or mainly on enforcement are destined to fail (Section 268).*[42]

The scale of that failure and the asymmetrical benefits from this illegal trade were brought to our attention by global drug policy analyst Ricardo Soberon whom we met while filming.

> *Drug trafficking moves around $300 billion a year. Most of the money remains in the northern part of the world. Less than one per cent of that money stays in the Andean region where most of the coca leaf is produced. Those who are trying to eradicate coca in order to defend world health, they are confusing the target. The coca leaf is part of life, is part of culture. What we find is a terrible contradiction between treaties, policies and people.*

None of this will be tackled, Soberon claimed, until the issue of poverty is tackled. Poverty, he maintained, is the driving force of production. Over two million people are forced into this business because they simply have no other option.

Defiance

With two hours' daylight remaining, we started filming our first illegal grower. We didn't have time to eat. It was three o'clock in the afternoon and we hadn't shot a single frame all day. Crew anxiety levels were rising by the minute. This was pressure.

Feliciana's crop had just been eradicated. Specially trained and well-armed guards were flown in by helicopter and they didn't ask any questions. They just dug up and then cut everything in sight. A whole harvest that was to provide for the most basic needs of these peasant farmers was just dug up and cast aside. Bereft and angry, all the *cocaleros* could do was look on. Today's eradication means no food tomorrow. By then the helicoptered eradicators will have moved elsewhere. Feliciana lives with her husband and five children in very poor circumstances in a highly inaccessible part of the jungle. Yet the eradicators found her. Clearly distressed, and with her newly born baby at her breast, she told us what happened.

> *I heard the helicopters. Then in a few minutes, they were here. They told me that they were sent by the state. 'The government sent us to pull out the coca,' they told me. We told them that we have no money, that we have nothing else to plant. I begged them but they had nothing to say.*

Everywhere we looked we could see the result of their handiwork. Dry, shriveled coca plants with their roots turned to the sun. The family had tried to pick some leaves from what remained, but this would not yield any serious income. They had nothing and the future looked more than bleak for them. Others would tell us similar stories.

Feliciana was more helpless than angry. Her children very visibly hungry and undernourished, her spirits deadened.

But it was defiance that greeted us on arrival at Nancy's village in the jungle valley of the Huallaga River where we met with illegal coca growers. Defiance and palpable anger at the destruction of their coca crop and the threat to their very existence. With no legitimate market, these farmers must sell to drug traffickers to make a living; in turn, this becomes the cocaine that is sold on the streets of cities like New York, Cape Town and Dublin. There was no doubting their absolute determination to continue with coca production. We were invited to a public meeting of about fifty *campesinos* who trenchantly defended their right to produce the coca leaf as they have done for centuries beforehand with no adverse effects, something even the World Health Organization acknowledges. Nancy Obregón was passionate in her defense of the centuries-old Andean way of life, blaming white people for corrupting their coca leaf, extracting its malign spirit and using it as a key ingredient in the manufacture of cocaine.

> *When the white man came to Peru and transformed the coca leaf, bringing harm to humanity. We indigenous are not to blame.*

*I tell you comrades we will never bow again. They eradi-
cate us today, tomorrow we sow. Enough! We are looking
for seeds to go back and sow. I am a farmer. I was born a
peasant. I tell you, we peasants have power. And we will
have more power!*

Her rallying cry to protect the coca leaf against forced eradication was taken up by others, among them illegal coca grower
Genaro Flores whose crop was eradicated shortly before our arrival.

*They left nothing, not one plant. This was to maintain my
children. We farmers are ill-treated and abused. We are
accused of being drug traffickers and terrorists and we are
none of these. The US is the principal consumer of drugs.
Why don't they eliminate their consumers instead of our
coca leaf?*

*If they continue to eradicate our coca, our lives will be
completely different. Our biodiversity will be completely
destroyed and we will be condemned to a slow death. Effectively it will make the indigenous peasantry disappear. The
State is trampling the constitution for foreign interests.
All joined together, we can beat this injustice.*

Another man said what was happening to them was humili-
ating, claiming that they have been abandoned and attacked by
their own government who view them as terrorists. Another man
pointed to where he had been shot in the head and where a piece
of his skull is missing.

Concluding the meeting, Nancy Obregón declared:

*We have heroes and martyrs now, but we have to continue
to resist. We will not leave our villages. This is our land.
The bloody government knows we are rebels and we will
continue to rebel.*

'We will sow again, Yes or No?' Nancy asked her late night
audience. 'Yes' they all cheered as they drifted into the night.

A Way Out

It was virtually impossible to be untouched by the raw emotion of the night. It had been an incredibly long, arduous day and it was eleven o'clock that night when we sat down for dinner. We were out of power. Our batteries had run dry. Eleven o'clock and we hadn't eaten or checked into our hotel. We poured beer and rice-chicken into ourselves and as we are wont to do on occasions bought a packet of cigarettes for after dinner relaxation. We needed all the fortification we could get because we hadn't yet seen the hotel. Perhaps hovel would be a better description.

An immaculately nail-polished young woman in the less than prepossessing reception area decorated with erotic images of male models meticulously recorded all our passport details. The contrast between her striking appearance and the squalor of her surroundings couldn't be more pronounced. Such was the level of detail she recorded that we jokingly wondered what her next question would be given her preference in office décor. And then she brought us to the rooms. The filth. Cockroaches everywhere. Apparently, tropical cockroaches can be up to nine centimeters in length but we didn't stop to measure them. One toilet that was overflowing with what we didn't wait to find out. Rooms with no natural light. As for the beds, and the well-slept sheets, we didn't dare peer too close.

The drivers had made a bolt for it. They were fast asleep in their locked cars and couldn't or wouldn't be woken. So we stripped the beds and used whatever we would subsequently wash at first opportunity to sleep on. Then the chorus started. Outside our rooms were crates of cockerels and hens stacked one on top of the other. Crate upon crate. At the first glimmer of light, the dawn if not the pre-dawn chorus started and they continued as they started. This was a different cacophony from the late night restaurant of the previous evening. Sometimes situations like this are funny. This was not one of those times.

Emotional and physical journeys have that effect. The following day we were to leave at midday but the power of the testimony of one of the previous evening's *campesinos* had us up at six o'clock the following morning. We could grab five hours of his time and witness the devastation of the coca eradication he had experienced. Without breakfast, we were all were running on empty.

I went in search of food. I found a local café not yet fully open and wheedled my way in. I asked for chicken and bread and as soon as it was ready I was in the kitchen with them hurriedly buttering bread, making sandwiches with whatever fillings I could find. Perplexed and bemused might have been the café owner's reaction to the early and unexpected appearance of this Gringo in his kitchen.

We had to be gone by eleven at the latest if we were to get the plane from Tarapoto before a flight to Lima, but before that we had that seven-hour journey ahead of us. This time we knew what to expect. Expectation did not make it any easier. The storm clouds were gathering and we worried about rising river levels, but we knew that eventually we would weather the storm. We were certain in the knowledge that for us there was a way out. For the *campesinos* we were leaving behind, life was not so certain.

Bolivia

From Grainy Images

For the *campesinos* of Bolivia, however, life has become more certain since the dramatic election of Evo Morales in January 2006, the first indigenous president in the country's 470-year history. In a country and on a continent where an extermination of genocidal proportions was perpetrated against the indigenous people, Morales' victory was as symbolically important in Bolivia as was the election of Nelson Mandela in South Africa. The ill-treatment of indigenous people of Latin America was as profound as was the ill-treatment of black African people in South Africa, yet it never quite caught the imagination of Northern Europeans to the same extent that the South African apartheid system did. There were, of course, some notable exceptions, and as a teenager I was the beneficiary of one of those exceptions.

My experience of Leaving Certificate Geography in the mid-1970s bucked the disinterested trend and gave me my first glimpse into the darkly oppressive world of South American mining. Even in that pre-visual age, barely discernible photocopied images from an old *Gestetner* of ant-like tin and silver miners swarming all over places like the Cerro Rico in Potosí made a striking impact. Those of us who sat in Father Pat Malone's classroom were swept up, however momentarily, in his passion for South America and with a curiosity about the revolutionary figure of Simón Bolívar. This very mainstream Catholic cleric, while gasping for breath from his lifelong addiction to cigarettes, planted a seed. That seed led us underground in the mines of Potosí in Bolivia. Perched at 13,000 feet above sea level, Potosí is the highest city in the world. In a curious twist of fate, while there we too found ourselves gasping for breath. But ours was altitude, not cigarette, related. Had he been with us, it surely would have tested Father Malone's strained lungs.

Our first stop was the rebel city of Cochabamba, Bolivia's third largest city and the centre of the country's 'water war' that thrust the city and the country onto the international spotlight as a disparate coalition of grassroots organisations won the battle to de-privatise the local water company. Five years prior to Morales's election as President of Bolivia in 2000, the World Bank threatened to withhold badly needed loans if the government did not agree to privatise public services. In a textbook case of how international conglomerates swoop on critical utilities in the Third World, a consortium led by London-based International Water Limited (IWL), which is jointly owned by the Italian utility Edison and US-based Bechtel Enterprises Holdings, purchased the city's water utility for $200 million. The consortium immediately raised consumers' rates by up to 35 per cent. The government may have capitulated to World Bank demands, but not the people of Cochabamba. They had other ideas.

That price hike sparked six months of street protests led by the Coalition in Defense of Water and Life, a broad-based organisation including environmental groups, economists, lawyers, labor unions and local neighborhood organisations. Confronted by the anger of its citizens, the State did what states invariably do in such circumstances: they declared a state of emergency. And that's exactly what former dictator and then President Hugo Benzer did. Pitched battles broke out between the police and the protestors. On 4 February 2000, two protesting youths were blinded by police fire. Then, on 8 April, seventeen year-old Victor Hugo Daza was shot thorough the face and killed. Protest leader Oscar Olivera remarked in the aftermath of his death, 'The blood spilled in Cochabamba carries the fingerprints of Bechtel'.[43]

Eventually the government caved in. The law to privatise water was rescinded and to this day water remains a public utility. Their success was hailed as a major triumph by street activists throughout the world. This indeed was a rare victory, the will of the people in a city of one of the poorest countries in Latin America winning out over the demands of office-based bureaucrats in one of the most powerful international financial institutions in the world and one of the United States largest engineering firms.

The people of Cochabamba did not fully solve their water problems as the city struggled to provide water to many of the city's residents, but they and other social movement activists learned invaluable lessons in how to challenge not just their own state but powerful external institutions. The chief lesson was that sometimes the poor win, and sometimes what appear to be unassailable citadels can be successfully challenged.

Scholar, writer and activist Linda Farthing was 'our woman in Bolivia'. Her husband Benjamin Kohl also shares her passions and research interests. In *Impasse in Bolivia: Neoliberal Hegemony and Popular Resistance,*[44] they describe the aftermath of the water war.

> *This success heralded a turning point and had an enormous psychological impact on grassroots and popular organizations in Bolivia. It gave resistance movements the voice they had lost after fifteen years of continuous, unsuccessful opposition. Bolivia's status as a poster child of neoliberalism for the World Bank and the International Monetary Fund (IMF), which had widely touted and copied its policies in other low-income countries around the world, had ended (p. 167).*

These resistance movements helped to catapult Evo Morales into the presidential office. We had hoped to meet him but first had to gain entry into the country. Prior to our arrival in Bolivia, Morales had gotten himself into a spat with the US government about visas and entry requirements for US citizens coming into the country. For decades, the United States government had put all kinds of restrictions in place on the people of Bolivia and other Latin American countries entering the United States. In contrast, entry to Bolivia for United States citizens was relatively easy. So Morales thought what is good for the Latino goose is good for the Yankee gander. The days of easy access for citizens of the United States were over, and so it would appear for other Gringos as well, ourselves included.

Securing visas and permits for filming in countries is an ex-
hausting and patience-sapping task, and one that routinely falls
to my colleague Mick Molloy. The journalist Robert Fisk often
writes about his utter exasperation with custom and emigration
officials, so we were in good company. We had secured every con-
ceivable document for entry to Bolivia. Mick had even taken the
precaution of flying to London to meet with embassy officials
to ensure that everything was in order. But between the time we
secured the documentation and our arrival in the country, the
regulations had changed. The official in Cochabamba was un-
sympathetic. We didn't have the required papers so we wouldn't
be allowed into the country. '*¡No pasarán!*' Four hours we spent
squatting in the official's office – Mick Cassidy, Ruth Meehan,
Philip Graham and myself.

The airport police were called. Senior immigration officials
were summoned. We refused to leave adopting our own policy
of '*¡No pasarán!*' Stalemate. Radios crackled. Officials came and
went. We remained rooted to the floor of the small, sparsely furnished office close to the cooling whirring fan. Philip Graham's
quiet, understated ways have a steadying effect in these situations. We told them we had an interview with the President.
Even though it wasn't confirmed, we thought that might swing
it for us. It didn't. The same positions were endlessly repeated.
'We have the correct documents,' we asserted. 'No you don't,' was
their summary reply.

Eventually, they relented, and with surprisingly good grace.
They were adamant at all times in the position they adopted but
were always respectful. There was never any question that money
should change hands, not that we offered, and in fairness to the
officials, it was never intimated to us that greasing the point of
entry was an option. We may not have appreciated it at the time,
but I believe that this was an honourable official doing his job to
the letter of the law. There was, however, a fundamental irony
in our being holed up at Bolivia's borders on a trip that began in
Argentina. Simón Bolívar had envisaged a unified and integrated
single territory of Latin America. No borders. No passports. It
was not to be. Fragmented and broken by the colonial system,

Latin America, like Africa, emerged as a series of disconnected and competing countries. With the emergence of the new generation of left-leaning politicians, that dream is being revitalised but its realisation remains a very long way off.

Notwithstanding the delay, we eventually did get to Potosí.

Deep Down on the Top of the World

The city's story is deeply troubling. If we ever need examples of human callousness towards the sufferings of others, and sadly there are no shortage of examples, Potosí's mining history stands as one of the most potent. Bolivia has always been defined by mining. Even before the Inca invasion in the fourteenth century, archeological evidence unearthed mining operations there. Since its discovery by the conquistadors in 1544, the Cerro Rico Mountain, which overlooks the city of Potosí, has yielded a river of riches that has produced over 70,000 metric tons of silver, permitting the colonial Spaniard aristocracy to live in exquisite opulence. Even the horses were reportedly shod in silver in Potosí's heyday. Local legend has it that they extracted enough silver to build a bridge of silver from Potosí to Madrid.

As for the price of extraction, well, at the time nobody thought to ask. The miners were non-people, soulless Indians all. Pope Paul III may very well have declared in 1537 that Indians were 'true men', but few including many senior figures within his own church were willing to accept his view. A Spanish theologian, Juan Ginés Sepúlveda, argued that the indigenous population deserved the treatment because their sins and idolatries were an offense to God. A fellow confrère argued that, like the Jews, they were lazy, did not believe in the miracles of Jesus Christ and were ungrateful to the Spaniards for all they had done for them. A French naturalist concluded that no activity of the soul could be observed.[45] Even respected philosophers of the Enlightenment fed the dehumanisation narrative. In his essay 'Race and Racism in the Works of David Hume' (2002),[46] Eric Morton had much to say about the eighteenth century Scottish philosopher, regarded as one of the most important figures in the history of Western philosophy.

> *Hume played a major and conscious role in the institutionalization of the hatred of blacks. In Hume's moral universe, racial subordination is depicted as the sole factor shaping the choices and actions of blacks and Indians. European domination is to be viewed as a 'cure' for the inferior species by providing them with colonial structure, assimilation, evolutionary up-grading or, in some instances, blessed extermination.*

Alas extermination, blessed or otherwise, of genocidal proportions was the fate of millions of indigenous people. The Spaniards' insatiable hunger for the wealth of Latin America took an enormous human and environmental toll, none more so than in Potosí.

Life expectancy in the mines averaged six months. The miners were simply expendable objects. Writer Eduardo Galeano estimates that in three centuries, eight million people lost their lives in the Cerro Rico, and to this day painful and premature death continues to stalk the mountain. The Cerro Rico, it seems, is deserving of its nickname – 'The Mountain That Eats Men'. But statistics rarely capture the human cost. Eduardo Galeano recalls the system in all its grotesqueness.

> *The labour system was a machine for crushing Indians. The process of using mercury to extract silver poisoned as many or more than did the toxic gasses in the bowels of the earth. It made hair and teeth fall out and brought on uncontrollable trembling . . . It was common to bring them out dead or with broken heads and legs (pp. 40-41).*

This was a wholly exploitative, dehumanising edifice constructed by the few for their own personal enrichment, based on the mass oppression of generations of indigenous people, without mercy, without empathy, without compassion. This was raw exploitative capitalism at its worst. In *Capital Vol. 1* Karl Marx wrote as follows:

> *The discovery of gold and silver in America, the extirpa-tion, enslavement and entombment in mines of the ab-original population, the beginning of the conquests and looting of the East Indies, the turning of Africa into a war-ren for the commercial hunting of black skins, signaled the rosy dawn of the era of capitalist production (p. 915).*[47]

Not a lot has changed from those dismal days, at least not until Evo Morales came to the presidency. Although silver depos-its have significantly decreased from the enormous richness that characterised the early days, finding a rich silver seam within the Cerro Rico remains the holy grail of mining. Day after day for six days a week, between 15,000 and 20,000 men go deep into the mines hard-grafting for this increasingly elusive ore. All in search of *El Dorado,* a colonial term meaning 'City of Gold', ad-mittedly not used by the miners themselves. And death contin-ues to stalk the men who work the Cerro Rico.

Ruth, Linda, Mick, Philip and I went down the mines with Basilio Mach'ala and his son Carlos. Prior to going down we asked him what a typical day entails. Very matter-of-factly Basi-lio told us that every day is the same.

> *Well I get up at 5.00 in the morning, get ready, cook, come here, I chew some coca and I go in. That's it. The coca gives us courage to work, it makes us work with a will, that's why we chew. It stops us being tired: inside the mine chewing coca gives us courage. And you don't get either. We spend all day in the mine with nothing to eat until the evening, sometimes for eight, nine or twelve hours, some-times twenty-four hours with nothing to eat but coca, that's the way the coca helps us. If it's a twenty-four hour shift we come out to eat. If it's a twelve-hour shift we don't.*

Fortified with bags of coca leaves that were intended to help us cope with the high altitude and airless conditions deep in the bowels of the earth, we strapped on helmets and headlights and followed them into the darkness.

The first fifty meters seemed very straightforward. We could walk upright and even with our gear it all seemed very doable.

Creeping complacency soon gave way to the hazards of jagged rocks and lowering rooftops. Crouching and gasping for breath with sweat tricking between our shoulder blades and blinding our eyes, we were forced to shout stop every twenty metres or so. Without turning round, Basilio and Carlos waited silently, their hollow expressionless faces remained fixated on the barely illuminated darkness into which we were descending.

Eventually, we arrived at where they had left off the previous day. They stripped to the waist, Basilio indifferent to our presence, Carlos more taciturn, and went to work. Their tools: hammer, crowbar, chisel and shovel. We asked them what was the most difficult part of their work.

> *Well, the hardest work here in the mine is the work of the drill operators and after that the work of hauling the rock, because the drillers inhale a lot of dust, and then the machine is heavy, it shakes you. And then hauling means you have to go up and down the steps with heavy loads: that's the hardest work in the mine, drilling and hauling.*

Not a lot had changed in 500 years. Each blow of the hammer was followed by a grunt from their taut, sinewy and surprisingly not very muscular bodies and the strike-grunt, strike-grunt, strike-grunt rhythm soon echoed round the glistening hollowed rock. Our grasping for the thin air was further compromised when they stopped for a smoke and to take time out to venerate *El Tío*. Miners have a unique belief system, a blend of Catholicism and indigenous belief. The Virgin rules over the outer world while *El Tío* rules over the underworld and is central to their belief system. By venerating him, dressing him up, gifting him with cigarettes, alcohol and coca leaves, as Basilio explained, they believe that he will ensure their safety.

> *We talk to El Tío, we talk to him, so that he'll help us with the work and so that nothing happens to us. And that he will give us mineral ore. El Tío doesn't say anything; El Tío doesn't ever talk, but we always talk to him. We go close to El Tío to drink when we are tired. When we are alone we go close to El Tío and we tell him everything, if we are sad.*

We ask him not to let anything happen to us, to look after us, to give us ore, that everything will go well.

It is not a failsafe system as Margarita Cañaviri explained to us. Her husband, who started working in the mine at the age of fourteen, died at the age of thirty-eight from silicosis, a lung disease caused by the inhalation of mineral dust which affects all underground miners. He had been ill for four years before he died, during which time he was unable to work. In graphic detail, Margarita detailed her husband's final days.

I saw his body . . . little by little . . . his skin got darker and darker. His lips went red, then purple. He couldn't do anything for himself. If you put his poor hand out in the sun, it looked as though the light passed right through it. He would take two steps and have a rest. He'd cough phlegm and in the end he was bringing up pus. In the end his lungs burst. He started to vomit pus mixed with ore from the mine. It's a terrible disease. It was a terrible end.

As Colum McCann recalls in *This Side of Brightness*,[48] it is the same for miners the world over as evidenced in his account of tunnel digging under the Hudson River in New York.

If they could reach down into their throats, they could chisel out diseases from their lungs. The tar and filth would could come away in their fingertips. They could hold a piece of flue-coloured tissue and say: This is what the tunnels have done to us (pp. 5-6).

Faced with mounting debt arising from her husband's illness, along with her daughters, four-year-old Abigail and twelve-year-old daughter Julia, Margarita was forced to work as a hand-picker sifting through the discarded debris outside the mine for nuggets of ore that might have been missed by the miners.

I was left with four children. Well, two of my little ones died. I had six. I had no way of earning money. There was nowhere to turn. I had no financial support. We gradually used up the little we had saved, everything until in the end my husband died. I had a debt with two banks. The debt was what I worried most about. I couldn't pay it off. I couldn't pay the rent or even pay for food for my little ones. My little girl is a witness. We would collect rubbish from one o'clock in the morning. We would collect waste food and wash it to survive for the week.

Bereft and bereaved, Margarita began the search for work.

I walked all over looking for work and that is how I found this work as a hand-picker. I have to be the breadwinner and I struggle to have to look after them. I am the only support for my family.

Julia told us what it is like working beside her mother.

It's heavy sometimes, when you carry the sacks (of stone) on your back. With a sore back, you can't do anything. Above all, why I'm here is to help my mother.

Much to her added grief, her seventeen-year-old son had just started work in the mines. With a hammer and a sack she and her daughters spend much of their days breaking rocks, examining them closely and then filling the sack with bits they think might be of value. Even at their young age, her daughters have become very adept at recognising real from illusory ore.

We met other miners. Newly married with a young baby, Grover Montes Coria feared the dreaded silicosis disease. His doctor had warned him that he was in real danger of contracting it if he didn't give up the mines. He felt he had no alternative but to continue and so every day, like so many other men, he entered the death chamber that was his only source of livelihood. His brother Wilzon had been injured in a mining accident and could no longer work. Once a strongly built, good-looking man, he now dragged his injured body along, his chances of marrying, having a family and an independent means of livelihood in ruin. Grover felt a responsibility towards him and to his own family, one more reason for going into the mine.

There are about three or four accidents a month, and the reasons for accidents vary. People have accidents with ex-

plosives, people get trapped by rocks when the roof caves in. There are cave-ins and there are inexperienced people who don't know the terrain. But it was not like that with Wilzon. We worked side-by-side. We knew how to cooper-ate like brothers.

Grover also had an acute understanding of how the mining industry operates.

Well, I think those who get the least benefit are those who do the most work. And they earn the least. We make a lot of sacrifices to get the ore out and the buyer pays us whatever they want. All the profits are invested outside the country. I feel really bad about it because a lot of the prof-its are being taken out of Potosí, out of Bolivia.

They looked to Evo Morales to lift them out of their precari-ous existence, and Morales seemed, to us at least, to be the real deal. Unlike other false dawns it seems as if he wasn't in it for his own personal enrichment and aggrandisement.

Throughout our time in Potosi, Linda worked the phones in Bolivia to secure an interview with the still new president. We re-ally wanted to get a sense of the man and of the profound change that was still in its infancy. For six months prior to our arrival in the country, we had been negotiating with various officials and nothing was confirmed but neither had they dismissed our re-quest out of hand. Where there was no refusal, there was hope. Then, just as we were ready to leave Potosí and head for the capital La Paz, word came through. We had the interview.

Playtime in the Palace

We were scheduled to be at the presidential palace at three o'clock the day after the message reached us. That meant an eight-hour bus journey to the capital city of La Paz – or as it was named by the Spanish colonists when it was founded in 1548, La Ciudad de Nuestra Señora de La Paz (The City of Our Lady of Peace). We drove through the Andean mountains in what we had been told was some of the most amazing scenery in the world, but we would have to take the guidebooks' word for that. Darkness falls early in the Andes and we only caught fleeting glimpses of the countryside before we settled down to the cold of the night in a bus that had no heating.

At the presidential palace, we had to report to the main door an hour beforehand for what were efficient but relatively relaxed security checks. Front door entry for all is important for Morales. No more skulking around the back. Enough of that in the past. And then the long wait in the long Rococo state room. One hour came, then two became three and three became four. We stretched, yawned, stretched and yawned again. We were waiting for a president after all, and we had more disposable time than did he. We set up shop and paced the grand hall. There were a few false alarms but nothing came of them. Traditional coca tea was served several times.

At one stage, Mick Cassidy and I stood and looked out from the balcony from where Evo and his Vice President Alvaro Garcia greeted the still disbelieving and jubilant multicoloured indigenous and mestizo people on the night of their inauguration. Like the two amigos that we are, we half-sheepishly waved to the few going about their business below. They dutifully ignored us. Bloody Gringos! Having failed to interest the people below, Ruth, Philip, Mick, Linda and I took turns on the presidential chair beside the flag – it must always be to the right and slightly behind the president – and took each other's photographs. Playtime in the presidential palace.

Then, virtually unannounced, he entered. We were almost caught off-guard. He had to be the tieless one among them. He graciously, and in our view unnecessarily, apologised for keeping us and took his just evacuated seat. So what did it feel like to be the first indigenous president of Bolivia? It would appear that the shock at being elected was still very real. He told us that his mother, a low-sized, bowl-hatted, rural indigenous woman, had previously not even been allowed into the central square, the Plaza Murillio, where the palace is located, and now here he was, her son, sitting in the president's chair.

My mother, rest in peace, used to tell me that she did not have the right to enter the city. She could not walk in the footpaths, much less in the main square of the city. During the colonial period, we were literally considered savages, animals. The extermination of the indigenous people was carried out in order to plunder our natural resources.

Morales is deeply conscious of his heritage. He had an indigenous ceremonial inauguration as well as a state one. Proud, certainly, but he is no narcissist. Authoritarian yes, according to those who have worked with him, with a streak of Latin American machismo to boot, but an incredibly hard worker. Certainly he is no vainglorious lout like many South American presidents of yore. He rises at 5.00, starts work at 6.00, and finishes sixteen hours later. That is his schedule six days a week. Every day, two teams of civil servants are required. The first clocks in at 6.00 in the morning and finishes at 2.00 in the afternoon when the second shift kicks in. Even Sunday is a work day. He travels to different rural parts of the country each Sunday where he chews the traditional coca leaf and inaugurates everything from hospitals to soccer fields. His embrace of coca, which is excoriated by those outside the country who fail to understand the sacred, medicinal and social role of the leaf in the Andes, is wholehearted and total.

Morales is unfazed by North American and western criticisms. Supremely confident in his own indigenous skin, he wants to carve not just a new narrative for his people but also a new economic order. He recounted with some glee his first meeting with representatives of the International Monetary Fund and the World Bank. On his way to meet with their representatives shortly after his election, Morales quipped, 'well, let's see what they make of this little Indian'. Not only has the man a sense of humour but he also has a sense of style. Even on inauguration day he did not wear a tie and his casual but beautifully tailored alpaca jacket always carries some distinctive indigenous design.

Morales is not interested in the politics of optics. He doesn't wear his politics on his sleeve, which is just one of his many distinctive trademarks that stand him apart from previous Bolivian presidents. His is a deliberate ground-breaking presidency that puts indigenous rights centre stage. One of his first acts as president was to announce a fifty-seven per cent salary cut for himself, his ministers, vice ministers and all high-ranking officials and consultants, with the consequent savings going to improve conditions in health and education.

His critique is clear. Capitalism has failed, he argues, not just the people of Bolivia and South America but also more fundamentally it has failed the planet. His message to those who want to hear, and there are many, is simple.

> *Bolivia has key mineral resources and we are prepared to trade but only at a fair price. The days of feudal servitude are over. No more masters: only partners.*

If meaningful change in the wholly iniquitous global economic order is to come, he argues, it will come from South America, and that change has already begun. His is a simple, clear, confident, unambiguous message. Then, twenty minutes later, the interview is over.

Would he stay for a photograph, and would it be okay to give him a present from Ireland, we anxiously ask. The previous year we had made a documentary on the *cocaleros* in Peru and we'd like him to have a copy. He accepts and asks how we got on. The former coca farmer, local soccer star and union leader has never forgotten his roots. After a quick and somewhat chaotic flash from the cameras he was gone. We gather up our gear and leave. On the way out, Mick Cassidy asks me what I thought of him. 'Some little Indian,' I self-consciously reply, wondering if it was now okay to use that term given that Evo Morales has given it his imprimatur.

Probably not. Context and ownership are everything.

Argentina

It Says in the Papers

*T*he (London) *Independent* is a reputable newspaper. After all, Robert Fisk writes for it and that in itself is a pretty strong recommendation. So when I saw a headline on its 22 September 2007 edition extolling the green credentials of clothing magnate Luciano Benetton, whose empire stretches across 120 countries, whose personal fortune is estimated at €2.1 billion and is ranked 463 on the Forbes rich list, I could not resist reaching for it. About a year earlier, I had read an article written by Tomás Bril Mascarenhas,[49] then a research fellow at the University of Buenos Aires, in the *New Internationalist* on the privatisation of Patagonia that featured a somewhat less flattering profile of Signor Benetton. The *New Internationalist's* article was the catalyst for making a documentary on Benetton, land ownership and the indigenous Mapuche people.

Another coincidence. Around the same time as I read Tom's article I stumbled across *Bombón: El Perro*, a gorgeously observed film about a Patagonian man, his dog and his dreams by Argentinean director Carlos Sorin, set in the beautifully bleak landscape of Patagonia. While Tom's article evoked the splendor of the landscape of Sorin's film, it also highlighted the way in which some of the world's wealthiest people had swooped vulture-like on Patagonia, and in the process displaced the Mapuche people, one of twenty-five indigenous groups in the country. Mapuche presence in Patagonia, as explained to us by Chacho Liempes, a man who had a deep reverence for the Mapuche way of life, long pre-dated Spanish colonialism and, like the Hebrews of the Old Testament, their existence in the area owes its origin to a flood.

Our ancestors tell how many years ago there was a great movement. The mountains sank and the planes rose up: there were great floods. Together the Mapuche helped each other to climb the mountain to seek protection and were saved. All the elements of the environment helped them to survive – all the weeds, all the plants, all the animals.

Chacho explained to us that in their own language *Mapuche* consists of two words *mapu* (land) and *che* (people), so they see themselves as people of the land. That was also one of their recurring themes when we were eventually to meet with them – 'without our land we are a lost people'.

Also included in Tom's article was Ted Turner, worth $2 billion and ranked 634 in the Forbes rich list 2012,[50] who had acquired 55,000 hectares of Patagonian land. Douglas Tompkins, self-styled environmentalist and founder of the *North Face* clothing company, does not make it into the Forbes list but nonetheless was able to afford the purchase of 800,000 acres, some of which were located in Chile as the Mapuche territory is no respecter of colonial drawn borders. Likewise, the actor Sylvester Stallone, rich but not rich enough to make the listing, and his Hollywood colleague Michael Douglas, also rich, were named in Tom's article. But writ large ironically enough in green lettering above all of these was the name of Luciano Benetton, cited in Forbes as worth $2.1 billion, along with his sister Giuliana who is equally wealthy. The older Benetton topped all foreign acquisitions with the purchase of 900,000 hectares, equivalent to half the area of Wales. It was not the kind of green write-up that Luciano Benetton would have wished for. Not like the article in *The Independent*.[51]

By any yardstick, *The Independent* article (and its later companion piece in *The Financial Times*) was a piece of publicity that is hard to come by. Two full pages with glowing tributes and equally glowing photographs. Signor Benetton, 'The Green Billionaire', tall, bespectacled, white-haired, was photographed receiving his 'Green Star' environmental award at the Monte Carlo Yacht Show for his new fifty-metre luxury yacht that accommodates eight people. There were also the *de rigueur* pictures of the smiling multiethnic Benetton models.

'This is not a ship,' eulogises Peter Popham in the article, 'it is the drawing room of the gracious home of a man of wealth and taste. The ceiling is more than two metres high, floors are carpeted, furnishings offer no concessions to maritime etiquette. The huge double bed in the master bedroom has no grab rails and the room is equipped with a grand piano. Bathrooms have severe modernist lines,' waxes Popham, 'jacuzzis, polished marble floors. The galley is a large and a luxuriously appointed kitchen ('I intend to cook,' says Luciano) features a machine for slicing prosciutto . . .

In keeping with good taste, the literal rags to riches billionaire was modesty personified about his yacht. 'I have no interest in fashions in yachts,' he insisted. 'I chose this design because it is suitable for trans-oceanic voyages, and allows me to live on the water day after day following the sea's natural rhythms.'

Popham is not alone in his adulation. Rachel Sanderson in *The Financial Times* similarly soft-pedaled her profile of Alessandro Benetton, scion of the 'bespectacled (why do these correspondents make such a fetish of wearing glasses?) *primogenito* of the Benetton clan'. Mr. Benetton, Sanderson informs us, is 'frank, softly spoken and disarmingly at ease'.[52] He may be part of the rich elite, but Mr. Benetton is keen that we all know that his rich background did not protect him from coming up the hard way. 'I was cleaning the air conditioners in the factory when I was ten,' he informs Sanderson.

Frank he may very well be but that frankness did not extend to his business dealings in Patagonia. Nothing in either article made any reference to Benetton's very publically contested landgrab in Patagonia, a story I had been diligently researching for over a year following on from Tom's article. There was nothing about the very public opposition of the Mapuche people to that land grab, or about the long-running court battles within Argentina, or indeed about the increasingly vociferous international campaign that was all over the Internet. It wasn't as if Popham or the editors at *The Independent* could not have been aware of this long-running controversy.

The day after I read Tom's article, I contacted him by e-mail. I wanted to make a documentary about this story and wondered if he would help me? His reply was immediate and unequivocal. Yes, he would but could he involve Sebastián Hacher Rivera? Thus began a trans-oceanic friendship and collaboration involving a new learning curve that immersed me not just in the Benettons' involvement in Patagonia but Argentina's recent economic upheavals. As was the norm, prior to making any documentary, a 'treatment' (essentially a long essay) that outlines all the contextual and personal details that will frame the film was crafted. The background to the Benetton purchase of land in Patagonia is based on that collaborative document written by Tom and myself over a number of months.

Neoliberal's Yo-Yo Puppet

From 1989-1990, Argentina experienced staggeringly high rates of inflation, one of the highest hyperinflations that the world had witnessed since 1956, although it was subsequently outdone by Zimbabwe. During his ten-year tenure in government, the President of Argentina, Carlos Menem, embraced the free-market monetarist policies espoused by Milton Friedman.[53] According to Friedman's analysis, inflation is always linked with excessively expansionary monetary policies. To off-set that he advocated cutting public expenditure and privatising public utilities. His views were the flavour of the 1990s decade and have cast a long shadow over global economic policy ever since. These policies coalesced around three key ideas in what became known as the Washington Consensus, since they expressed what were perceived as common sense policies of multilateral agencies based in Washington in 1990. Robert Gwynne, cited in Peadar Kirby's *Introduction to Latin America* (pp. 55-56), outlined these objectives as follows:

> . . . trade liberalization and easier foreign direct invest-
> ment . . . reduce direct government intervention in the
> economy through privatization . . . introducing fiscal dis-
> cipline . . . balanced budgets and tax reform . . . increase

the significance of the market in the allocation of resources and make the private sector the main instrument of economic growth through deregulation, secure property rights and financial liberalization.

In the fervour to free-up the Argentinean market, nothing was spared. Electricity, telephones, railways, the national oil company, the post office and airports were all privatised. The government trenchantly cut its social welfare programmes. It privatised a significant share of the pension system. In addition, there were mass public sector layoffs.

Free-market policies were not just confined to social policies, but also affected land ownership. Prior to the adoption of the free-market policies by the Menem administration, it was very difficult for non-Argentine citizens to buy land, particularly areas near the coast and along national frontiers. By the 1990s, all that had changed. Now the state adopted a classic laissez-faire policy. Land, with the exception of a mere six per cent of national and provincial parks, and other areas that were designated of historic, culture or environmental importance, would now go to the highest bidder.

Feeding the avarice of local and foreign elites became the new imperative. Menem personally invited foreign investors to take advantage of one of the least regulated land ownership policies in Latin America, arguing that Argentina had 'too much land' and that it needed foreign investment. Naturally, the indigenous communities were totally overlooked; Patagonia was ripe for the taking. Sites for Sale. This seemed like a win-win situation for international and domestic elites, while Menem personally received most of the tycoons and offered to help them if bureaucratic meddling endangered their investments.

The Patagonian paradise at the end of the world was now an even more attractive proposition. In 1997 Benetton paid $50 million for his 900,000 hectares – $55 a hectare, a snip for someone on the Forbes rich list. For other wealthy magnates watching from the sidelines, Benetton became an icon of the *extranjerización* ('foreignization') process that was well under way in Patagonia. Menem and his political allies at home and away were suspected of having benefitted enormously from these land transactions and are accused of having millions in Swiss bank accounts. However, despite several lawsuits, nothing has been proved and he has never been sentenced.

The Barbed Wire World of Patagonia

Patagonia in Argentina is one of the wildest places left on earth. It is a land made famous by writers such as Bruce Chatwin (*In Patagonia*, 1977)[54] and Paul Theroux (*The Old Patagonian Express*, 1979).[55] I came across a copy of Chatwin's book in a second-hand bookshop on Valentia Island off the coast of Kerry. Chatwin's book lived up to its dust-jacket blurb with incident, anecdote and the oddest of facts. But by page thirteen, it was clear that Chatwin's Patagonia was a desert place peopled only by colonisers, Welsh, English (Charles Darwin included), Italians, North Americans, South Africans, Lithuanians and more. Not a mention of the indigenous Mapuche people, who lived in this region for thousands of years and who recoil at reference to it as a desert.

He did, however, capture the physical beauty of the place. Deep blue lakes, swirling rivers, endless plateaus, rugged snow-capped mountains. No wonder it tempted the world's wealthy elite. As we were to discover, its vastness is immense, the scale of its beauty bewildering. We flew from Buenos Aires to Bariloche, high up in the Andean mountains close to the Chilean border, a journey of about two-and-a-half hours, and from there we drove south to El Bolsón, a further two hour journey and close to the area where the Welsh settled in 1865. This took us into the heart of Benetton's bolt hole, his 'get away from it all hideaway'. 'Patagonia gives me an amazing sense of freedom,' said Luciano Benetton on the purchase of his *estancias* in 1997. But Benetton was not prepared to extend that sense of freedom to others, certainly not to the people who had lived on this land for thousands of years prior to his arrival. Benetton had the whole estate fenced in – or out, depending on one's perspective.

Cristina Rodriguez at the site where she lost forty members of her family during Hurricane Mitch, which struck Nicaragua in 1998 (Nicaragua, 1999)

Hands across the Equator – Molly O'Duffy with Fidel Aquinda Mastracón, leader of the Cofán people of Lagro Agrio (Ecuador, 2004)

Doña Sanchez who could not afford a wheelchair for her 16-year-old daughter Irma, disabled by meningitis (Nicaragua, 1999)

Achuar chief 'Sindico' Wampash Muquink opposes oil exploration on ancestral land (Ecuador, 2004)

Curious to know what Ken was viewing through his lens, Wampush goes behind the camera while another member of the Achuar takes to the mike (Ecuador, 2004)

*Peadar King, Sadhbh Ni Donnabháin, Rosalynn Carter, Jimmy Carter,
Gerry Nelson, Mick O'Rourke and Mick Cassidy (USA, 2006)*

*Walter McMillian with Bryan Stevenson and supporters following his release
in March 2003 having spent six years on death row (courtesy of Equal Justice Initiative)*

Robert Tarver (left) as a young man with friends (courtesy of Ethel Ponder)

Robert Tarver just before his execution, 2002 (courtesy of Ethel Ponder)

Congresswoman and illegal coca grower Nancy Obregón (Peru, 2006)

Julia Cahuana, legal coca grower (Peru, 2006)

*Mick Cassidy, Javier Molina, Peadar King, Evo Morales, Linda Farthing,
Ruth Meehan and Philip Graham (Bolivia, 2008)*

Basilio Mach'ala and his son Carlos in the Bolivian mines (2007)

Peadar King with Margarita Cañaviri and her daughters Abigail and Julia as they sift through discarded waste from Potosí mines (Bolivia, 2008)

Atilio Curiñanco and Rosa Naheulquir on Mapuche land claimed by Italian clothing magnate Luciano Benetton (Argentina, 2008)

Rogelio Fermin, community leader and campaigner against the Benetton land claim in Patagonia (Argentina, 2008)

Sebastián Hacher Rivera, Peadar King and Tomás Bril Mascarenas (Argentina, 2008)

Chacho Liempes, defender of the Mapuche way of life (Argentina, 2008)

In a deeply poignant observation, Chacho Liempes, a man who had an ingrained reverence for the Mapuche and for their inheritance, lamented:

> Today, one looks with pain, with sadness, at the barbed wire fences around all the fields. Wire is one of the elements that comes with prosperity. One cannot pass through. In the past, my parents crossed those fields freely and today it all belongs to the big estates. Today we are prisoners in tiny pieces of land.

I've never viewed barbed wire in the same way since. We conducted the interview in his car as he drove through flat Patagonian countryside. As he spoke passionately about the land, we could see stretching before us for what appeared to be miles and miles of perfectly, though menacingly, constructed taut barbed wire fences. But theses people's voices simply do not count. Benetton was the purchaser and the power of money would establish his rights. For him, what was yet another transaction should be plain sailing. That is until he came up against the determination of Atilio Curiñanco, Rosa Nahuelquir and other Mapuche people.

If Tom gave us some intellectual ballast in our exploration of the internecine machinations of the Argentinean political system and land policies that facilitated the purchase of vast tracts of land by extraordinarily wealthy businessmen with no prior connection to the country, Sebastián Hacher Rivera provided us with an entrée to the Mapuche people. A photographer and activist, he has enormous credibility with the Mapuche and other indigenous people.

Legal title to land is not something that the Mapuche people have ever considered. The land is the land and the people walking on it are only transient caretakers whose footprints eventually fade. With Sebastián as our interpreter, Segunda Huilinao, now fondly referred to as the 'old lady' of the resistance, explained.

> Being Mapuche means that we are people of the soil, since we live on the land. When we die, we will go back to the soil. We love the land, and we were born here. The white people can say, 'I have title to the land, I have the deeds'.

But they do it through paper, of course. They measure it in hectares or meters. They have it all in numbers. How much, what's it like, what it can produce. What it is really like. That is not our way.

Twenty-two-year-old community leader Rogelio Fermín, whose community is surrounded by the Benetton estate, agreed.

Being owner of the land and being part of the land are two very different things. We are not the owners of the land. We are sharing it and living side by side with it. We do not have a piece of paper that says: 'we are the owners of this land, or of any area.' For other people, the most important thing is ownership. But for us it is completely the opposite.

He took us on an amazing tour. But first, a diversion.

For good reason I now have an aversion to the word 'remote'. I once wrote an article about a local saint whose presumed likeness is cast in stone in what I then described as a 'remote' place on the border of the parishes of Kilkee and Doonbeg in West Clare, no more than two miles from where I was born. That was until my father looked up from what I had hoped was a promising first draft and simply said, 'remote, and where are you coming from now that this place is suddenly remote?' He had lived all his life in that area, as had many of our neighbours, and neither he nor they had any sense that this was a 'remote' place. It was in fact the centre of their world. So while two hours on horseback through the spectacular Andes to where Rogelio and his family lived certainly *felt* remote to us, it clearly did not to them.

To get to his community we followed him on horseback in single file. Philip first with camera strapped to his back. Tom, Sebastián, Ruth, Mick and I followed with various bits of equipment strapped to ours. Two hours on horseback through some of the most stunning scenery on the planet. Towering mountains, plunging valleys and narrow winding pathways. Our plodding horses were surefooted as ballerinas. For them, this was a journey like all others: they walked heads down, nonchalantly negotiating the rough terrain. Ours was a mixture of fear and awe. Awe at the sheer beauty, fear at the dramatic drop, stretching in places to hundreds of feet below us, where one equine miss-step would have resulted in certain death. But these were old stagers, and I had at least some level of comfort on a horse having learned to love riding in my twenties. It was different for Mick Cassidy. He had never been up on a horse before and his comfort zone was further jolted, as was ours, by having to make the return journey lighted only by a half-crescent moon. This time shadowed valleys and silhouetted mountains were our only bearings. For Mick this was a particularly memorable first outing. As we reached the end of the return journey, the horses, sensing home, took off. No more plodding gait. Shouts of anxiety mixed with nervous laughter were the only break in what had hitherto being the sublime silence of the Andean night. An edgy coming and going we might have had, but the welcome on arrival was equally memorable.

All the while Rogelio rode along side us with a deftness of touch that came from generational familiarity with this unspoiled land.

Roast goat, freshly killed, greeted us on arrival. Rogelio's extended family, no more than twenty people in all, were our hosts. The welcoming of strangers is central to Mapuche tradition, as it once was to ours before we thought to commodify it and market it as a way of taking money from others. This was a welcome uncorrupted by commerce. As one of his family members told us:

> This is what makes us Mapuche – we have to give a very good welcome to the visitor and share what we have with them.

We sat around the log fire that burned brightly in the open air and drank tea through a silver stem from the communal pot. Communal tea-drinking is one of the few traditions that the Mapuche share with all Argentineans. The host handed the pot to each one of us and we sipped from the stem and passed it back to the host who then gave it to the nest person and round and round it went. And then we ate meat from the bone with its juices dripping down our chins, mopped up with freshly-made warm crusty bread. Even for those of us in the group who were rare carnivores, this was sweet eating. The only discordant moment was when we noticed, at too close quarters for comfort, the severed head of the goat on a stick, eyes fixed reproachfully it seemed on us.

Rogelio's community was spread over a hundred-mile radius, its sense of identity and cohesion belying its dispersed nature. We listened through Sebastián's translation of their fears for the land. What became clear to us was not only did they *talk* about the land in a way that was very different, but possibly more importantly they *thought* about the land very differently. What was equally clear was that they were not being listened to, not by their own government and most certainly not by the latest manifestation of conquistadors' greed. Not only are the Mapuche wedded to the land but to the other elements of the earth as well. Prior to telling us about their struggle with Luciano Benetton, Rosa Rua Nahuelquir and her husband, Atilio Curiñanco, had earlier told us about their way of life.

> We are the primitive inhabitants to our core. That is why we are able for all this living with the snow, the ice, with the wind, with the intense heat that sometimes comes. For us every element of nature is part of life. Our bodies contain every element of the natural world. Our life is made from the air of these mountains and from these territories.
>
> We plant by the waning moon so the plants will produce, if we sow the plant under any other moon, they might grow and grow and grow and not produce anything. So, these are all the things that our grandparents, my mother, all of them, took very seriously.

Rosa and Atilio had been victims of the Argentinean crash and so they decided to move from the city back to the country, to their natural home. In 2002, having secured permission from the local land office, they decided to set up home on unoccupied Mapuche land. What neither they nor the local land office realised at that point was that this land had previously been purchased by Benetton. Thirty-eight days after setting up their home at Santa Rosa, a complaint by the administrator of the Benetton estate resulted in Atilio and Rosa's eviction. Rosa described for us what happened.

> *We were evicted on 2 October. We got up early as we do every day. I heard some voices, some noises. I went out to see what was happening, who was coming. It turned out the police were coming, all armed. They were coming with dogs, rifles, everything as if they were coming after major criminals. They began to tear everything down. They tore the house down. They started to dig up all the plants.*

The eviction catapulted Atilio and Rosa's plight into an international conflict with one of the wealthiest landowners on the planet. But their story was not unique. What happened to Rosa and Atilio was happening to others, but their case became a cause célèbre. Adolfo Pérez Esquivel, winner of the 1980 Nobel Peace Prize for his defence of human rights in Argentina, accused Benetton of having the 'same mentality as the conquistadors' in a letter published by Italian newspaper *La Repubblica* on 14 June 2004. 'If we don't stop this intrusion, we will live forever in exile in our own land,' he claimed.[56]

Worried about the impact that Esquivel's intervention might have on his wholesome 'United Colours' advertising slogan, Benetton met with Rosa, Atilio and Esquivel in Rome in October 2005. In a public gesture, he offered 7,500 hectares of land elsewhere in Patagonia, of which 95 per cent was unproductive, but repeated that any access or rights to the ancestral land were nonnegotiable. Rosa and Atilio rejected the offer.

In 2007, fed up with protracted negotiations, Rosa and Atilio decided to return to the land from which they were evicted five years earlier. They re-built their wooden house, and had just planted corn by the waning moon by the time we arrived there later that year. Banners bearing slogans like *Territorio Mapuche Recuperad* and *Basta de oppression fuera Benetton* hung from the timber fencing they had constructed around their home and plot.

On a bitterly cold October morning, they welcomed us with the traditional tea. They welcomed us with the kind of customary hospitality that we had come to know from other people, other communities, in the welcoming warmth of their wooden house. As we sat by the fire Rosa Rua Nahuelquir's demands seemed imminently possible.

> *All we are claiming is the recognition of our rights to live on Mapuche land. The recognition that we are descended from this place and its ancestors. That does not mean that Benetton has to leave Argentina. All we are asking of Benetton is to recognize that. The same way he says that colour makes no difference. Now he has the opportunity to show that colour and race make no difference. This is his opportunity.*

As she and Atilio told us their story, I couldn't help thinking of Luciano Benetton in his green award-winning yacht. He claims, as do other 'investors' in Patagonia, that they are here to protect the land. Their claims are underpinned by a double discourse that is utterly contradictory. One the one hand they claim they are entitled to purchase anything, anywhere in this global open-ended market economy, irrespective of the wishes and histories of local populations. But at the same time, they claim that certain lands need to be protected and that the only way to do this is for people with no connection to the land to parachute in, elbow out the people who have lived on it for centuries, and cordon it off with barbed wire fencing.

People like Atilio Curiñanco, Rosa Rua Nahuelquir, Rogelio Fermín, Segunda Huilinao and Chacho Liempes. People whose only desire is to live with the wind, the rain, the sun and the snow.

Endnotes

[1] Neruda, P. (1975) *Selected Poems.* Penguin Books. London.

[2] Galeano, E. (1997) *Open Veins of Latin America,* New York: Monthly Review Press. p. 38.

[3] Guatemalan Commission for Historical Clarification (1999). Guatemala Memory of Silence: Report of the Comission for Historical Clarification. Conclusions and Recommendations. http://shr.aaas.org/guatemala/ceh/report/english/toc.html

[4] Chomsky, N. (1993) *What Uncle Sam Really Wants.* Odonian Press. This book is currently out of print but can be access for free at http://www.cyberspacei.com/jesusi/authors/chomsky/sam/sam.htm.

5 http://liturgyhouse.blogspot.com/2008/03/archbishop-oscar-romeros-letter-to.

6 *The Economist* 'Corruption in Latin America: Harder Graft' 7 April 2004. http://www.economist.com/node/2576104

7 Rodriguez, C. *Cristina Rodriguez: A Nicaraguan Story.* The Nicaraguan Return Visit Committee. Dublin.

8 Adès, H. and Graham, M. (2004) *The Rough Guide to Ecuador.* Penguin. London.

9 Ibid..

10 http://www.amazonwatch.org/amazon/EC/burling/index.php?page_number=99

11 http://www.br-inc./com/community/community_ecuadorfaq.asp. At the time of going to print, this web-page was no longer active.

12 http://www.ilo.org/indigenous/Conventions/no169/lang--en/index.htm.

13 http://www.br-inc.com/community/community_ecuadorfaq.asp.

14 http://www.conocophillips.com/EN/norwaycareers/graduates/company_reports/documents/06_Fact_Book.pdf.

15 Ecuador Indians sue Texaco over polluted water http://www.planetark.com/dailynewsstory.cfm/newsid/20745/story.htm.

16 Hurtig, A-K., and M San Sebastían, (2004) 'Incidence of Childhood Leukemia and Oil Exploration in the Amazon Basin in Ecuador in *International Journal of Occupational and Environmental Health* http://chevrontoxico.com/assets/docs/childhood-leukemia.pd

17 San Sebastien, M., Armstrong, B. and Stephens, C. 'Outcomes of Pregnancy among women living in the Proximity of oil Fields in the Amazon Basin of Ecuador'. *International Journal of Occupational Health*, Vol. 10 No. 3 (2004).

18 Klasfeld, A. Chevron Shareholders Want Oil Giant to Settle. Courthouse News Service. Thursday 26 May 2011. http://www.courthousenews.com/2011/05/26/36880.htm.

19 Prejean, H. 'Death in Texas'. *The New York Review of Books.* http://www.nybooks.com/articles/archives/2005/jan/13/death-in-texas/.

20 U.S. Department of Justice Office of Justice Programs Bureau of Justice Statistics, 'Correctional Population in the United States, 2010' December 2011, ncJ 236319 http://bjs.ojp.usdoj.gov/content/pub/pdf/cpus10.pdf.

21 Carter, J. (2006). *Palestine: Peace and Apartheid.* Simon and Schuster. New York.

22 http://www.eji.org.

[23] Zimring, F. (2003). *The Contradictions of American Capital Punishment*. Oxford University Press, Oxford.

[24] Cassidy, L.M. and Mikulich, A. (eds.) (2007). *Interrupting White Privilege – Catholic Theologians Break the Silence* Orbis Books, Maryknoll, New York.

[25] http://www.deathpenaltyinfo.org/u-s-supreme-court-roper-v-simmons-no-03-633

[26] Stevenson, B.A. 'Testimony on Criminal Justice for the United Nations Special Rapporteur on Racism.' 26 May 2008.

[27] See http://www.deathpenaltyinfo.org/intellectual-disability-and-death-penalty.

[28] http://www.eji.org/node/734.

[29] Wallace, G.C. The 1963 Inaugural Address of Governor George C. Wallace. January 14, 1963 Montgomery, Alabama http://www.archives.alabama.gov/govs_list/inauguralspeech.html.

[30] www.eji.org.

[31] Lee, H. (1997). *To Kill a Mockingbird.* Arrow Books. London.

[32] *Robert Lee Tarver, Jr. v. State*. CR-99-1379. April 13, 2000. http://caselaw.findlaw.com/al-court-of-criminal-appeals/1096202.html.

[33] United Nations (1950) 'Report of the Commission of Enquiry on the Coca Leaf' Economic and Social Council. Official Records Fifth Year. Twelvth Session. Special Supplement No. 1. New York. http://www.druglawreform.info/en/issues/unscheduling-the-coca-leaf/item/995-report-of-the-commission-of-enquiry-on-the-coca-leaf.

[34] *The Guardian*: Nixon's 'war on drugs' began 40 years ago, and the battle is still raging. http://www.guardian.co.uk/society/2011/jul/24/war-on-drugs-40-years.

[35] Davenport-Hines, R. (2002). *The Pursuit of Oblivion. A Social History of Drugs*. Phoenix Press. London.

[36] King, P. (2003). *The Politics of Drugs: From Production to Consumption*. The Liffey Press. Dublin.

[37] Veillette, C., Plan Colombia: A Progress Report 17 February 2005. Congressional Research Service The US Library of Congress. http://assets.opencrs.com/rpts/RL32774_20050217.pdf.

[38] Chomsky, N. (2000). *Rogue States* Plan Colombia http://www.chomsky.info/books/roguestates08.htm.

[39] http://www.ukcia.org/pollaw/lawlibrary/singleconventionon narcoticdrugs1961.php

⁴⁰ Bewley-Taylor, D. and Jelsma, M. Jelsma. 'Fifty Years of the 1961 Single Convention on Narcottic Drugs: A Re-intrepretation'. Series of Legislative Reform on Drugs Policies Nr. 12 March 2011.

⁴¹ http://www.un.org/ga/20special/poldecla.htm.

⁴² The Home Affairs Committee. 3rd Report. Home Affairs Select Committee 2001-02. HC. 318-I http://www.publications.parliament. uk/pa/cm200102/cmselect/cmhaff/318/31803.htm.

⁴³ Shulk, J. 'Water Fallout: Bolivians Battle Globalization'. *In These Times*, May 2000 http://www.ratical.org/co-globalize/linkscopy/ waterfallout.html.

⁴⁴ Kohl, B. and Farthing, L. (2006). *Impasse in Bolivia: Neoliberal Hegemony and Popular Resistance.* London: Zed Press.

⁴⁵ Galeano, E. (1997) *Open Veins of Latin America.* Monthly Review Press. New York. (p. 41).

⁴⁶ *Journal on African Philosophy.* ISSN: 1533-1067 (online). Editor: Olufemi Taiwo.

⁴⁷ Marx, K. *Capital* Vol.1 [1976]. Harmondsworth: Penguin. New York.

⁴⁸ McCann, C. (1998). *This Side of Brightness.* Bloomsbury. London.

⁴⁹ Bril Mascarenhas, T. 'The privatization of Patagonia'. *New Internationalist* August 2006.

⁵⁰ http://www.forbes.com/billionaires/list/#p_1_s_ao_All per cent20industries_All per cent20countries_All per cent20states_ted per cent20t.

⁵¹ Popham, P. 'The Green Billionaire' *The Independent* Saturday 22 September 2007.

⁵² Sanderson, R. 'Scion of clothing empire' *The Financial Times* Monday 14 November 2011.

⁵³ Friedman, Milton (1980). *Free to Choose: A Personal Statement.* London. Secker and Warburg.

⁵⁴ Chatwin, B. (1977). *In Patagonia.* Summit Books. New York.

⁵⁵ Theroux, P. (1996). *The Old Patagonian Express.* Penguin Books. London.

⁵⁶ The 14 June 2004 letter was published by Italian newspaper *La Repubblica.* There is a reference to the conflict in Omero Ciai, 'Benetton, restituisci la terra agli indios', in *La Repubblica,* Rome, 12 July 2004. To read the correspondence between Luciano Benetton and Adolfo Pérez Esquivel, visit the Patagonia Talk section of Benetton's site www. benettontalk.com.

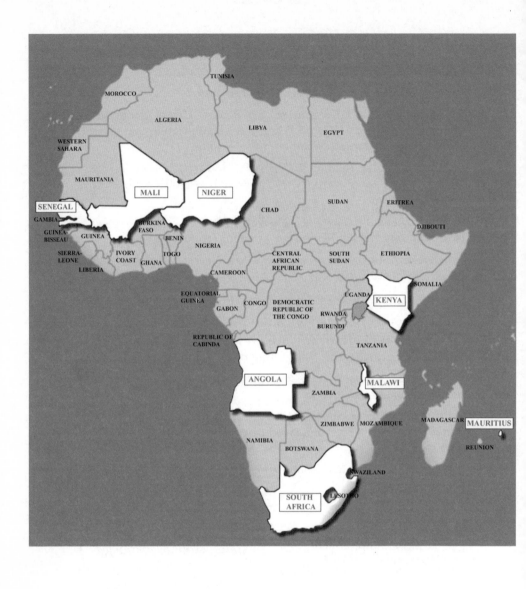

Section Two

AFRICA

I am apt to suspect the negroes and in general
all other species of men (for there are four or five
different kinds) to be naturally inferior to the whites.
There never was a civilized nation of any other
complexion than white, nor even any individual
eminent either in action or speculation. No ingenious
manufacturers among them, no arts, no science.
– *David Hume*[1]

Introduction

'Africa is close,' writes Richard Dowden in the opening chapter of his compelling book *Africa: Altered States, Ordinary Miracles*.[2] 'I have watched the sun set, shrunken and mean, over a cold, drab London street and stood outside a mud hut next morning on a Kenyan hillside and seen it rise in glory over the East African plains' (p. 1), he writes. But for many people in Ireland, particularly those over the age of forty, Africa is close for an altogether different reason. Like other people growing up in Ireland in the sixties, I had a cousin, a nun, who worked in Kenya. About every five years she returned home, smiling and bronzed. All the cousins were visited and she regaled us with stories of missionary work. Heroic deeds in an exotic world. After supper she produced her guitar and sang 'Michael, Row the Boat Ashore' in our sitting room. Flooded by the setting summer sun, we could in our childish imaginations easily picture her protected from the blistering hot African sun as she sat under some shady tree surrounded by a slew of admiring black children.

This was not a unique experience in the Ireland of the 1960s. In an article in *The Sunday Business Post in 2008*,[3] Father Eamon Aylward, formerly Director of the Irish Missionary Union, remembers as a child waving from the edge of the East Wall dock in Dublin as he watched a boat carrying his aunt, Sr. Frances Clare, out to sea. She was making her way to Africa to work as a missionary nun. 'I thought I would never see her again. It was a moving experience that stuck with me; this sense that she was travelling to a far-off place to do God's work,' he says. Eamon was to spend fourteen years working as a missionary priest in Mozambique, no doubt influenced by the stories he heard from his aunt. When I rang Eamon to talk about his aunt, he had, by coincidence, that very day attended her final obsequies in Birmingham. She died at the age of ninety-two.

We were, I imagine, not alone in our familial contact with Africa. In 1965, there were over 7,000 Irish priests, brothers and nuns in Africa, Asia and South and Central America, 4,122 of whom were based in African countries. Currently, there are fewer than 2,000 Catholic missionaries in Africa. It wasn't just Catholic missionaries who were working in Africa in huge numbers as there were also significant numbers of Anglican, Presbyterian and Methodist missionaries, though the precise numbers are less clear. There were also large numbers of Irish aid workers. Concern, the largest of the non-governmental organisations working in Africa, estimate that there were 450 Irish people working in Africa at peak levels, while the APSO (Agency for Personal Services Overseas) had over 620 Irish-funded volunteers at its peak in 1986.

For all the contact and all its closeness, Africa remains an enigma, as inscrutable as ever to the outsider. The closer you get to the continent, the further away it seems to slip. Perhaps that is as good a starting point as any. To believe that one can easily get a handle on such a vast and populous continent is to blunder into all kinds of error, which essentially is what Europeans have done since they first touched African soil. What many fail to comprehend in their reductionist prescriptions is how geographically vast, varied and socially and politically complex Africa is.

Stretching from thirty-four degrees north of the equator to twenty-five degrees south, Africa consists of 53 countries excluding the disputed territory in the Western Sahara. It also has a number of island groups including the Chagos Islands. At 30,301,596 square kilometers, it is bigger than Western Europe, the United States, China, India, Argentina, Britain and Ireland combined.

In Sub-Sahara Africa, there are forty-one separate and distinctive countries. In all of Africa, there are an estimated 1,000 indigenous languages. Africa also has the world's fastest growing population. In 1950, Africa's total population was less than half the total population of Europe: 221 million as compared to Europe's 547 million. Over sixty years later, the population of Africa had risen to over one billion while the population of Europe has slipped to 738 million. While not an exact science, and population projections are constantly being revised, it is expected that by 2025 Africa's population will reach 1.184 billion and by 2050 it will hit 1.994 billion. In contrast, it is expected that Europe's population will dip to 736 million by 2025 and will contract further to 702 million by 2050.

Not only is Africa's population enormous and increasing, but it is highly complex. Where pre-colonial Europeans might have only seen, in the words of Joseph Conrad, 'the blankest of blank spaces on the earth's figured surface',[4] there were about 10,000 independent kingdoms in Africa prior to colonialism. Over a twenty-year period in the late 1800s, these were merged into forty states, thirty-six of which were under direct European control. That merging was agreed at a major 'Scramble for Africa' conference in Berlin in 1884-1885, hosted by German Chancellor Otto von Bismarck. Foreign ministers from fourteen European powers and the United States established ground rules for the future exploitation of the 'dark continent'. Not surprisingly, Africans were not invited, or indeed even informed of the outcome.

Essentially, the Ministers took slide rulers to the continent and straight lines were drawn. Territories were bartered in a great trading game. Afterwards, some of the participants admitted that they didn't even know the location of some of the places they were trading. Their handiwork can still be seen in the current political map of Africa. If not one colony for everyone in the audience, then at least there were enough to go around for the big players. The French secured most of West Africa, and the British were given East and Southern Africa. The Congo became a personal fiefdom of Belgian King Leopold II, before it reverted to Belgian control. The Portuguese held a small colony in West Africa and two large ones in Southern Africa. The German territories were scattered throughout the continent. Russia was excluded from the conference, as was Turkey. Forty new colonies emerged from the bartering. Only Ethiopia was left standing. The motto of the conference could very well have been, 'let the exploitation begin'.

Perhaps partly because of the Berlin conference's unwillingness or inability to see Africa as anything more than a blank map on which it could superimpose whatever arrangements it wished, Africa is often seen as a unified country with a homogenised society. Nothing could be further from the truth. It is a highly diversified continent. That reading of Africa has been re-enforced by, amongst others, classics by European authors such as Conrad's *Heart of Darkness,*[5] *and* Isak Dinesen's *Out of Africa.*[6] These and other books have certainly framed our understanding of Africa. Even the title of Conrad's book, *Heart of Darkness,* has become a kind of metaphor for Africa – dangerous, dark and disturbing. Tim Butcher's remarkable account of his extraordinarily courageous epic journey through the Congo River tells a very different story. As even indicated in the title of his book, *Blood River: A Journey to Africa's Broken Heart,*[7] it is Africa's rather than the colonialists' heart that has been broken. The whole colonial experience was, as Marlow said:

. . . just robbery with violence, aggravated murder on a
great scale, and men going at it blind . . . the conquest
of the earth, which mostly means the taking it away from
those who have a different complexion or slightly flatter
nose than ourselves, is not a pretty thing when you look
into it too much.

While Africa cannot be summed up in a pithy phrase, there were moments, not withstanding the distinguished Nigerian writer Chinua Achebe's characterisation of the Conrad's classic as a racist text,[8] when I could empathise with Colonel Kurtz's exclamation in Conrad's book, 'The horror! The horror!' We felt the horror of African hunger on our arrival in Lilongwe, the capital of Malawi, in the spring of 2004, the first African stopping off point in *What in the World*? The horror was in the normality of it all. Everywhere we turned, our eyes would settle on gaunt, shadowy, raggedly-clad figures, all of whom seemed to move silently through the streets. It was the end of Ramadan and the people were queuing for alms at shops and businesses run mainly by Lebanese and Indian people. Mick Cassidy and I walked silently through the crowds, conscious of, and embarrassed by, our own hunger. Ours would be easily sated, but not so for the multitudes crowding the streets of Malawi's capital city. While hunger in Africa is the most seductive of all images to convey to western audiences, despite the strong resistance from many, including many Africans, it remains a reality. It's not the only reality – certainly Africa smiles as well – but that evening hunger was very much in evidence.

South Africa

Ricocheting around South Africa

Gerry Nelson, Mick Cassidy, Mick O'Rourke, Rodney Rice and I spent a grueling twelve-day shoot in South Africa. We were making a documentary on ten years of democracy in South Africa and had crisscrossed the country at breakneck speed. Having arrived in Johannesburg, we travelled to Pretoria, flew to Leboeng in the Northern Province not far from the border with Botswana, then on to a one-night stopover in Durban on the Indian Ocean, on to Cape Town and back to Jo'burg and Pretoria.

On this helter-skelter trip we met with Kader Asmal, the Irish anti-apartheid campaigner and two-time minister in the post-apartheid government, along with fellow cabinet colleague then Defense Minister 'Terror' Lekota – Mosiuoa Gerard Patrick 'Terror' Lekota to give him his full title. Like Mandela and other leaders of the African National Congress (ANC), he served time on Robben Island prison for 'conspiring to commit acts endangering maintenance of law and order'. However, the name 'Terror' apparently had more to do with his reputation on the football pitch than his involvement in armed struggle. Subsequently disillusioned with the African National Congress, Lekota resigned from the ANC and was a significant player in the formation of the new political party COPE (Congress of the People) of which he is now President.

Kader Asmal, whose death was announced on 22 June 2011, just as I was working on a draft of this, was under no illusion about the kind of challenges that the new South Africa faced.

The nature of the struggle has been such that change and transformation has to be telescoped. How do you lift peo-

ple living in abject poverty? How do you lift people who were invisible before? To do all of this in ten years. It is not possible in ten years.

How do you ensure that the rich economy develops further while at the same time work hard on the principles of justice, freedom, equality and dignity?

Other iconic figures from the resistance era included people like Brian Molefe, Baraney Pityana and Fatima Meer. Of Indian origin, Meer was one of the most formidable leaders of the anti-apartheid movement and a visit to her home in Durban provided an early dilemma for us. On our arrival at her house, we were greeted by visibly armed men in suits and dark glasses, all in what appeared to be an uncompromising mood. We were kept well away from the house and told we had to wait, though wait for what we were not so sure. It transpired that Fatima Meer had a guest and we were to be kept well back. That guest, it subsequently materialised, was Winnie Mandela, then out-of-favour with the ANC establishment but still hugely popular with the millions of blacks for whom the newly independent South Africa was a major disappointment. Mandela, who had been given a six-year jail sentence, later reduced to a fine, for her involvement in the abduction and death of fourteen year-old Stompie Moeketsi, still held the affection and esteem of those who continued to be dispossessed.

Despite all the allegations that were swirling around her, including ones of diamond smuggling, Winnie Mandela and Fatima Meer remained friends. An hour later, splendidly dressed and with tremendous poise, she walked out of the house and passed in front of us. It would have been tempting to greet the woman once dubbed 'Mother of Africa'. Even if we wanted to, she made the decision for us. It was not that she averted her gaze as she walked past, more like we simply did not exist as her body-guards sprung into action and she was whisked away.

In contrast, the welcome we received from David Diholo was all-embracing. Diholo was then deputy-principal and now principal in Senaone Senior Secondary School in Soweto, where I spent a very brief period teaching on my first visit to South Africa in 1996. While Kader Asmal struck an optimistic note about the prospects of substantial change coming to the black poverty-stricken people of the country, David was more despondent.

> *We serve kids from the squatter camps in the old Soweto where we still have two-roomed houses filled with families of ten, sometimes more. Some parents are not working and some kids stay with their grannies. Sometimes they have only one meal in a day and sometimes they don't eat for two days.*

We also met with Gertrude Fester from the Gender Equality Commission, and others such as Yani Momberg, Pinkie Morena and Dublin-born and educated Sherry McClean. McClean was married to the late ANC activist and Afrikaner Marius Schoon. Afrikaners who backed black emancipation were particularly vilified for what white people regarded as their treachery. Shoon's first wife and their six year-old daughter Katryn were both killed in front of the then three-year old Fritz in 1984 by a parcel bomb sent by South African security police spy Craig Williamson. We also interviewed the now adult Fritz and his adopted brother. All of these people were willing to talk to us, not just because of Rodney Rice's involvement in the anti-apartheid movement and his engagement with African politics, but also because of the enormous support that existed in Ireland for the struggle of the black majority in South Africa. Two decisive events crystallised that support. The first was the 1969 protest against the rugby Springboks tour to Ireland.

Leaving Apartheid Behind

That rugby game became hugely controversial, as did the 1974 Lions tour which was captained by Irishman Willie John MacBride. Further tours followed, including one in which the then out-half and now rugby commentator Tony Ward took part. A couple of year ago, in an altogether different context, I asked Tony about his decision to go to South Africa in 1980 and his subsequent decision to boycott a South African tour. This is what he had to say.[9]

> *I went to South Africa in 1980 and I didn't think about the boycott or the politics of going. I had tunnel vision. All I wanted to do was get on the plane and go. When we arrived in Johannesburg airport I came face to face with the reality of apartheid when I went to the toilet and saw the sign 'Whites Only Toilet – No Blacks'. Despite the fact that we got red star treatment, I was really upset by what I saw. The following year when I got the opportunity to go again, I thought, 'hold on – rugby represents white oppression of the black people and the only way I have of saying that I don't agree with this is not to travel'. I know there is an argument that you should keep up contact and try and change things that way but in 1981 it was clear to me that it would have been wrong to travel. I wasn't the only one – Moss Keane, Hugo McNeill, Ciaran Fitzgerald and Donal Spring didn't travel either. OK, it cost me two caps but I'm now glad we did it.*

The second key event was the Dunnes Stores strike in 1984. Twenty-one year-old Mary Manning, working as a cashier in Dunnes Stores in Henry Street, refused to handle fruit and vegetables from apartheid South Africa. She was immediately joined by nine other women and one man, all members of the MANDATE trade union, who refused to handle South African goods. The strike lasted for two-and-half years. Dunnes sacked the workers and the strikers took to the picket line in solidarity with the dispossessed and disenfranchised black people of South Africa. The dispute ended when the Irish government banned all fruit and vegetables from South Africa until the apartheid regime was overthrown. The strike reverberated across the world. The strikers were fêted by Archbishop Desmond Tutu and international human rights groups, the British Trade Union Movement, the South African Trade Union Movement and the South African Council of Churches. Nelson Mandela said that their stand helped keep him going during his imprisonment. Today a street in Johannesburg is named after Mary Manning and in 2008 a plaque to the bravery of those strikers was erected on Dublin's Henry Street.

We were conscious while filming in South Africa that we were walking in their shadows. From the wine lands of Stellenbosch to the townships of Cape Town and Soweto, to Durban on the Indian Ocean and the farmlands of the Northern Province and what seemed like all points in between, we were the beneficiaries of other people's commitment to the cause of South African freedom, and that included Rodney Rice who travelled with us. Rodney knew South Africa like few other Irish journalists. For ten years, from 1981 until 1991, he was refused a permit to cover South African politics from within the country. But partly because of his anti-apartheid activism in Ireland, and partly because of his work in covering African politics from outside the country, he had built up a significant network of contacts. Wherever we went, he was warmly embraced. An old comrade comes home. In the film, Rodney succinctly describes the apartheid architecture that was in place all those years, an architecture he along with very many others in this country worked to undermine.

> *Blacks and whites lived lives apart, unable to use the same sections of beeches, busses or trains.[10] They were barred from sharing a drink or meal in a public place. The Land Act[11] reserved almost nine-tenths of the country for the white minority. The Group Areas Act[12] corralled the black majority. The Population Registration Act[13] framed the residential restrictions. Pass Laws policed the streets and the Bantu Education Act[14] ensured a third rate and distorted education for the majority.*

There were others, too, such as the 1949 *Prohibition of Mixed Marriages Act*, the 1950 *Immorality Amendment Act* and the *Suppression of Communism Act* of 1950. By the time we got to South Africa, all of that has been swept away. In its place stood 'The Rainbow Nation'.

Lest we ever forget the horror of that apartheid era, we only have to read Alan Paton's searingly painful account of the apartheid era in his extraordinarily beautifully written *Cry, The Beloved Country*,[15] in my view one of the most profound books of the twentieth century, or look back to the Truth and Reconciliation Commission and hear again the pain and deep-seated trauma that was inflicted on the majority black population.

But what were we to make of it, this rainbow nation? Notwithstanding the many gains at that mid-point in the Mbeki presidency, and there were gains – nine million people with better access to clean water, seventy per cent of people with electricity, two million homes built – there was also ample evidence of abject poverty, with people still living in shacks, forty per cent unemployment levels and the land issue largely unresolved. We saw terrible poverty, but we also felt hopeful that the ANC could yet deliver. In retrospect, I realise that whatever about others in the crew, I was overly optimistic in my assessment of the changes that had taken place in South Africa. The reality is that much of the first term was a lost opportunity.

Nelson Mandela was at that stage unquestionably the most revered global figure, a status that continues to this day. His stature was unrivalled – his grace, poise, discipline, playfulness, authority, vision, energy, integrity, generosity, intellect. Even his shirts were admired. The way he moved, walked, danced, smiled, talked drew spontaneous approval from his adoring followers. These characteristics, allied to what he experienced, what he suffered, plus his ability to understand and ride the tide of history, added to the glow that followed him.

Long after Mandela's release from prison, National Party Justice Minister Kobie Coetsee, a member of the hated apartheid government of P.W. Botha who initiated secret talks with Nelson Mandela five years before his release, was asked in an interview by John Carlin what Nelson Mandela's greatness consisted of.[16]

> *Some years ago, long before he became president of this country, I was asked a similar question by the media. I said to them that I studied Latin, Roman culture, Roman literature and now for the first time I've met a man whose*

qualities have explained to me what the Romans meant with 'onestas gravitas dignitas'.

Unlike any other revolutionary political party coming to power, the ANC could draw on that stature and goodwill to bring about a transformation to the oppressed people of South Africa. Not only that, but the ANC had for decades planned for this moment. Intellectually and organisationally they were better placed to implement policies than were others who were suddenly catapulted into power. Its 1955 *Freedom Charter*[17] spelled out in clear, unambiguous terms what it would do once it had achieved power. 'The people shall share in the country's wealth,' it boldly declared.

With democracy came a new parliament. Gone were the old days in which grey men in grey suits talked to other grey men in grey suits about the unachievable desires of the black population and the never-ending needs of the white people. The sole exception to that white male monopoly was the exceptional Liberal Helen Suzman. The only woman representative between 1961 and 1974, she was courageously and unequivocally opposed to the apartheid regime. For the first time in the country's history, the new parliament looked like its people, and for the first time it was anticipated that its legislation would reflect the needs of its entire people.

Organisationally, too, this new parliament and government were well equipped to implement these policies. The African National Congress included the Congress of South African Trade Unions (COSATU) and the South African Communist Party (SACP), radical left-wing organisations with a mandate to implement pro-poor policies. If ever a party was ready to implement radical economic policies, it ought to have been the ANC.

But while Nelson Mandela was deeply loyal to COSATU and the SACP, by his own acknowledgement he did not share their economic views, and he made this patently clear in the lead-up to the negotiations with his then adversaries in the National Party, which led to the establishment of a transitional government. Speaking to what Mr. Mandela refers to as an Eminent Persons

Group – heads of state drawn from the British Commonwealth of Nations – he detailed his political and economic position in plain language in his extraordinary autobiography *Long Walk to Freedom*.[18]

> *I told them I was a South African nationalist, not a communist, that nationalists came in every hue and colour, and that I was firmly committed to a nonracial society. I told them I believed in the Freedom Charter, that the charter embodied the principles of democracy and human rights, and that it was not a blueprint for socialism (p. 629).*

While Mr. Mandela was adamant that he was not going to shed the SACP as a revolutionary partner in securing a free democratic South Africa, he simultaneously put clear blue water between his position and theirs.

> *They maintained that the Communist Party dominated and controlled the ANC. I then explained at great length that the party and the ANC were separate and distinctive organizations that shared the same short-term objectives, the overthrow of racial oppression and the birth of a nonracial South African, but that our long-term interests were not the same (p. 642).*

Mr. Mandela's clear priority, again spelled out in the most unambiguous terms in his autobiography, was reconciliation between whites and blacks.

> *I knew people expected me to harbour anger towards whites. But I had none. In prison, my anger towards whites decreased, but my hatred for the system grew. I wanted South Africa to see that I loved even the enemies while I hated the system that turned us against one another.*
>
> *I wanted to impress the critical role . . . of whites in any new dispensation. I have never tried to lose sight of this . . . Whites are fellow South Africans and we want them to feel safe and to know that we appreciate the contribution*

*that they have made for a democratic, non-racial South
Africa (p. 680).*

Without a shadow of doubt, Nelson Mandela succeeded in
doing that. Every opportunity, most notably the Rugby World
Cup final in South Africa, was carefully choreographed to convey that message. When Nelson Mandela turned up to that final
wearing a Springbok rugby shirt, he tore another hole in the fabric of apartheid, and when World Cup-winning South African
rugby captain Francois Pienaar handed Mr. Mandela his jersey
at the end of the game against the Australians, it unleashed an
extraordinary wave of emotion. This was one much longed-for
but yet wholly unexpected symbol of reconciliation.

As Michael D. Higgins pointed out, that was his contribution. If Nelson Mandela missed the opportunity to open up new
economic frontiers, Higgins was not blaming him for that.

> *In fairness to Mandela, one of the things that history will
> tell me is that different leaders deliver different moments. I
> would be very slow to (criticize Nelson Mandela); the wit-
> ness of his life . . . the stone he had to push up the moun-
> tain seemed to be an enormous one. He had to dislodge
> an awful lot so it was up to his successors and others who
> didn't have to pay such a huge price in their personal biog-
> raphies to actually bring it on to the next stage.*

President Higgins was acutely aware of the difficulties of
bringing it to the next stage.

> *There is a huge difference between the act of independence
> and the transformation of the society. And we realise this
> ourselves here in Ireland in that while we achieved formal
> independence, if you look at the language of the people
> from 1890–1910 and you move on then to the 1920s and
> 1930s and there is no comparison between the conservative
> institution and the behaviour and the twenties and thirties
> and that which brought our state into existence. So the
> moment of independence and the movement towards inde-
> pendence can in fact have rhetorical flourish and can even
> be delivered but the process of transformation institution-*

ally, delivering the different society, isn't ever easy. It is in
fact the challenge to intellectuals and it is the challenge
to me and to scholars and the people who are outside to
actually direct their attention and their writing into that
vacuum taking account of the indigenous aspiration.

Yet as Naomi Klein points out in her book *Shock Doctrine*, the ANC failed to implement the economic reform they had so long called for. From the beginning, they implemented mainstream policies. The new government inherited a chaotic financial and fiscal mess, including a debt of almost $25 billion,[19] the bulk of which was incurred by the apartheid regime in bolstering its grip on power. Given its status as the newest and brightest democracy in the world, many believed that it would simply renege on the debt and that those who were owed it would not challenge the new government. That did not happen. Instead, the government steadfastly re-paid the debt even while its citizens continued to live in desperate poverty. Mandela satisfied himself with broad brush-strokes economics. The detail was left to Mbeki. Despite his Communist Party past, Mbeki soon divested himself of Marxist ideology and joined the mainstream.

After all the toil, after all the suffering, after all the rhetoric, to fall so meekly into line? The really puzzling question is where and how did the imagination and creativity that brought them so far dissipate and disappear so quickly? Naomi Klein takes the view that ANC were caught off guard, that caught up as they were in the politics of democracy and national reconcilliation they failed to concentrate on the politics of the economy. The outgoing De Klerk administration had bought into the Washington Consensus and wanted to protect a low-spending, business-friendly environment. ANC economist Vishnu Padayachee told Klein that caught up as the ANC were in the buoyancy of the negotiations something had to give, and the negotiators conceded economic policy to the old guard in return for political transformation.

From Padayachee's point of view, none of this happened be-
cause of some grand betralal on the part of ANC leaders
but simply because they were out maneuvered on a series of

issues that seemed less than crucial at the time – but turned out to hold South Africa's lasting liberation in the balance.[20]

As distinguished South African journalist Allister Sparks ruefully noted in his *Beyond the Miracle: Inside the New South Africa*, 'it's not as if nothing has changed but that things have not changed for enough people'.[21] While a somewhat meandering if moderately useful account of the early days of post-apartheid South Africa, it does not compare with his grippingly superb *Tomorrow is Another Country: The Inside Story of South Africa's Negotiated Revolution.*[22]

I have a very tentative connection with one of the first people to give testimony to the Truth and Reconciliation Commission, and whose story was very familiar to me long before the Commission began its work. During my first visit to South Africa in 1996, I stayed briefly with Peggy Calata, sister of Fort Calata, one of what became known as the Craddock Four. In June 1985, Fort Calata and with Matthew Goniwe, both teachers in the Sam Xhallie secondary school in the dilapidated black township of Lingelihle, along with Sparrow Mkonto and Sicelo Mhlauli, were killed. Mhlauli had been stabbed more than thirty times, his throat slit and when found his right hand was missing. Mkonto was shot in the head. The four bodies were mutilated and burned to prevent identification. Fort Calata's widow, Normonde Calata, was one of the first to give evidence following the opening hearings of the Truth and Reconciliation Commission on 16 April 1996. Allister Sparks describes what happened in the courtroom the morning of Normonde's evidence.

> *At that moment of the telling of her story Normonde Calata disintegrated. She threw her head back and let out a terrible cry. 'A primeval and spontaneous wail from the depths of her soul,' is how Boraine, who was on the panel of commissioners hearing her testimony, described it. 'It was a cry from the soul that transformed the hearings from a litany of suffering and pain to an even deeper level. It caught up in a single howl all the darkness and horror of the apartheid years.' (p. 162)*

It's a sterling reminder of the shocking past South Africa has left behind, the extraordinary bravery of those who brought about change and of the grieving families they left behind.

Misplaced Optimism?

As we left South Africa in 2004, Thabo Mbeki was re-elected president but his second term in office ended prematurely and in disarray. Crime, poverty and HIV/AIDS all led to his undoing, as well as his perceived patrician attitude. His Achilles heel was the HIV/AIDS pandemic. His inability to acknowledge the connection between HIV and AIDS was incomprehensible, as was his Health Minister Manto Tshabalala-Msimang's assertion that a cocktail of garlic, lemon, olive oil and beetroot could stave off AIDS' deathly calling card. Disparagingly nicknamed 'Dr. Beetroot', she died at the age of sixty-nine on 16 December 2009 as a result of complications arising from a liver transplant. Speaking at an international conference in Toronto in 2006, UN Special Envoy for HIV/AIDS Stephen Lewis described South Africa's policies as 'more worthy of a lunatic fringe than of a concerned and compassionate state'. He characterised the South Africa's policies as 'obtuse, negligent and dilatory'.[23]

At the end of Mbeki's tenure as president of South Africa, an estimated 300,000 people had died from AIDS – up to 1,000 deaths a day. What promised so much in the after-glow of the Mandela presidency, in which Mbeki was a key player, ended in his abrupt and ignominious rejection by his own party. For Mbeki it was a personal tragedy, but his personal indignity pales in comparison with the scale of suffering and death that occurred on his watch. So much so that there are now calls for him to be charged with crimes against humanity or even genocide for his wretched negligence. At the very least, many expect an apology though to date none has been forthcoming.

Initially, his nemesis and elected successor Jacob Zuma seemed to offer little hope of a breakthrough on the critical AIDS issue. Infamously, he once asserted that he couldn't contract AIDS as he had showered after having sex. Eventually, he rejected that characterisation of safe sex and agreed to take an HIV test, before going on to promise that all HIV-positive babies under the age of one would receive anti-retroviral drugs as part of a huge expansion of treatment.

Not for the first time this change proved illusory. Change that people can believe in still hasn't come to South Africa, or at least not to all the people of South Africa. At the end of the first decade of this third millennium, unemployment has remained stubbornly high – just slightly below the forty per cent level we found in 2004. All the old indicators of poverty are still intact. Almost half the population still does not have enough money for essential food and non-food items. Rural households are at greater risk of poverty than their urban counterparts, as are households headed by women and households headed by older people.

The fears that David Diholo starkly expressed when we met him in his school in 2004 have come to pass.

> *I believe the economy is still going to be in the hands of the white people. We are still going to be beggars.*

At the time, I simply did not believe that could be possible. Not after all that had happened. Not after all the goodwill. Not after all that terrible suffering. But David was right. For the majority black population, little if anything has changed. An OECD report, *Trends in South African Income Distribution and Poverty since the Fall of Apartheid,*[24] tells the depressingly grim news.

> *In addition to high poverty levels, South Africa's inequality levels are among the highest in the world. Furthermore, levels of poverty and inequality continue to bear a persistent racial undertone. Blacks are very much poorer than Coloureds who are very much poorer than Indians/Asians who are poorer than Whites (p. 9).*

And the situation is getting worse as the report highlights. In 1993, one year before the ANC came to power, per capita income for black people was 24 per cent of white people's income. In 2008, this had decreased to 23.2 per cent (p. 13).

But that assessment of Mbeki's term in office as President of South Africa was to come later. At the time we were filming in South Africa, he has just completed his first term and was a shoo-in for a second. Certainly we had seen the poverty but it was viewed, by me at least, through the lens of what was possible, of what was to come. Mbeki had often spoken of an African renaissance and now that he was politically secure he could deliver in his second term. We had seen the emergence of a black middle class and where they had gone others, I naively thought, might soon follow. The old apartheid regime had been swept away. New systems had been put in place. New people at the helm. This was after all the Rainbow Nation, confident in its new-found status. Or so I thought at the time.

Malawi

For all the deprivation we experienced in South Africa, and clearly that wasn't the whole story, from the moment Mick Cassidy and I arrived in Malawi, we seemed to have entered a different world. This was poverty without an out, without the hope I had presumed to exist in South Africa. Prior to our arrival, director Ruth Meehan had been doing a 'recce' with a priest from St. Patrick Missionary Society, otherwise known as a Kiltegan Father. Pádraig Ó Máille knew Malawi intimately in the way that Rodney Rice knew South Africa. It was only after we had made the documentary that I had the opportunity to read his account of the end of the Banda years. His book, *Living Dangerously: A Memoir of Political Change in Malawi*,[25] reminded me yet again of the role many Irish missionaries played in the political life of their adopted countries.

Philip Graham, who was the cameraman on the shoot, was to arrive the following day. For the moment, though, Mick Cassidy and I had the town to ourselves. Having booked ourselves into Hotel Lilongwe, we walked through the city centre. It was on a Friday and we could not help but notice the number of people queuing in front of shops. Mostly men – thin, older men, many slightly stooped, most with threadbare clothing, signs of atrophied lives. Some turned their attention to us. Not sure of our surroundings we kept going, heads down, eyes averted. Later we learned that because it was Friday and many of the businesses where these half-emaciated people were queuing were owned by members of the Muslim faith, many were giving alms to the poor. Eventually, we went into an Indian restaurant. Here there was no shortage of food, and we had no shortage of money.

We were here to shoot a film on food security, that is, hunger, meet some people for whom food insecurity was a daily reality and ask why. From the very beginning, we had an overwhelming sense of pessimism, something that was not unique to first-time visitors to those parts of Africa where hunger still stalks the land. Again, though, it is not the whole story.

Patrick Chabal counsels Westerners against an all-embracing 'Afro-pessimism' consisting of fatalism, inevitability and intractability.[26] Our first day was certainly marked by pessimism. Among those who contributed to those feelings were Francis Kamwenda and his wife Gloria Elizabeth Kumwenda, Agnes Lekitala and her husband Scotland Kasala and Alena Monosile, amongst others.

Fifty-seven year old Francis Kamwenda, a father of six, was a civil servant. Unemployed since 1991, he lived in a block house on the outskirts of the capital Lilongwe. From the outside it looked substantial. On the inside it was practically bare, a few meagre furnishings on an earthen floor. Like all Malawians, maize was essential to Francis' diet but land was in short supply and so was seed and fertilizer. In 2004, there was a chronic food shortage in the country. Francis knew hunger and deprivation. A religious man, hunger had driven him to question the existence of God.

> Hunger is something that can make you ask God and say:
> 'Why you make me live, why you make me see this world
> when I don't have something to eat?'

But in a delicate balancing act of providing for one's family and feeding oneself, inevitably something has to give. There was a dignity and plaintiveness in the way he told his story.

> It is very difficult to send our children to school. But I
> would rather send my kids to school than, you know, have
> food. I sometimes stay two days without food just for my
> kids to be educated. You have the money, you just keep it,
> keep it to you know, it makes school fees.

His wife, Gloria Elizabeth Kumwenda, worked in a primary school. The school had no furnishings and consisted of a small cluster of roofless buildings. 'The children I teach are from wealthy families,' she told us. Clearly, wealth is a relative concept.

> *If I just stayed at home, how would we get something to eat . . . or put our own child through school? I charge twenty-five cent per month for each child. Although it's far, I always walk to work . . . because the bus costs too much money.*

The day we were there she had about twelve children in her classroom. At that rate she would earn about $3.00 a month.

Alena Monosile too knew hunger. An AIDS widow she had five children. We asked Alena to show us how to make *nsima*, a pasty porridge-like staple made from maize, which provides the illusion of a full stomach, but not a balanced diet. With hunger a constant, *nsima* offers a mirage of satisfaction. There was an awkward silence. Alena looked directly at the translator and then turned away embarrassed. She had no maize that day. Nothing. Not a morsel. It was our turn to be embarrassed. We bought it. She cooked it. We went off to buy her sacks of *nsima* – enough to do her for a couple of weeks. We realised that what was but a film prop for us was a lifeline for her. It was not the first food-linked embarrassment we had that day.

Earlier, when we were in Francis' home, he did not have food either and, given the time we would lose if we all decamped to get something to eat, I decided to go and buy for the crew and the household. I came back laden with rice, chicken, beef and the real luxury, large bottles of Coca Cola, or cold drinks as they are constantly referred to throughout Africa. What I had not anticipated was how the crowds of people who had been milling around all day watching us would react. As soon as I left the truck to walk the twenty metres to the house, the aroma from chicken and rice wafted through the crowd and they began to press in on me. The driver tried to protect me and there was nothing for it but to put my head down and get through the crowd as quickly as possible. It is an image that has remained with me. Earlier that day, we found a bag of sweets in the car and nearly created a riot when we began to pass them out. Normally, we would eat our food outdoors under the shade of a tree. That day we hid ourselves away.

'When there is no food for the children, I get very distressed,' Alena told us.

> If their father were alive, he would help us to get food for them. Sometimes they go to their friends' houses and envy them eating. As a grown up, I can bear hunger but the children can't . . . the little ones cry because they are hungry.

That year, 2004, was tough in Malawi, but three years earlier in 2001 it was even tougher. Famine conditions prevailed. Agnes Lekitala described how she coped.

> Myself and the children had absolutely nothing. We suffered from malnutrition . . . and our bodies started to swell from it. I had to get roots and leaves for us to eat.

Alena was preoccupied by the prospect of her own mortality and the consequences for her children, but she was determined to go on.

> If I die, my children won't have the love or support of parents. I can't give up or my children will be too weak to go to school. To get on they must go to school and they must eat. I will try to find a way to keep going.

On and on the stories went. Heartbreaking as they were, we felt we needed to know how such deprivation was possible, so we asked Collins Magalasi, a member of the Malawi Economic Justice Network. Certainly Malawi in 2004 was in a pitiful state. Then ranked 162 out of 175 by the United Nations Development Programme (UNDP), life expectancy was thirty-eight years of age, but the hunger that plagued Malawi at that time was by no means inevitable.

Much of that deprivation Collins Magalasi claimed could have been averted if the correct policies had been put in place, policies that favoured the poor of the country. But that did not happen. The scandal of the starter pack was a case in point.

In 2000, the government provided each farmer with a 'starter pack' of seeds and fertilisers to kickstart the path to food security. But then the World Trade Organisation stepped in. Starter packs were a state subsidy and this subsidy broke international trade rules, which marked the end of the starter packs. The United States and the European Union could keep their massive subsidies in beef and dairy production, but Malawi, which depends on aid from these rich countries for 60 per cent of its budget, must not provide a subsistence farmer with a pack of seeds and fertiliser. And there was more.

In keeping with the Washington Consensus, the International Monetary Fund (IMF) advised governments to privatise the agricultural marketing board, thereby putting food security into the hands of private traders. The government refused as they felt that it was not in the country's best interests to privatise its food distribution systems. The IMF then suspended the Poverty Reduction and Growth Facility (PRGF). External structural pressures piled on internal difficulties. It was a mess. When we left Malawi in 2004 we were in a despondent mood. Afro-pessimism was the order of the day.

Years afterwards I often wondered what had become of Frances, Gloria, Agnes, Scotland, Kasala and Alena, and when in 2011 we decided to do a *What in the World?* special on the UN Millennium Development Goals, I decided to go back to Malawi and see if I could meet with all or some of those who featured in the 2004 documentary.

I was, to say the least, quite apprehensive about our return visit to the country. Alena had been fearful about the impact of HIV and AIDS on herself and on her family, and there was the very real possibility that she may not have been alive. Frances and Gloria would by now be well over the average life expectancy and given his very difficult life I was conscious that he too may have died. Scotland and Kasala lived in the south of the country so we would not see them.

That apprehension turned to relief and delight when I heard that all three were well and that they would be happy to meet up with us again. That was the good news. Alena was delighted to meet with us and remembered us well. She immediately asked for Ruth Meehan who was not on this trip. She was doing very well. Her four children had grown up and all were healthy. Her older son had even gone to a third level college to study agriculture thanks to a grant from the local Catholic Church. She had found work in the city, which enabled her to extend her home and provide a more sustainable living for her children.

> I am now able to buy some fish, eggs and vegetables and my children go to school and one is in college and another is in technical school. My daughter is working in somebody's house.

Frances too was well-pleased to meet with us. On the surface he also appeared to have done well. He had extended his house, he had his small pension from his years in the civil service and he did some part-time work in the local Catholic Church. Nonetheless, he was in a despondent mood. His wife Gloria was very ill and could no longer work. He was worried about the medical expenses. He worried too about what the future held for his son who was mentally disabled. Also, the plot on which he grew his maize had been taken from him. He now grew maize in a much smaller plot over which he had no ownership. Effectively squatting on public land, he could be evicted at any time.

> I had a piece of land across the road, which was but two acres when you were here last but the Church bought that land and I came here to find this small piece of land, which is a quarter of an acre , which will give me maize for three months. Next year I will have no land to cultivate as this will be used for housing. I will have to look for land elsewhere.

But witnessing the partial and uneven changes that had taken place in the country, particularly seeing how well Alena if not Frances was doing, was somewhat encouraging – sufficient to shift some of the Afro-pessimism that gripped us on the first day we arrived in the country in 2004.

Kenya

Beacons of Hope?

If Richard Dowden takes a more optimistic view of Africa, I think it is fair to characterise Martin Meredith, another great chronicler of Africa, as somewhere on the pessimist end of that spectrum. Disillusionment and despondency fills many of the pages of his scholarly *The State of Africa*.[27] But even he recognised that there were times when beacons of hope shone on newly-found independent nations on the continent. Both Kenya and Senegal were included on the list of one-time hopefuls. In the case of Kenya, that was before the arrival of Daniel arap Moi who came to power on the death of Jomo Kenyatta in 1978. Famously, Kenyatta once quipped in what is now an often-quoted observation:[28]

> When the whites came to our land, they had the Bible, we had the land; they taught us to pray closing our eyes. When we opened them, they had the land, we had the Bible.

Kenyatta may have been flawed, detached in his old age from the affairs of the nation and happy to indulge a small circle of advisers while enjoying indigenous culture, however Moi was a different proposition altogether. Famously, he once remarked: 'I would like ministers, assistant ministers and others to sing like a parrot after me. That is how we can make progress.'[29] Between 1978 and his death in 2002, he oppressed, tortured, assassinated, intimidated, looted, obliterated, muzzled, gerrymandered and swindled his way through nearly three decades of power. Even the more optimistic Dowden despaired of what happened under Moi, as did virtually every other international commentator.

By the time we got to Kenya in 2008, Moi had been succeeded by Mwai Kibaki. Like all leaders, he offered a glimmer of hope.

Surely this couldn't be as bad as before? The constitution was re-written, the power of the Presidency curtailed and the position of Prime Minister was created as part of the new system of checks and balances. Once elected, Kibaki reneged on the deal to reform the Presidency. Why would he? He was now the President and there was room for only one strong man in Kenya.

That was the backdrop to our arrival in Kenya. But while the story of corruption in Kenya as in Africa is an easy one to tell, it is never the whole picture. We were here to cover a story about corruption, but from the perspective of European complicity. The searchlight would be on European rather than just African greed and, as we discovered, not everyone in Africa is corrupt.

I carry large amounts of cash with me on my travels, thousands of Euros. I have (thankfully) never been robbed and I've never paid a bribe, that is until I went to the Democratic Republic of the Congo in 2012, the first country of almost thirty in which I was forced to do so. And apart from the Congo, I have never been asked. Securing permits and visas does bring one into contact with officials, none of whom in my experience has ever asked for a bribe, however securing these permits can take up inordinate amounts of time and require endless patience with a global bureaucracy, not all of it Africa-based. Tim Butcher complains of having to 'stomp sweatily up to the ministry's seventeenth-floor offices in a government building where the lifts had not worked for years' before he could secure his transit papers for his epic journey up the Congo River. I know that feeling too.

We had done the paper work on the permit for Kenya but for some unexplained reason we could not send the fee through electronically. Clearly, four billion dollars could be fraudulently moved in and out of the country at ease by Moi and his cronies, but we couldn't send €1,000 to Nairobi from Cork through the international banking system. For three weeks this sum of money was held up in a London bank.

So we agreed to pay the sum in cash on arrival. On the Nairobi side they were concerned that this might be perceived as an under-the-counter payment and were anxious to reassure us that this was not the case. The plan was to meet at the airport and make the payment outside the terminal building lest we draw un-warranted attention on ourselves. So I brought Mick O'Rourke for cover and we made the payment. To the outsider this looked dodgy to say the least: passing amounts of notes to a Kenyan woman in a car with blackened windows in an airport carpark. But not so. Of that I am convinced. More documents were signed and stamped and weeks later copied by email to me. This was an honourable woman doing her job by the book. Not so those who were involved in the construction of the Turkwel Gorge Dam. For that story we have to go back in time, but first, Fr. Gabriel Dolan.

Spreading the Word

Fr. Gabriel Dolan, a Kiltegan Father originally from County Fer-managh, met us off the plane and that evening talked us through the current turmoil in the country. Consistently, Fr. Dolan has been a strong advocate of human rights and a public thorn in the side of the Moi and Kibaki governments. He served time in a squalid, over-crowded prison in 2005, a year before we arrived, for his searing indictment of systemic human rights abuses that con-tinue to plague the country, the Turkwel Gorge Dam included. Yet for all his seriousness about his work, Gabriel was remarkably light and buoyant company. In terms of the shoot, our biggest concern was getting access to the Gorge. He dismissed our anxi-ety mischievously, suggesting that 'it is easier to ask for forgive-ness than for permission'. It became known as Dolan's dictum, and we invoked it several times over the next few years.

We flew from Nairobi to Eldoret and from there we had a six-hour, crater-filled journey to the Turkwel Gorge. Journeys like that one, and we have had many, are filled with debate and dis-cussion, card games and blackjack, with long looking-out-the-window silences and some reading. I had brought along John le Carré's characteristically gripping *The Constant Gardener*,[30] in which he explores the exploitatively murky world of corrupt pharmaceutical corporations operating in Africa. As in the story we were pursuing, that corruption had its genesis in Western capitalism. I felt a certain symmetry in reading le Carré's novel about western complicity in the corruption of Kenyan ministers and officials set in the Rift Valley, all to the detriment of the poor of the country. Fiction mirroring fact and fact mirroring fiction.

As we left Nairobi, a largely uninviting city that held little appeal, what struck us most forcibly was the way in which Pentecostal Evangelical churches have come to dominate its streetscape. Church after church, huge sparkling citadels, many built amongst the squalor of the city, their names evoking a hope for what are for many desolate lives: Champions of Christ's Temple, Maximum Miracle Centre, Winners' Chapel. Not only are Kenyans flocking to these and other evangelical churches in their thousands, but so too are other African people, and the same holds true in Latin America.

The extraordinary growth of these churches is guaranteed to spark huge levels of indignation in Mick O'Rourke. On the journey to the Turkwel Gorge, he recounts experience after experience from his extensive travels around Africa and elsewhere of what he sees as the mass deception and exploitation that these churches represent. On that we agree. I was shocked once when I attended one of these churches in South Africa. The centre piece of the three-hour ceremony seemed to be the collection and the pastor led a virtual bidding war in the church. The lead up to the bidding war seemed to me to be carefully choreographed hysteria. The tempo was ever so carefully ratcheted up culminating in a crescendo of high emotion. Quoting from the Acts of the Apostles (20:35), 'It is more blessed to give than to receive', the pastor began by asking for a donation of 500 rand. After several exhortations, one woman made her way to the top table to rapturous applause. The bidding ended at ten rand. As the only white person in the congregation, I self-consciously made my way to the top table to place my lowly contribution. And all of this in one of the poorest townships of Soweto. I have also been to the homes of some of these BMW and Mercedes-driving, pin-stripe-suited pastors, the lavishness of their houses reflecting the opulence of their temples. Meanwhile, many of the pastors of these inde-

pendent churches voraciously reject any hint of personal enrichment. I remain deeply skeptical.

The social conditions in which people live out their often
fraught lives are of little concern to these churches. Unlike Fr.
Gabriel Dolan. These churches have never produced clergy of the
stature of ardent anti-apartheid campaigners Desmond Tutu of
the Anglican Communion or the Roman Catholic Bishop Dónal
Hurley or his Brazilian counterparts Helder Camara, who under
the military dictatorship was identified as the 'red bishop' for his
defence of human rights and the Church's option for the poor.

Despite the criticisms leveled against them, independent
Pentecostal churches are growing at a phenomenal rate, eating
away at the membership of the traditional Christian churches.
They are sweeping the spiritual boards. Televangelism and what
is referred to as 'personal prosperity theology' (God will provide,
the more you give, the more you will receive and so on) have
transformed religious practice in Kenya and in Africa generally. Primarily sponsored by US parent churches, an individual-
ised model of salvation is what's on offer, in stark contrast to
the mainstream Christian churches where the social gospel and
collective values are central tenets of faith. On this Mick and I
disagree. I think there is a fundamental difference between what
the mainstream Christian churches have to offer and what these
new churches are doing.

Back and forth, Mick and I argue the toss on the way to the
Turkwel Gorge in the Rift Valley located in the northwestern part
of Kenya close to the borders of Uganda, Sudan and Ethiopia just
above the Equator. The Rift Valley is the cradle of humanity. Here
the oldest human fossils have been found. But like most conversations, ours drifts from religion to politics and in this case the
politics of the construction of the dam. I first heard of the Turkwel Gorge Dam when I came across a report by British academic
Susan Hawley.[31] 'The whitest of white elephants; a stinking scandal; the issue of indifference; and greed and the richest dirty deal
in Kenya's history' was how Hawley began her report.

The Turkwel Gorge Hydro-Electric Plant

Originally conceived in the 1960s, concerns were expressed from the very beginning. Hawley claims that the dam was built on a major earthquake fault, even though other more suitable and cheaper sites had been identified. Initial feasibility studies raised questions about the reliability of the seasonal flow of the Turkwel River and potential detrimental environmental impacts downstream, particularly to forests that sustained the Turkana and Pokot people living in the area.

Without securing any international competitive tenders, without carrying out the feasibility study funded by Norad, the Norwegian government's aid department, and without reference to the findings from a European Community study, the Kenyan government awarded the contract to the French company Spie Batignolles for $250 million. British company WLPU, now known as Scott Wilson Piesold, were awarded a contract as assistant employer on the project. The $250 million was more than double the original estimate of $102 million.

Even the *Financial Times* was aghast at what happened. In March 1986, the paper stated that the dam was 'extremely disadvantageous for Kenya'.[32] From the very beginning, allegations were being made that this was a corrupt deal and that the President of Kenya, Daniel arap Moi, was at the centre of it all. *The Financial Times* claimed that Moi accepted the deal because it was to his personal advantage. These personal advantages were described in a British House of Commons Select Committee on International Development as follows:

> *In March 1986, an internal memorandum written by Achim Kratz, then European Commission delegate to Kenya, was leaked to the Financial Times. The memo stated that the contract price was 'more than double the amount Kenya's Government would have had to pay for the project based on an international competitive tender'. The memo continued, 'The Kenyan government officials who are involved in the project are fully aware of the disadvantages of the French deal . . . but they nevertheless accepted it because*

*of high personal advantages.' Kenyan observers say that
these 'personal advantages' included payments of millions
of dollars to Kenya President Daniel Arap Moi and to the
then Energy Minister Nicholas Biwott.*[33]

In 1991, the World Bank's East African Director, Peter Eigen, was so disgusted by the whole project that he resigned his job with the World Bank. He claimed that damming the river would destroy the river forests and endanger the livelihoods of the pastoralists in both communities.

The Turkwel Gorge Dam eventually cost $450 million to build, three times the initial estimate and nearly twice the contract price, which as outlined above was greater than the original estimate cost. No final audit of the dam has ever been conducted. Not only was the cost of the project exorbitant, but the manner in which the funding was secured was disadvantageous to Kenya. At the time, there was an informal agreement among European countries that they would pay for major projects in Africa with low-cost loans, and funding was available for this project on this concessional basis. However, this was not what happened. Instead, finance was secured at full market rates, adding yet another layer of debt on an already debt-ridden country.

But critically, the construction of the dam and the consequences in terms of water flow exacerbated the ancient conflict between the Turkana and Pokot people. Both eked out a living in what to us appeared to be an extraordinarily harsh and inhospitable land. Once described by a British travel writer Charles Miller as:

> . . . *a horizonless frying-pan of desolation: a sun-dried
> moon-scape of cracked earth harder than iron . . . vast
> plains of dehydrated thorn scrub, sightless deserts and
> scorched black mountains. Temperatures often climb to
> 120 degrees in the shade (when shade can be found). The
> country may have been described best by the late journalist, Negley Farson, when he called it 'as close as you can
> get to hell on earth' (p. 471).*[34]

The Turkana and Pokot People

For the estimated 650,000 Pokot and Turkana people, though, this is home. Both peoples are nomadic and pastoralists. More than anything else the rhythm of the desert determines their lives. They move when the need arises, always in search of new pastures for their herds. The nineteenth century political carve-up of Africa and the creation of artificial borders by the European powers have no standing with the Turkana and Pokot peoples.

Apart from that common way of life, the two peoples are quite different. The Turkana are exceptionally tall, very distinguished looking. With their partially shaved heads, their heavily elaborate multi-coloured beaded neck jewellery, with equally elaborate earrings and bracelets and their predominantly earth-red wraps, the women are stunning. The women were much more reticent than the men, covering up their bare breasts as soon as we arrived and keeping their distance from the cameras. The men are equally tall and wear a tunic-type wrap over the left shoulder. For Turkana men, the stick and stool, which they receive during initiation rites into manhood, remain potent symbols of their culture and identity. Everywhere they travel Turkana men carry their stick and stool. The stick straddles both shoulders and the stool is used for sitting on and as a headrest at nighttime. They live in what appears to us flimsy one or two-roomed circular huts made from sticks and palm fronds, covered in cloth or goat skins.

In contrast, the Pokot are smaller and less elaborate in their dress and jewellery, but their houses to our untrained eyes seemed more robust. The Pokot men are more likely to dress in western clothes while the women wear a mixture of western and traditional dress.

Depending on the seasons, the Pokot and Turkana peoples move their cattle and goats from one grazing area to another, often bumping up against each other, each accusing the other of invading their space. The conflict centres on cattle and access to grazing grounds and water. The construction of the dam exacerbated those tensions as an engineer working at the dam, who prefers not to be named, explained to us.

> *When the dam was built some of the people along here who had lived uninterrupted lives for centuries were forced to move to the mountains or further along the river below. The drop in the water level has affected the living conditions of the people.*

David Okosing, a settled Pokot and our fixer and translator, told us that neither the Pokot nor the Turkana peoples were consulted about the construction of the dam.

> *The people were not consulted at all when the company was coming to build the dam. They took it as a no man's land.*

A Pokot chief, Domonyang Lopuslo, told us of what happened. Remarkably, we were the first white people he had ever spoken to, despite white people working on his doorstep for twenty years.

> *One morning, cars entered from up stream, constructing the road. We asked ourselves what were these people doing. There was no chief to tell us what was happening. We could not understand their language. I never talked to a white person. Even when they were working on the dam, they never talked to me. Today is the first day I have ever spoken to white people.*

The irony is that while electricity is generated in the area, there is none for the local people, nor did the company honour its commitment to compensate them for the loss of their water supply, as Domonyang told us.

> *The company has done nothing for us. They promised us irrigation and we have waited and waited, but nothing has been done. We are just left without anything. Before the dam we used to get water from the natural river. Because of the flooding of the dam, we have to move up into the hills. We lost all the land that we used to till for maize, leaving us without food.*

Human rights activist Maina Kaia put what happened more forcefully.

This dam had absolutely no consultation. It was rammed down their throats. They displaced quite a number of people in that area. They took away a lot of land that was used for grazing by both the Pokot and the Turkana. And the consequences since then have been disastrous.

It also exacerbated the historical tensions between the Pokot and the Turkana. When the dam was built, both sides thought that the other side was benefitting.

The dam may not have been the trigger for the conflict but the proliferation of AK47s, a spillover from conflict in neighbouring Sudan and Uganda, and originally sourced in the former Soviet Union and Eastern European countries, has brought the conflict to new heights. There are now an estimated 65,000 weapons in circulation.

Domonyang's wife Helen was injured in one of those conflicts.

The Turkana raided my animals. They shot my wife and she lost her leg. At the moment, there is calm but we don't know if it will last. There is still need for guns because the conflict isn't over.

One young AK47-armed Turkana man took a strong exception to our presence. It was our first experience looking down the barrel of a gun. Heads down and silence was our instinctive response to his outburst, followed by furtive looks at our hosts. His was serious power, and to treat it otherwise would have been foolish in the extreme. A tense stand-off ensued before, to our immense relief, older and wiser counsel prevailed and he walked away. What was for us a momentary and frightening confrontation is a regular reality for both the Turkana and Pokot peoples.

The river's waterflow is now determined by the needs of engineers and production of electricity at the plant, and not by the farmers. Now their cattle, camels and goats are thinner; there is less food for the people and inter-tribal tension is on the increase. That is the real legacy of western attempts to shoehorn a river into something that nature never intended.

According to Kaia, the construction of the dam marks the beginning of serious corruption in Kenya.

> *The Turkwel Valley dam is really the beginning in this country of really big-scale grand corruption. Without any tendering without any environmental assessment. This is during the time of Daniel Moi. This was single sourcing, without any tendering. The eventual cost was more than four times the original estimate.*

Maina Kaia's comments about the construction of the dam, made in 2006 when the Celtic Tiger in Ireland was in full voice, were extraordinarily prescient not just for Kenyans but globally.

> *We need to start together to open up the banking systems that are based in the West. We need to know who is banking money from Africa in Western countries. The businessmen, they do their deals in London, they do their deals in Dublin, they do their deals in Paris. Corruption like we have seen here in the Turkwel Gorge thrives on lack of transparency, on darkness. We don't want conmen in this country. It is incumbent on the West to take control of their own people, to make them accountable. There are pliant and pliable officials in Africa and there are greedy companies in the West that are facilitating and palming African officials. Corruption in Africa cannot happen without the complicity of Western companies and banks. The West needs to know that and hold such companies to account.*

The dam still stands though the amount of electricity it is producing has never met with the initial deliberately exaggerated claims. Meanwhile, the conflict between the Pokot and the Turkana still rumbles on. Those who made fortunes on the Turkwel Gorge dam have long since moved on to other projects. Perhaps it's not the Turkana and Pokot peoples who are the ultimate nomads in search of new grazing grounds and fresh watering holes, but rather those in search of a quick buck who can move money in and out of pliant and pliable global financial institutions while simultaneously leaving a trail of destruction in their wake.

Senegal

Our Own Melting Pot

If we were dazzled by the texture and richness of the Turkana people and their landscape, our aural and visual senses, as well as our sense of smell, were blown away on the beaches of Senegal. This was our first experience of Francophone Africa and it was also my first time meeting Bob O'Brien, who was subsequently to become a critical member of the *What in the World?* team. We met him at Dakar airport, he arriving from Belfast, Mick O'Rourke, Mick Cassidy and I on our way from Nairobi. Bob's arrival in Senegal was a real baptism of fire. Not fully appreciating the brittleness of our white skin and the need to protect every exposed part, the back of his neck cracked under the baking African sun leaving him battling pain and discomfort for days.

Crewing together is a strange experience. Living cheek-by-jowl for sixteen hours a day and sometimes more. Cramped and crammed, time-pressured lives. Different lives. Different personalities. And then added to the mix were people from other countries as well as the host country. In this case, we were travelling with Sylvain Le Roux, a French PhD student from Paris, who was doing research on the fishing industry in West Africa, and our Senegalese translator Diop Mor Talla. Tall, thin, cerebral and a devout Muslim, Talla was initially diffident and reserved, but as the shoot progressed and he got more accustomed to our way of working, he relaxed, opened up and was brilliant company. That is one of the joys of doing this kind of work: meeting people as equals, sharing insights into private and public worlds that would be strictly off-limits if we were just passing tourists.

Thrown together from our diverse backgrounds, we were our own small melting pot, our own motley crew.

Maybe Talla's initial reserve was rooted in French formality as the French colonial footprint on Senegal is very strong, using the formal *vous,* for example, and it's not just the language. Baguettes and jam for breakfast. Patisseries on every street and those distinctive blue street signs that one sees in Paris are also on every street corner of Dakar, Senegal's capital city. But what was most striking from an Irish perspective was the strong attachment to France and all things French. Unlike our complex relationship with our former colonial master, the Senegalese are actually quite proud of their French connection. We found the same in Niger and Mali. The French colonial enterprise differs significantly from that of other colonial powers, though it would be untrue to suggest that it was more benign.

While the British, Belgian, German and Portuguese favored a somewhat semi-detached model of governance, using preferred ethnic groups to impose their imperial writ, the French sought – to corrupt a phrase from the Irish colonial experience – to ensure that Francophone Africa became as French as the French themselves. That benign attitude was of course wholly dependent on these countries remaining loyal to the French project. If, as in the case of Algeria, they were to assert any independent line, then the full weight of French colonial might would be brought to bear. The Germans favoured the Mwami in Rwanda and later the Belgians favoured the Tutsis in the same country. While the Portuguese claimed to have acted with an even hand in Angola, their abrupt handover of power in 1975 favoured the Kimbundu people, or at least the Ovimbundu people thought so. In contrast, 'we are all French people now' was the assimilationist French cry, up to a point.

None more so than on the first Senegalese President, poet, teacher and intellectual Léopold Senghor. Born in the fishing village of Joal, our third stopping off point, he was educated initially by Catholic missionaries in a predominantly Muslim country, and later in the Lycée Louis-le-Grand in Paris where George Pompidou, French President from 1969–1974, was a classmate.

Senghor taught Latin and Greek in a Parisian lyceé in what was an unheard of role for a black African at the time. Prior to independence, and again unlike the British model (with the exception of Ireland where the 1801 Act of Union abolished the indigenous parliament resulting in the creation of 100 seats for Irish MPs in Westminster), a select elite from the French colonies were represented in the French National Assembly. He was first a member of the French Constituent Assembly from 1945 to 1946, and from 1951 to 1955 he was member of the French National Assembly. But he was as influential on the cultural stage as on the political one.

A contemporary of existentialist philosopher Jean-Paul Sartre, he was very much part of that group of francophone intellectual writers and politicians who developed the concept of *negritude* that extolled pride in all things black and African, partly as a reaction to French assimilation policies. The movement also included Aimé Césaire, Léon Gontran Damas and Frantz Fanon, among others. In one of our meandering conversations, I asked Talla what he thought of *negritude*.

> *What was positive in negritude though, was that it gave some of us Africans who went to colonial schools and universities, full awareness and pride. I remember when we used to say while in secondary school, 'Black brother, be proud of your black skin'.*

Not everyone was comfortable with Senghor's philosophy of *negritude*, as many found it too contemplative and theoretical. The great Nigerian intellectual and Nobel Prize winner for literature (1986) Wole Soyinka, in a wonderful play on words, once remarked 'the tiger doesn't have to boast its tigritude; it just jumps on its prey, kills it and eats it' (p. 2).[35]

Still, Senghor is the Africa we don't often hear about. Notwithstanding his unease with official French colonial policy, he remained loyal to the French integrationist project in Africa and initially supported a French African zone as opposed to outright independence. As the winds of change were sweeping the continent, a phrase coined by British Prime Minister Harold Macmillan in 1960, Senghor was later to change direction and fell into the independence line.

On Senegal's Beaches

So this was a very different Africa to the part we had left behind us in Kenya. Visually, though, it was equally stunning. On the evening we arrived on Kayar's teeming beaches Mick O'Rourke, Mick Cassidy and Bob O'Brien threw themselves into the throbbing crowd with abandon. Hundreds of people thronged the beaches as the boats disgorged their daily catch and those on night duty prepared to set sail. The noise was as deafening as the colours were loud. Even if we did not understand the Wolof tongue, we could detect, as is often the case in these kinds of scenarios, the meaning in the shouts and counter-shouts.

I stood and watched and caught the occasional glimpse of Mick Cassidy's boom-pole and their bobbing heads. Mick, Mick and Bob appeared to be little more than bits of flotsam on a frantically turbulent sea of colour, their white faces surfing occasionally like bits of foam above a blue-black sea. There were times when it was difficult to know where the beach started and the sea ended such were the numbers of people thronging around. It was exhilarating, thrilling non-stop action. There were wonderfully painted wooden boats known as pirogues, sea-sky intense blues, streaks of sunset reds, sun-scorched yellows. Colours were replicated in the clothes worn by the women. These and the lime-green, dazzling white, rust-brown and azure blue *kaftan* or, in the Wolof language, *mbubb* full-length robe worn by the men. The very name of the country comes from these small wooded dug-out boats. Senegal is formed from a contraction of the Wolof *sunu gaal,* meaning 'our pirogues'.

Men in green and yellow waterproof overalls hurriedly disembarked from these pirogues. Equally hurried men met them with multi-coloured plastic containers into which the fish were poured. For people who think that Africa moves slowly, not here: Kayar proves them wrong. The weighty containers were then lifted on to the heads of the men who carried them to the waiting women. Wrapped in the most colourful of clothes that even rival those of the Turkana women, the women sort the fish so they are ready for export. Meanwhile, Mick, Mick and Bob weave their way through the throng, caught up in the exhilaration of the moment. Later, when I asked Mick O'Rourke what it was like, he replied, 'Easy, there's was nothing to it, you didn't have to think, everywhere you pointed the camera something extraordinary was happening before our eyes'. Modesty aside, he was right.

Gathering Storm Clouds

From a distance, it all seemed like an idyllic life. Since time immemorial, men have cast their nets at sea. This centuries old way of life that was unfolding before our eyes conjured up biblical images, but this was no first-century parable. These fishermen have to survive in a globalised, twenty-first century world and fish plucked from the sea were their route to survival, an essential lifeline for these coastal communities generating and enmeshing them into a capitalist economy that educated their children.

Exporting the fish is the problem. Behind the façade of light and jollity on the beaches of Kayar, a darker story lies. Fish have become a much sought after and increasingly scarce commodity. Wealthier nations in Europe and elsewhere have near exhausted their own reserves and have turned to Africa for supply, much in a way that previous generations of predators have turned to Africa for everything from rubber to ore to the people themselves in an attempt to plug the holes in their own economies/societies. Fish caught today in Senegalese waters are more likely to end up in a European pan or a Japanese, Chinese or Korean wok. First shrimp, then tuna and even the fish of the poor, sardines, are now heading elsewhere. While there are some gains in the form of foreign earnings for a cash-strapped people, the long-term consequences of satisfying the world's insatiable desire for fish are seriously detrimental to Senegal's own strategic interests.

Whatever about Senegal's strategic interests, for the irrepressibly gregarious Mati Ndaw, the president of a local women's cooperative who dries fish on Kayar's beaches, fish exporting is her family's lifeline.

> *We process all the products from the sea and dry them. When the fish is unloaded here it is scaled washed and salted. Afterwards we leave it here for two days, then wash it and dry it for export. With the money we get, we help in the upkeep of our families, help our husbands. The change is noticeable in our homes. With the money we are earning, we are changing society. Women can now pay for everything, starting from school stationery to medical care.*

When we met her husband, Mandiaye Diop, later that evening, he was less sanguine about the country's fishing industry.

> *Each fisherman has a lot of people to feed. Those who have small pirogues feed up to twenty people. For the big pirogues, it's up to 100 people. Where once you could catch fish within ten kilometers, now you have to go up to thirty kilometers. This, combined with the higher cost of running engines, adds to our overall costs.*

Those who used to go out to fish for one or two days now spend six or seven days at sea. Far beyond the horizon, out of sight of local fishermen, large factory ships are hovering up Senegal's increasingly depleting fishing stocks. Nobody knows for sure how much fish is being taken from the sea. None of this fish is landed but is exported directly to Asia and Europe. In an effort to compete with these large fishing trawlers, local fishermen are forced to invest in new technologies, like GPS systems, and to go further out to sea and for longer. When the catch is good, it is worth their while. Those who can't afford to invest in these new technologies or in more seaworthy boats are being forced out of the industry. And all of this is in direct violation of the UN Convention on the Law of the Sea, which states that foreign fishing activities should disrupt neither local fishing nor national food security.[36]

Local food security is indeed under threat. As fish become increasingly more scarce, the price increases. Increased prices might bring benefits to some but it hurts the poor, and the price of fish is on the up in local fish markets. Not only that, but the quality of fish in the local markets is deteriorating. The pick of the crop goes for export, the runts for the local market. In Dakar's fish markets mothers seek out the best pickings from these left-overs. One of these mothers, Aminapa Gueye, told us that five years previously one could buy good quality fish for ninety cent. Now it only buys low-quality fish.

> It makes me sad because I would like to buy good quality fish for my family but this is all I can afford. It is so small it is difficult to cook. It disintegrates too easily. My fear is that fish will get more expensive and things will get worse.

Yet again the poor have to make do with the leftovers from their rich neighbours' tables. Despite this potential source of wealth, Senegal remains a poor country. Ranked 155 out of 182 countries by the United Nations' Human Development Index,[37] about half of its thirteen million population are on or below the poverty line, and child malnutrition remains a problem.

Senegal once saw the ocean as its yellow-brick road to fortune, its *El Dorado*. Senegal had fish. Europe and the world wanted fish. A marriage made at sea. In the 1980s, people fled from the drought-ridden countryside to the coast – over eighty per cent of the people live less than 100 kilometres from the sea. Now, forty years later, Joal's fishing port manager Biguiry Cissakho is in a despondent mood.

> It is true that we did sign fishing agreements with lots of countries – Spain, Portugal, Greece, Italy, France, in the 1970s. But we did not look at the impact of this on the future. Today, Senegal once abundant with fish has become a sea of scarce fish.

Give a man a fish and you feed him for a day, we used to presume to tell African people, teach a man to fish and you feed him for life – not understanding that fishing was already an integral part to their centuries-old way of life. It is a supreme irony. Western governments and the fishing business they represent

have taught themselves to fish in African waters, leaving malnourished coastal communities struggling to feed themselves
for the day.

Mbaye Sene, who is now an economic refugee in Europe,
was disconsolate about the future of fishing in his home country
when we met him in Senegal prior to his abandonment of his
inherited family tradition.

> *I stop go to school until I was twelve because I wanted to
> help my father and my mother. That's why I am a fisher-
> man. It's a problem most of my friends come across. Ten
> years ago there would be many many boats in the sea.
> Look at this kind of fish we catch now. It's not good. It's
> not very good. In ten years, we catch big fish, many big fish
> but now they are no fish.*

> *Now, if you go far out in the sea, you find there a lot of big
> boats coming from Europe and from Japan. And they take
> all the fish they find there.*

> *I think in the next years we are going to have nothing to
> fish. I wonder what we will have to do when we cannot go
> to fish.*

> *I wonder.*

And so did we.

Niger

It was virtually impossible to resist asking my Bible-reading, baby-carrying travelling companion on the flight from Paris to Niamey, Niger's capital city, on 4 November 2008 about the election of Barack Obama. Children at the best of times are good conversational catalysts, and cooing looks at a six-month-old are hard to resist. 'So who do you think will win?' I asked. The exit polls were indicating that Obama was going to make it. 'Obama,' she said without a doubt. Looking at the Bible, I asked somewhat brazenly if that were an outcome she would welcome. None of my business of course – just natural curiosity. It was then she told me very conspiratorially that she had voted for him. She waited for my reaction. I waited for her to go on. 'Don't tell my husband,' she somewhat worriedly added. I didn't think I was going to be meeting him so I didn't feel it necessary to reply. 'The sky didn't fall in?' I asked. 'No, but it might have if I told my in-laws.' They were, it would appear, Bush's natural constituency and they were content to pass their allegiance to John McCain. Well, if not wholly enthusiastically to McCain then at least to Sarah Palin.

The question is, where to go in a conversation like this? The Bush legacy? Iraq? Weapons of mass destruction? Abu Ghraib? No, unfair, and anyway too confrontational in such a confined space. So what would have been the in-laws' reaction? 'They wouldn't have believed it.' A silence followed. I wondered if she felt she had revealed too much.

There is a predictability about the 'where are you off to, for how long and to do what' travel talk. We settled into that, now that the very discretely breast-fed baby had settled into its post-feed sleep. 'And you,' I asked when the first opportunity arose.

'I am going to join my husband,' she told me somewhat stiffly, I thought as much a marker of our conversation as letting me know the reason for her trip.

Her husband was a Pentecostal missionary and they were going to build a church in Niamey. So this was the kind of church and missionary activity that had so exercised Mick O'Rourke and me on the road from Eldoret to the Turkana Gorge in Kenya. Mick O'Rourke was out of earshot. I would tell him the story later. Where to go with this conversation? Her husband had been in Niamey for three months at this stage and had, like all good Biblical stories, gone ahead to prepare the way for mother and child. He was starting from scratch. Now she would too. From the comfort of Texas to one of the poorest countries on the planet. So how would she manage the transition? 'The Lord will provide,' she said. I looked at her. I couldn't help but feel that her reply was just too neat, too pat and that she knew that herself.

I was curious to know how one starts a missionary church. How do you overcome cultural and linguistic barriers? How do you maintain your own motivation? As a woman do you expect to have any difficulties adjusting to life in a Muslim country? This was for me the *Poisonwood Bible*[38] come alive. Her husband had a base in the city and his job was to build on that. Her job was to support him. I told her about an article I read years ago in the now sadly defunct *The Word* magazine about a group of bachelors, including a religious minister, who were asked to describe their ideal wife. The religious minister said that *poise* and *deportment* would be a critical characteristic in any aspiring wife of his. I asked her if that was what was required of a pastor's wife. She laughed, but did not answer. 'So how do missionaries build churches? I asked. It's actually pretty straightforward. Pastors go into villages, sit under trees with pots of tea and church literature. They play church music and wait for people to approach them. Then they ask if they would like to be saved in Christ Jesus. And that's it. On to the next village.

'How would US-inspired Pentecostalism be accepted in what is a largely Muslim country, and how would a woman used to western norms adjust?' I wondered. Very well according to John

Micklethwait and Adrian Wooldridge in their somewhat wry but fact-packed book *God is back: How the Global Rise of Faith is Changing the World.*[39] Pentecostalism is, they claim, 'growing like crazy' worldwide and not just in Africa. It is, they claim, the great religious success story of the twentieth century. There are more than 500 million 'renewalists' or members of Pentecostal denominations in the world. Africans are embracing this new renewalist religion with open raised arms and lots of Halleluiahs.

Driven by US-style swish marketing tools and a stripped down version of Christianity that emphasises not just personal relationship with Christ Jesus but salvation in the next life, and a better economic life in this one, the message is simple and compelling. An estimated 30 per cent of the population of Nigeria and about 50 per cent of Zimbabwe have joined. In South Africa, there are 900 congregations in Soweto alone, three of which I attended at various times and at two of which I was invited to speak. While the focus is on the global reach of Islam, Pentecostalism is growing apace far away from the glare and scrutiny of most media, partly because they have steered clear of mainstream media and created their own powerful and wholly effective version. It is expanding twice as fast as Catholicism and three times as fast as traditional forms of Protestantism. It is even outstripping Islam.

Recent US attitudes to the Muslim world certainly complicated the work they do, my travelling companion conceded, but again she invoked the Lord as her guide and saving grace. As for herself, she too would have to make sacrifices. She had been told in advance that at times she would be expected to walk behind her husband and not at his side. She didn't like the prospect but was prepared to reluctantly accept the given norms whatever they might be.

I couldn't help but marvel at her life. This beautiful woman with her new-born baby was leaving what I imagined was a cocooned world for the harsh world of Sub-Sahara Africa. She was leaving home comforts for a strange unknown world. This was after all an utterly decent, sincere woman who was making a tremendous sacrifice for her beliefs. Easier options beckoned. It was a reminder yet again that we can fundamentally disagree with each other while simultaneously recognising each other's sincerity. We wished each other well as we disembarked. I often wondered about her afterwards. How did this young woman and her child settle in Africa? Did she learn to carry her baby on her back? Did she sit in the shade of a baobab tree under African skies serving tea to the sound of 'Precious Lord, take my hand'?

As we were about to leave the plane, she told me of a party that was taking place the following day in the US embassy to celebrate the election of the forty-fourth president of the United States. She would be there. Would we like to come? Would we what! Late the following afternoon we turned up at the embassy. I tried to blag our way in, but I should have known better. US embassies don't do blagging even when the official's name is as Irish as it gets. In any case, the party was over. For us too it was back to work. The tragic face of poverty in Africa beckoned.

When confronted with human tragedy, the temptation is both to stare and to look away. We are invariably caught between these contradictory impulses. We slow down at car crashes while we walk briskly past homeless drunkards stretched on the pavements of our streets. Our eyes are drawn to what we perceive as different – skin pigmentation, appearance, dress code, types of behaviour – and then lest we are seen staring we hastily look away. Decorum requires that we don't gawk, that we avert our gaze, and at times that is as it should be. An awful power imbalance exists between those who hold the gaze and those at whom the gaze is directed.

But the averted gaze remains deeply embedded in our interactions with each other. In this celebrity-obsessed world our gaze is drawn to the endless parade of the famous and the infamous. Our consciousness and knowledge of these tiny elites increases and multiplies as if by an inverse relationship to our consciousness and knowledge of the poor, the disfavoured and the excluded of the world. The reality is that we are happy to avert our gaze from the world's poorest, particularly now that we have our own troubles at home.

However that is not the sole reason why we are reluctant to face Africa's daunting poverty – abject poverty is not a pretty sight anywhere – and none more so than for the sufferers of Noma in Niger in what has become known as the Noma belt that stretches across Sub-Sahara Africa from Senegal in the West, through Burkina Faso, Niger, Ethiopia and into Egypt.

I first read of this disease in an Irish newspaper article written by Maggie O'Kane over ten years ago.[40] The images of deeply scarred children never left me. Mick O'Rourke, Mick Cassidy, Stephen O'Connell and I prepared in advance as well as we could for our meeting with children with Noma, but nothing can prepare you for face-to-face confrontation of this disease's insidious impact. Eyes, nose, mouth and chin are all Picassoesque-like thrown out of shape. The skin is blotted and blackened, not from natural pigmentation but from cellular degeneration.

Also known as grazers' disease because of the way it eats facial tissue, Noma leaves a terrible trail of destruction on children aged between two and six. Tissue degeneration begins on the inside of the mouth and by the time it comes to the attention of parents, it is often at an advanced state. A hole appears on the outside of the cheek which very quickly spreads and engulfs the whole cheek. As the facial muscles degenerate, the jaw often locks and as a result children are unable to eat and quickly die from starvation. As these children await their untimely death, the pain is often excruciating.

Dr. Issa Eohamady, a surgeon who treats Noma, explained its scientific etiology.

> *Noma or cancrum oris is a gangerous infection, which starts in the mouth and the gums. It spreads very rapidly and necrosis sets in to all soft tissue of the mouth and can reach the bone. It spreads rapidly and is often fatal. Ninety per cent of children who contract Noma die. Those that survive and often have severe facial deformities. It is an infectious process. The pain of flesh Noma is very severe. It is a really difficult pathology. The proof is the number of patients who die.*

The cause of this horrendous disease is malnutrition and poverty allied to poor hygiene, as Dr. Issa Eohamady explained.

Studies have shown that malnutrition is a major cause of Noma. At a time of low resistance, these germs turn on us. That's what causes low immunity. This happens in the course of a viral or bacterial pathology such as malaria, measles and always in a malnourished person.

Nobody knows for sure why some child-ren succumb and others, even within the same family, do not. This is not a high profile disease that attracts research grants and university-led investigation. Pharmaceutical companies simply do not want to know. While nobody knows for sure, epidemiologists estimate that eighty per cent of those who contract the disease die from it. Ostrasisation and stigma are often the fate of those who do not surrender to death's calling card. For the few survivors, the physical scarring often masks deep psychological trauma. Many of those who contract the disease are hidden away, others are often demonised.

Last seen in Europe in the concentration camps in Europe, it is now mainly confined to Sub-Sahara Africa, but there are Noma black spots in Asia and in Latin America. Isolated cases have also been reported amongst HIV/AIDS sufferers in Italy, Scotland, Portugal and the US, but these cases are extremely rare. While a clear causal relationship between extreme deprivation and poverty have been established, many sufferers still rely on myth to explain the onset of the disease.

Mother of five Habiba Maman is unusual in that she is a Noma survivor. But her disfigured face tells its own story.

The Noma began when I was a little child. The sickness began with a small acne on my lip. With time an evil genie entered the acne. That was how my sickness started. The evil that entered made my wound really painful.

Now, thirty years later, tired of the furtive and undisguised gazes, she has decided that she wants reconstructive surgery. Poignantly though she tells us that her husband has never made an adverse comment on her appearance. 'My husband loved me,' she matter-of-factly tells us.

Filming such physical degeneration poses its own difficulties. As a two-year-old child's facial wounds were being dressed, his screams chilled our spines as his frail legs curled up in pain as if in slow motion. Despite the enormous difficulty, Mick O'Rourke held his gaze, while Mick Cassidy did not flinch from the amplified sounds of the child's screams in his headphones, but their gaze was neither prurient nor voyeuristic.

There were other heartbreaking scenes. We interviewed Sanda Abdou and Rakia Ousman, grandparents of two-year-old Sani Yahaya who had died from Noma. When we called Sanda and the other men of the village were at prayer. Sitting outside their mud home out of the glare of intense sunshine, with resignation that only comes from those who have no choice, they recalled Yahaya's dying days.

> *His name was Yahaya. He was two years old when he died. He cried a lot all the time, and it was hard for me. I didn't like it. I had pity on him. He suffered one month before he died. We think about him. We can't forget him. Each time we think about him. I think about my little son. We pray for him all the time. It's the will of Allah. Today one dies and next time it will be the turn of another. It's life. It has begun with my little son. Some die after they are one day old, one month or one year old.*

A simple antibiotic costing no more than ten euro could have saved his life. Proper nutrition and good oral hygiene would have ensured that he never contracted Noma. Had he lived, he would now be four years of age. Instead, another child of African soil dies prematurely.

As we were filming Stephen O'Connell, who was directing this documentary, caught sight of a four-year-old child out on his own away from all the other village children. It was almost as if this child suddenly appeared against the broad flat expanse of the African landscape as the embodiment of the dead child. In the final version of the film, Stephen held that shot for over twenty seconds in the film – an inordinately long time in the world of television. We discussed this shot at some length as we wrestle with many aspects of how we tell the stories we tell. This is Stephen's rationale.

> *I chose the extended length of the shot of the boy to counteract the normal speed and pace of everything else. To make you pause. We're conditioned to receive and digest images very quickly. And I think that while that reflects on us well, evolving at great speed, details are lost. And it's hard to get the viewer to explore below the surface – often because we don't give them the chance. We're speed learning too much.*

> *It's easier to make a film with 500 edits than it is with 50. Some day, I'd like to make a documentary like this in one or two shots, but getting everything in, that you would in a conventional form. It would be cheaper and more interesting.*

> *I also chose to desaturate the two documentaries from Africa as we have an image and recollection of places that does not always correspond to the reality. Africa, we think, is colourful. It is, but in a dirty colourful way. It's a bit like referring to Africa as the 'developing world' when clearly it's not - it's a lie we tell ourselves, to comfort us when feeling guilty of human neglect.*

> *To me, the grade reflected my own experience there and, by not blowing the colours out, exposed a layer of detail that lies hidden beneath. You see more. More skin tones, more mid tones and a more sensual and realistic experience.*

For me, at least, the impact was powerful. Gazing at that unknown child one couldn't but be more aware of the child whose death we were just mourning. Momentarily, he seemed to capture all the lost children of Africa.

Mali

Environmentalists in Mali tell us that eighty per cent of its fif-teen million people are at risk as a result of the drop in water levels of the Niger River. Eighty per cent of twelve million people. That's a lot of people. The truth is that the Niger River is chang-ing, changing utterly. Mali's great lifeline is slowly dying. Its once great vitality gone, most fear forever.

For the foreseeable future, the world will be faced with three liquidity problems – finance, oil and water. If oil was the catalyst for war in the twentieth century, then water could very well be the trigger for the twenty-first century. The reality is that fresh water on the earth's surface is fixed. The planet holds approximately 1,386 million km³ of water, of which 97.5 per cent is salt water. It cannot be increased or decreased. Consequently, as populations grow, more and more pressure comes on this most precious of resources. And increasingly, we are consuming vast quantities of this liquid. Twice as much water was used worldwide in 2000 as was in 1960. As a result, rivers are shriveling, water tables are shrinking and wells are drying up.

'Repeated blows are being dealt to a hydrological cycle that has continuously renewed and replenished Earth's water flows since time immemorial,' warns Robin Clarke and Jannet King in their attractive and persuasive book, *The Atlas of Water*.[41] Wa-ter watchers are united in their view that by the middle of this century half of humanity will experience water shortages. But in Mali in Sub-Saharan Africa that future is now.

Mali is hugely dependent on the Niger River, which curls around the shoulder of West Africa starting in Guinea and snak-ing its 4,400 kilometre-way through Burkina Faso, Niger, Mali and flowing into the Atlantic Ocean in Nigeria. The river has been called the umbilical cord that joins together the urban centres of Mali. Its impact is felt not just in these six countries, but in Algeria to the north and Cote D'Ivoire in the south. The Niger has the world's ninth largest river basin, a stunning miracle of nature that feeds these five water-starved countries and, when it is in full flood, feeds an estimated 110 million people. Environmentalist Sounfountera Salahina told us of the river's importance.

> In Africa we have three big rivers – the Nile, the Congo, and the Niger. The Niger is the one we have in Mali – so those rivers are very, very important. They are crossing lots of countries and most of the people – the whole population – live on this river . . . because we have different populations using this river: the fishers, the farmers, and also the herders. All these people need the river – for different reasons . . .
>
> In one word I can tell you that these rivers are not only the arteries, and the veins, but the soul of the countries – this is what we used to say. The Niger for Mali is the soul of the country. So if these rivers disappear so it's like the countries are dead: people will really suffer and 80 per cent of the population will not survive without this river. If we don't do anything about desertification, this Niger river will disappear in twenty-five years.

Those who live on and off the river are the true bellwethers of its state, none more so than elder Kono Famanta, a member of the Bozo tribe. The Bozo people, unfairly caricatured here and elsewhere as the clowns of our circus world, are deadly serious about the impending implosion of their world. Nomadic fishermen, they follow the seasonal migration of various fish pulling into ports along the way to sell their catch in exchange for other basic staples.

> The river gives me everything in my life and I want to take the river and protect it. A Bozo's life is water and fish. Nothing else describes a Bozo except water and fish. Bozo people are born in the water, we are circumcised in the wa-

Rodney Rice at the Hector Pieterson Memorial site in South Africa (2004)

Alena Monosile and her children in Malawi (2004)

Peadar King with Francis Kamwenda on his return visit to Malawi in 2011

Turkana women in Kenya building their home (2006)

Pokot house building with Chief Domonyang Lopuslo in yellow t-shirt (Kenya, 2006)

A Turkana woman and her child (Kenya, 2006)

Senegalese fishermen put out to sea (2006)

Mbaye Sene in Senegal (2006)

Diop Mor Talla in Senegal (2006)

Sani Yahaya's grandfather, Sanda Abdou, and grandmother, Rakia Ousman in Niger (2009)

Children with Noma in Niger (2009)

Mick O'Rourke at the Great Niger River in Mali (2009)

Fody Walett, a member of the Taureg group, insisted on playing for us as she sat outside her tent on the outskirts of Timbuktu (2009)

Ould Saleh el Hadj who told us the story of Timbuktu (Mali, 2009)

Aurelie Talate, who was evicted from her beloved Chagos home in Mauritius (2008)

Centenarian Felice Maudarin was 60 when she was evicted from her home in the Chagos Islands in Mauritius (2008)

Ansie Jaffer tends the graves of Chagos people who never made it home (2008)

Children like these in Angola face a bleak future despite the country's enormous wealth from oil (2008)

Fishermen in Angola, Felipe Mbongo in yellow (2008)

Mateus Lopes in Angola (2008)

*ter, grow up in the water, die in the water. Our whole life is
just that. Everything we do, we do it with water.*

Preoccupation with water and the decline of the river is also a
central concern in the music of internationally renowned Malian
guitarist and singer Afel Bocum, nephew of Ali Farka Touré. Irish
filmmaker Dearbhla Glynn made *Dambé: The Mali Project*[42] with
Afel and not only did she generously pass on her contacts to us
but travelled to Mali with us as well. Afel's band is called Alkibar,
which translates as 'messenger of the great river'. Afel invited us
to his home to meet his band and also internationally renowned
singer and drummer Fadimata Walett Oumar, otherwise known
as Disco. The music they played for us was spellbinding, Afel's
gentle melodies accompanied by light drumming, hand clap-
ping and that ever distinctive African ululating.

Africa's musical heritage is extraordinary. African rhythms
have infused practically all contemporary music: jazz, rock,
soul, reggae, hip-hop, rap and rhythm and blues. Names like
Yossou N'Dour from Senegal, Fela Kuti from Nigeria and Miriam
Makeba from South Africa have become well known to music afi-
cionados everywhere. What has always amazed us in our travels
around Africa is how quickly and easily Africans will spontane-
ously break into dance and song, and how intense these perfor-
mances can become. From the fisherwomen in Senegal at the
end of their day's work to the late evening jump-dance of the
Turkana, the toi-toi of South Africans to the drumming of the
Bozo music we have been privileged to witness such a wealth of
music. When we visited Fody Walett in her Taureg tent, all she
wanted to do was perform on her homemade stringed instrument for us.

In Mali it was the intensity of the late evening drumming and
dancing of the Bozo that remained long after we had left them.
All day they had talked about the decline of the river, the erosion
of their way of life and the long-term loss they faced. As we were
about to depart, the music began. It was as if all that intensity
of feeling could only be fully expressed in the music. The power
of the music, the mesmerising intensity, the physicality of the

dance created a greater sense of cultural distance than I had ever previously experienced.

The Bozo have the reputation for being loud, gregarious, extroverted people. Some reputations are deserved and this is a case in point, and that extrovert nature extends to their dress sense – stunning pink, lilac and lime green turbans, and that is just the men. But beneath that façade, that jostling, bustling, vibrant exterior, many Bozo people are deeply worried not just about their short-term economic prospects but about the imminent loss of an ancient way of life. Exuberant spirits are being quietly stilled. Doubt has replaced a sense of impunity from change. Year-on-year fish stocks are decreasing, and the fish that are caught are getting smaller and smaller. The shrinking of the fish stocks mirrors their shrinking sense of their own invulnerability. Bozo chief Kono Famanta welcomed us, anxious that the outside world would see what was happening to them.

The Bozo don't stay in one place. The great work of the Bozo is found where the tributaries meet and where there is lots of water, when there is grass, they fish with great nets from morning till night. The Bozo move around according to the rhythm of the fish. The Bozo move like the Fulani herders move.

This way of life is now under serious threat.

In the past and today is very different, many things have changed. Fishing the big fish is very rare today, this river does not give us the big fish anymore, now it is just the little fish. In the name of God, this is true. The water is diminishing is the cause of all this. Today there are carpe, capitane, ntimbim, congom, saleh, wulu djeguae and tninin these fish are still there. The kundo, the kologana, the poli and the fono, the fono exist but it is very rare. We never find it the Sana and the Pinu. These are the Bozo names. I know no other.

Today, there is not much to eat. Before the Bozo were strong. Now people don't eat well, they eat little cakes, bis-

cuits and peanuts: this is not proper food for the Bozo.
There is not enough to eat.

The ruin of the river is not just measured in declining fish stock. While in other parts of the globe people are anxiously watching the rising tide that threatens to engulf them, forcing them to move not just to higher ground but also to other lands, in Africa it is the land that is threatening to engulf the river. As the water level continues to drop, islands are emerging out of the streams. Permanent homes for the Bozo and other tribes of Mali are now being constructed in what were once homes to an abundance of diverse fish stock, fish that remain critical to the life and well-being of whole communities.

The Niger River has been silted up by the relentless march of the desert, inching its way forward. The devastating drought of 1973 was a critical turning point. Sounfountera Salahina estimates that the desert is creeping forward at a rate of ten kilometres a year. None have experienced this more than the celebrated city of Timbuktu, once known as the gateway to the desert where the camel met the canoe, but the river no longer flows through this great city. The canoes have long since gone.

The great city of Timbuktu is a microcosm of what may yet lie in store for other African cities. Walking its now dry, barren, dusty streets, it was hard to imagine that children once played and swam on the banks of the river, that market gardens were fed from its waters. Ould Saleh el Hadj described the changes that have taken place in Timbuktu.

> *There used to be a canal, a big canal bringing water from the Niger to Timbuktu. At that time this place was a very lively spot. The entire population came here to do their laundry, to wash themselves. Children used to swim here. Fish were plentiful in this canal also. As well as people, aquatic birds came to this spot, birds such as storks and kingfishers. Animals too used this canal, cows, sheep and goats. The Tuareg came here to get water and there was grass everywhere. Better still, many people in the surrounding areas were market gardeners. Their produce in-*

cluded a variety of vegetables, salads, carrots, tomatoes, onions. All around the city there were market gardens and there was no shortage of water for them. That was how it had been for a very long time.

But from the 1960s the river has been in retreat.

That process accelerated from 1973, the year in which there was a much publicised drought. It increased at an even faster rate from 1982 onwards, so 26 years ago, water ceased coming into this canal. Now it is a sorry sight. It is really desolate. Fewer people come here now. There is only an odd tree here and there. Nature has died.

So too it would appear has Kono Famanta's spirit. Confronted with the steady decline of this once great river, and in the absence of any concerted human response to the impending doomsday scenario, Kono Famanta watches and prays. In keeping with ancient animist traditions, he pours a libation of badly-needed goat's milk on the river's waters. The river is his god and that god seems to be abandoning him, something that is more puzzling than that most precarious African thing, life itself.

I have come to offer you this sacrifice. Even the white people have come to talk to us about this problem. You need to help us with this problem. I ask you to do everything you can to help us have many fish, to have many fish, to have many fish, to have many fish. Don't be angry with us, we are from the same mother and father. I beg you to help us, help us have many fish. We are Bozo, help us to have lots of water.

Having poured his libation, Kono Famanta stares disconsolately at the stilled waters of the Niger River, hope evaporating for what he once thought of as an unquenchable way of life.

Mauritius

Death

From the moment we got on the 15.45 British Airways flight from Heathrow to Port Louis in Mauritius, the baby cried for the hour-and a half we sat on the tarmac waiting for take off. An hour and-a half delay is a hell of a wait when you are facing into an eleven hour flight. People have different reactions to crying children on such flights. Mick Cassidy, who was sitting beside me in the middle row of the packed Boeing 737, took refuge in his iPod. I took comfort from Conall Creedon's gripping Cork-based novel *Passion Play* and the wonderful world of Pluto, Tragic Ted, Georgie, Fatfuka and Pinko, not to mention Brenda, Herman, the Monk, Eddie de Nut and a host of other characters.[43] Mick O'Rourke and Jerry O'Callaghan were sitting further up the plane and how they were coping I could only guess. But our discomfort was insignificant compared with the eighteen month old baby's distress, not to mention that of her mother and grandmother who were oh so patient.

Earlier, I had taken the 07.40 flight from Cork to Dublin, and waited until 10.00 for the others to arrive. Over breakfast of eggs and toast in the departure lounge, I was joined at the table by an Irish priest from Kilkenny now working in the United States. He told me that he was home to see his brother who had just been diagnosed with terminal cancer. I listened, touched that he would trust me with his story, and as he left the table he asked me, a complete stranger, to pray for his brother. While at a loss on how to do that, I said that I would certainly try.

Coincidence or not, but death too frames Creedon's novel. His mother went down to Pope's quay, sat on a bench across from the Dominican Priory, took off her rings and shoes, walked down the steps into the river Lee and drowned herself. The flight took off, the child quietened and I was lost in the labyrinthine streetscape of Cork on my way to Mauritius.

Death and loss were to frame our work over the next three weeks. It was almost as if both the book and the priest were a prelude to what was to come. We were in Mauritius to hear about the plight of the people of the Chagos Islands who were forcefully evicted from their homes and island to make way for a military base in the Indian Ocean.

We arrived in Mauritius at 8.30 local time. Sleep did not come easily and my grogginess was not eased by the blast of heat – over thirty degrees on disembarking from the plane – followed by the inevitable queues for customs. Mick Cassidy, Mick O'Rourke, Jerry O'Callaghan and I were thrown together for the next three weeks, first in Mauritius and then Angola. Mauritius was about the size of County Dublin with a population of 1.2 million. A flat tropical island (with the occasional unlikely mountain formation) sprouted sugarcane on either side of us as we drove the forty-minute journey to the hotel. But even on this journey I'm back with Conall Creedon. Back in Cork traipsing past the South Gate Bridge, past Barrack Street on the left and Beamish's, tripping along Proby's quay, up to St. Finbarre's, around by Crosses Green, back to the South Gate Bridge again, into South Main Street, down the North Main Street and into the Coal Quay and all in the company of Mags and Pluto.

Eventually, when we got to the hotel, we were met by human rights activist and author Lindsey Collen who would be our guide for the next week. Even though we were desperately battling sleep deprivation, we sat munching toasted sandwiches and drank pots of tea as we planned the week's shoot before we hit the luxuriantly warm Indian Ocean. Its waters unwound our knotted bodies and for the first time since we left Dublin we could feel ourselves stretching, relaxing, floating, eyes shut, face to the sun as the water washed over us. We had arrived in Mauritius. Cork was but a dream away.

We started the shoot in a cemetery because we were in Mauritius to record an extraordinary story of loss, death and exile.

Not only physical death, but also the death and destruction of a community, and loss of innocence too in the political forces that govern our lives and whose crass self-interest ruin so many. Ansie Jaffer worked as a cemetery cleaner in Port Louis, the capital of Mauritius, where her mother is buried far from where she was born. Others from her community are also buried here, brought to this island over thirty years ago against their will and denied any possibility of going home. Later in the day we met with Aurelie Talate, who lost two of her children on their way here, and who along with her four remaining children was forced to move into the house of her brother who had six children in a slum area in Mauritius.

Aurelie Talate is an extraordinarily brave woman. Drawing deeply, yet lethargically, from her cigarette, she unflinchingly holds your gaze. Burdened by a lifelong addiction to nicotine – she started when she was fourteen – and a kind of pervasive sadness, neither of which she carries lightly, her frail frame belies a steely determination. Intermingled with sustained chesty coughs, Mrs. Talate's stark story involves political and military intrigue, geo-political maneuverings and fundamental violation of human rights. This was not just her story but that of a community displaced by bureaucratic and political apparatchiks unable or unwilling to imagine the shocking consequences of their actions.

Just south of the equator in the middle of the Indian Ocean lies the Chagos Islands. Diego Garcia, the largest of the 65-island archipelago, was the birthplace of Aurelie Talate. These islands have been at the centre of global power struggles for centuries. Wellington's victory over Napoleon at Waterloo in 1815 marked the end of French influence and the beginning of British colonial rule that continues to this day.

Death of an Island

In 1966, as Mauritius was about to assert its independence from Britain, Labour Prime Minister Harold Wilson, along with Defense Minister Roy Mason and Minister of State for Foreign and

Commonwealth Affairs Roy Hattersley, sold Diego Garcia, the most populated of the Chagos Islands, to the United States for a fifty-year lease with a further twenty-year option. From this base, the US launched the first Gulf war and subsequently the Afghanistan war. In return, the US government provided Britain with Polaris nuclear missiles, below the market value, missiles that are still in place today. Both the British and US governments connived in the fiction that the islands were uninhabited except for what one British official at the time said were a few Tarzans or Men Fridays and some contract labourers. They were anything but.

Simon Winchester, in his 1985 journey to the surviving relics of the British Empire, tried to land on the Diego Garcia where the bulk of the population on the Chagos Islands lived and was unceremoniously turned away by the US navy. Nonetheless, he was able to record life on Diego prior to the mass eviction.[44]

> *There was a flourishing, contented and permanent population on Diego Garcia and on half a dozen other islands in the group besides. There were towns, churches, shops, schools, prisons, farms, factories, docks, playgrounds, warehouses and a light railway. People had been living on the islands for the previous two centuries; there were graveyards, with stones inscribed in Creole and English and telling of a tradition of community and comradeship (p. 39).*

According to Winchester, the US wanted to build their base on Aldabra, but this island was home to the giant Aldabran tortoise that would inevitably be disturbed by the noise of the aircraft and by the construction work, and the Pentagon wisely decided not to pick a fight with the international tortoise lobby. So they settled for Diego Garcia and picked a fight with its human occupants instead.

Having decided to leave the tortoises to their own devices, the problem was what to do with the people on Diego. *Pretending* that people weren't on the island wouldn't solve the problem. If the US and British governments wanted to build their military base on the Chagos Islands, they had to induce or force the people off the island. They chose the latter.

Over a seven-year period, they threatened, coerced and cajoled the 2,000 islanders – poisoned their dogs, stopped their food supply, and denied them medical attention. If for any reason someone had to get off the islands, they were never allowed to return. Those that survived the initial onslaught were forcibly removed. By 1973, the islands were cleared of their people and a US military base was in place. Notwithstanding the sign that they erected stating 'Welcome to the Footprint of Freedom', apart from US military personnel and a few British officials nobody was allowed to set foot on the place. Meanwhile, the shell-shocked people from the Chagos were abandoned in Mauritius and in neighbouring Seychelles.

Mrs. Talate and her six children were among the 2,000 people forcibly removed from their homes and dumped in the squalid slums of Mauritius, 1,200 miles away. Her memories of life on Diego Garcia are perhaps understandably tinged with nostalgia.

> *I was born on Diego Garcia and I grew up there and it was there I bore six children. Prior to our deportation, my family lived on Diego for five, six generations. All my life was spent on Diego. My birth was there. My ancestors were from there. It was a paradise. You see it was a paradise that we have lost, when I was uprooted, forced to leave Chagos. Over there I lived like a fish in water.*

Auriele was pregnant when she was evicted from her home in 1973 and was gripped by what the islanders call 'the sadness' – a grief that found expression in dejection, disorientation and even suicide. Two of Auriele's children died shortly after her arrival in Mauritius.

Centenarian Felicie Mandarin, now blind, was over 60 years of age when she was forced out. She remembers a time of plenty – food, water, work and rest. Still defiant after all these years, she too wanted to go home.

Soon that pervasive sadness gave way to defiance and the islanders began to organise. The 1980s were marked by a series of hunger strikes and Mrs. Talate went without food for eighteen days. Then they took their campaign from the streets to the courts. They were convinced that their eviction was illegal and soon senior legal figures within Mauritius began to speak out. Former Chief Justice Rajsoomer Lallah was absolutely clear that the forced evictions were illegal.

> *What happened to the people of the Chagos islands was illegal. It was illegal according to international law. The United States of America and the UK government were complicit in this illegality . . . and they were removed in terrible conditions, their dogs were shot, their animals were shot dead and they were threatened with being deprived of food and were told that ships would no longer come there. What happened was gross intimidation, gross inhumanity.*

Death of Justice

Meanwhile, the international campaign began to gather momentum. Simon Winchester credits a middle-aged English teacher from Kent named George Champion as the instigator of that campaign. He changed his name to George Chagos and began a monthly vigil outside the gates of the Foreign Office. Others followed, including John Madley who wrote a report in 1982 that was picked up by every serious newspaper and journal in Britain.

The islanders took the British government to court in London. Sensationally, the court found that the British government had acted illegally. Led by Prime Minister Tony Blair, the government appealed the decision and in a stinging rebuke of government policies, the courts again found in favour of the islanders. In a last throw of the legal dice, the UK government appealed the High Court decision to the House of Lords. Forty years of resistance was determined by five law lords. Two – Lords Bingham and Mance – voted in favour of the islanders' right of return but, critically, three – Lords Hoffmann, Carswell and Rodger – voted against. Thereby hangs the fate of a people. Three to two.

And then, from the Chagos Islanders' perspective, came the galling, self-serving rhetoric of a third generation of Labour politicians. This time it was from David Miliband, British Foreign Secretary, later pipped at the post by his younger brother for the leadership of the Labour Party. There were the now-mandatory expressions of regret, but they cannot disguise the palpable sense of relief that underpinned his public utterances, not to mention his disassociation from the messiness of the past.

> Our appeal to the House of Lords was not about what hap-
> pened in the 1960s and 1970s. Rather, the government's
> decision was rooted in the defence/security of the archi-
> pelago and the fact that an independent study had come
> down heavily against the feasibility of lasting resettlement
> of the outer islands. [45]

Magnanimously, it would appear that Miliband wanted to protect the people from themselves. Such Orwellian justifications do nothing to diminish the bitter disappointment of the people of the Chagos who have struggled so valiantly over the last forty years.

Now, Mrs. Talate and others were left to contemplate their future. Maybe there are worse things than a lifelong addiction to cigarettes. Maybe it is not so much tobacco as the fickleness of politicians and the rulings of unelected elites that should carry government health warnings.

Of all the stories we have covered, this one has weighed heavily. This was not about the fickleness of nature, a chance happening, being in the wrong place at the wrong time. This was blatant, willful, self-serving disregard for the rights of people, and the British Labour Party was up to its neck in it. How could successive British Labour Prime Ministers – Wilson, Callaghan, Blair and Brown – connive and plot against such innocent people? If it was the Tories, Margaret Thatcher for example, it would be more understandable – reprehensible still but more understandable. And all the while Blair, Brown and Co. presented themselves as great advocates for Africa. By 2010, Blair seemed to have expunged the Chagos Islands from his consciousness. In his autobiography, *A Journey*,[46] there is no reference whatsoever to one of the greatest miscarriages of justice in recent British history, and one that continued to be played out on his watch. Nine years earlier, in 2001, Blair stated that 'the state of Africa is a scar on the conscience of the world'.[47] Well, he might ask Ansie Jaffer, Lindsey Collen, Aurelie Talate, Felicie Mandarin and Rajsoomer Lallah what they think.

Postcript

Sadly, Aurelie Talate died at the beginning of 2012. She never returned to the Chagos Island of her dreams. Rajsoomer Lallah, the former Chief Justice, died in the middle of 2012, after a fall in which he injured his neck very badly. A case is winding its way through the British courts. A mini-judgement within this case said that the Wikileaks documents could be heard as evidence. The case is also before the European Human Rights Court and the Mauritian Government has a case against the UK Government under the UN Convention on the Law of the Sea.

Angola

Whitewashed

If the story of the Chagos Islanders weighed heavily on us, so too would the story of Angola. Word from Kevin O'Sullivan, who was our fixer in Angola, was not good. Kevin was at the time a PhD student in Dublin. More than once he reminded me of former Taoiseach Brian Cowen's description of the Irish Department of Health as akin to Angola. Cowen didn't intend the comparison to be flattering to Angola. Compared to enjoying the warm waters of the Indian Ocean, he felt he had pulled the short straw. Communication between Angola and Mauritius was patchy at best. Telephone calls were breaking down and Kevin found it difficult to access internet lines. Worriedly, we learned that he had been held at gunpoint and robbed. Not so worriedly, he later commented, that it stopped us from luxuriating in the Indian Ocean.

Kevin met us off a flight from Johannesburg in Luanda's crumbling, dilapidated, international airport. He had in tow the worst translator/fixer we have ever encountered on our travels. The fixer and his sidekick had all the garish accoutrements of perceived success: the pinstriped if ill-fitting suit with pen *and* handkerchief in breast pockets, sunglasses which were worn indoors, heavily polished pointed shoes and what appeared to be empty briefcases. There was a certain swagger about their whole demeanor, the only thing missing being the Kojack-style toothpick in the mouth. And of course they had the ubiquitous mobile phones glued to their ears. In reality, they were caricatures of themselves. Diop Mor Talla they were not. But our fixer was also a modern African morality tale of a nation and a continent whose soul had been corrupted. This is what westerners had brought to Africa and this is what many Africans had presumed would impress us Europeans. Brash, bluster and brazen.

In that sense, our fixer had learned his lesson well. As he explained to us later, he was on the winning side in the civil war, now well connected to the government, his family all in the right places. His self-representation was a carbon copy of many post-independent leaders across Africa – Malawian president Hastings Banda's penchant for three-piece pinstriped suits complete with sunglasses and black homburg hat, the extraordinary self-aggrandizement of Jean-Bédel Georges Bokassa, who in 1977 crowned himself Emperor of the Central African Empire at a cost of $22 million in a country at the time of two million people. And perhaps the crown prince of them all was kleptocrat-in-chief Zairian President Mobutu Sésé Seko Nkuku Ngbendu wa Za Banga, to give him his full title, who chartered Concordes so that his family could fly to New York on shopping trips and whose day was not complete without his favourite tipple of pink champagne. Our guys were miniature mirror images of those they held in such high esteem.

Our fixer and his role models were of course a product of other white people, people who had sought to form them in their own likeness. Jean-Paul Sartre put it most eloquently in his Preface to Frantz Fanon's classic text on colonialism *The Wretched of the Earth*.[48]

> *The European élite undertook to manufacture a native élite. They picked out promising adolescents; they branded them, as with a red-hot iron, with the principles of western culture; they stuffed their mouths full of high-sounding phrases, grand glutinous words that stuck to their teeth. After a short while in the mother country, they were sent home, white-washed. These walking lies had nothing left to say to their brothers; they only echoed (p. 7).*

But confronted by all kinds of difficulties, I was at the time less than sympathetic to the etiology of our fixer's fixations. We had some major confrontations along the way, the first and only time I had such battles, not of the high volume stand-up row variety but confrontations nonetheless. The first was in Luanda airport on our way to Benguela. Another was when he would not or could not get up in the morning, leaving us stranded and the clock ticking. Plus there were the seemingly endless requests for yet more money to buy telephone credit. As is the way of these things, he would have a very different take on it all, and the irony of it all was that he could have been such a superb fixer. His translation skills were superb. He could be utterly charming and even disarming when he chose. Of course, that is also the irony of all the post-independent African leaders. It could have all been so different. They need not have succumbed to the corrupt inducements of their erstwhile colonists.

In rehashing these well-worn frailties and foibles of Africans and African leaders, I am conscious of how close to stereotypes they become. Of course we have had our own kleptocrats in the western world, and we have had our own leaders who have gone to all kinds of extremes to cloak themselves in the vanities of power. I also understand that many of these well-rehearsed litanies of African excesses are grounded in racism, colonialism and cultural superiority. But in my defense against accusations of yet another Western-inspired generalisation, the experience of that one fixer was the exception rather than the norm. While it would be grossly misleading to reduce the vast and sprawling continent of Africa to one stereotype, it would be equally disingenuous not to acknowledge that Africans, like the rest of us, are a mixed bag.

Unfortunately, in the heat of a shoot, there is little time for such equivocations. We had a feckless fixer and there was no time to try to locate another, but that was not the only difficulty we encountered in Angola. Immediately as we left the airport, we were stuck in rain-deluged traffic. Roads in Luanda, Angola's capital, are sorely lacking. Not just good roads, any roads. It has the worst traffic imaginable of any city I've ever seen. Kevin had put a timetable together for us for the week. 'All times are traffic dependent,' he advised us straight off. As well he might. It took us nearly four hours to travel fifteen pockmarked kilometres.

Colonialism's Legacy

We headed for the Boa Vista slum, a twenty-first century Dickensian world of ramshackle corrugated iron houses and open sewers in one of the poorest and most overcrowded, but not untypical, districts in Luanda. Boa Vista is home to about 50,000 people. On what passed for a road, there were craters that would swallow a small child. There were no drains, few if any latrines, no sewage systems, no access to safe drinking water. The rain churned up the earth and sewage into an ugly, gurgling mix. We slowly sloshed our way along. In a short time, the water was up to the door of our 4x4 wheel drive. People were scurrying from the rain and at one stage we saw a disabled woman dragging herself on her backside, using her hands to propel herself along. Mick O'Rourke had the camera on his shoulder, but on seeing the woman he put it down. To film her would be to heap indignity upon indignity.

This was the shocking and distressing reality of oil-rich Angola. But poverty and misery are never random. They don't just appear by accident. For centuries, Angola's wealth has been plundered by outside forces as have other African countries. First Portugal took what it could before it fled in 1975, and then Angola became the Cold War's hottest battle site in all of Africa. The Soviet Union, Cuba, the United States and South Africa were all scrambling for their piece of the action.

It all stemmed from the collapse of the Salazar dictatorship in Portugal which abruptly catapulted the country into independence. Unlike most other colonial powers who succumbed to the winds of change sweeping the continent of Africa, Portuguese dictator António de Oliveira Salazar was not for turning. For fourteen years, from 1961 until 1975, the Portuguese fought an unwinnable war against the forces of time, until the 1974 coup brought the Portuguese dictatorship to an end. Independence did not bring any respite to Angola. If anything the chaos deepened. Those Portuguese who had made their homes in Angola fled in a mass exodus in the midst of an apocalyptic atmosphere of well-grounded fear of impending doom, an exodus compel-

lingly captured in Ryszard Kapuściński's moving and astonishingly brave account of his time in Angola in *Another Day of
Life*.[49] Everything the colonialists could take with them, they did.
Overnight, contents of homes were emptied into huge wooden
crates.

> *Into these crates went whole salons and bedrooms, sofas,
> tables, wardrobes, kitchens and refrigerators, commodes
> and armchairs, pictures, carpets, chandeliers, porcelain,
> bedclothes and linen, clothing, tapestries and vases, even
> artificial flowers (I saw them with my own eyes) all the
> monstrous and inexhaustible junk that clutters every mid-
> dle-class home. Into them went figurines, seashells, glass
> balls, flower bowls, stuffed lizards, a metal miniature of
> the cathedral of Milan brought back from Italy – letters
> and photographs, wedding pictures in gilt frames, all the
> pictures of the children . . . everything and I mean every-
> thing . . . this case of wine, this supply of macaroni . . .
> the fishing rod, the crochet needles, yarn, (the) rifle . . .
> coloured blocks, birds, peanuts, the vacuum and the nut-
> cracker . . . the curtain rods. The house's striptease goes all
> the way (p. 14).*

Later, Kapuściński stood on the quay and watched the wood-
en city sail away.

> *It was carried off by a great flotilla with which, after sever-
> al hours, it disappeared below the horizon. This happened
> suddenly, as if a pirate fleet had sailed into port, seized a
> priceless treasure, and escaped to sea with it.*

> *Even so I managed to see the city sail away. At dawn it was
> still rocking off the coast, piled up confusedly, uninhab-
> ited, lifeless, as if majestically transformed into a museum
> exhibit of an ancient Eastern city and the last tour group
> had left. At that hour it was foggy and cold. I stood on the
> shore with some Angolan soldiers and a little crowd of rag-
> tag freezing children. 'They've taken everything from us,'
> one soldier said without malice. 'They've taken everything
> from us,' he repeated (p. 17).*

The irony of it all is that these wooden crates were piled up on the quays of Portuguese ports for months on end, abandoned by their owners. Nobody knew who owned what and many were eventually destroyed.

Their owners or their forebears may have come empty-handed to Angola but they weren't leaving empty-handed. The heavily-laden departure of the Portuguese marked the further unraveling of an already tattered nation in what the United Nations described at the time as the world's worst war, and what historian Paul Nugent called 'a seamless continuity from a colonial to a civil war (p. 287)'.[50] The civil war was indeed chaotic, bitter and brutal, perhaps even more so than most wars. Here there were no neat dividing lines. Ragged-trousered soldiers fought ragged-trousered soldiers. There were no uniforms to distinguish one army from another. The enemy was everyone and no one. There were no real territorial gains; the territory was too vast, the soldiers far too under-resourced to claim any piece of territory for long, though that did not stop the atrocities and the blood-letting. It was murderously messy. Horrifically traumatising tactics were employed by everybody. Forced recruitment of children, annihilation of villages, torture, looting and of course the ultimate weapon of war, the systematic rape of women. It was as if a killing stupor had descended on the country and those who were doing the killing did not know why.

If the internal dividing lines were lost in a haze of confusion, the international dividing lines were very clear. This was standard post-colonial chaos very deliberately ventilated by Cold War rivalry. The Civil War that followed the independence civil war pitched the Soviet and Cuban-supported MPLA (Movimento Popular de Libertação de Angola) against the US and South African supported UNITA (União Nacional para a Independência Total de Angola). Cuba sent 50,000 soldiers, the US and the Soviets sent weapons of war. Nobody knows for sure how many South Africans were operating in Angola. Apart from territorial superiority, oil and diamonds were the great prizes Angola had to offer. The Soviet and Cuban-backed MPLA had the oil, while the US and South African-backed UNITA had diamonds, but even these neat divisions had fault lines. The civil war threw up one of the greatest war-time ironies. Communist Cuba defended US oil facilities, the revenue from which allowed Angola to purchase Soviet weapons to fight a US-backed militia. But that wasn't the only conundrum that the Angolan war threw up. Zambian President Kenneth Kaunda supported UNITA, which in turn was backed by the apartheid government of South Africa. Yet at the same time, Kenneth Kaunda was host to Oliver Tambo, Nelson Mandela's former law partner in the first black legal firm in South Africa and President of the ANC, along with many other ANC leaders who were trying to overthrow the apartheid government of South Africa.

By 1991, when the Cold War ended, 100,000 Angolans had died on the battlefield, a further 700,000 were killed by landmines, famine and disease and almost one-third of the remaining population were displaced. In addition to this litany of woes, Angola has more amputees from the war than any other country. From 1991 until the assassination of UNITA's leader Jonas Savimbi in 2002, Angola's civil war dragged on.

The ultimate spoils of victory went to the MPLA, and for the rest of the century they were the custodians of Angola's extensive oil wealth. A Soviet-educated engineer, Edwardo dos Santos, took office in 1979 and has remained in power since. In another remarkable twist, the MPLA renounced Marxism in the new post-Cold War dispensation and the United States switched sides and backed them. Two years later, dos Santos was given the White House welcoming treatment by George W. Bush. Erstwhile enemies now forged a pragmatic alliance.

In power, dos Santos quickly distanced himself from his collective roots. Power and influence was centred on an estimated 100 families who became the sole beneficiaries of the country's enormous wealth, along with the predatory foreigners who have come to leech off Angola. While Angola retains the trappings of democracy, in reality these trappings are little more than a façade. The vast majority of those who fought in the wars of independence and the civil war were left outside in the cold. A new Cold War hit Angola but this time of a different kind. A small clique took control of the levers of power and the rest had to fend for themselves.

For a time, Mateus Lopes, whom we met in the Boa Vista Slum, was on the winning side.

> *I was simply a student when the Portuguese abandoned Angola. At the time of independence I was twenty years old. I was born in 1955. We couldn't come to an under-standing and what happened, happened. I fought with the MPLA who went for the socialist option. We were support-ed by the Russians, the Cubans as well.*

Living in a Fraudulent Fog

In telling of his experience of the war, Mateus' features were impassive, almost deadpan, as he recalled its horror. Like Mrs. Talate, he too held our gaze as he told us his story. He talked of Angola's pain but he did not show it. Even as he told us of how cheated he and others feel at what is currently happening in An-gola, his stoical expressions held. Apart from his words the only clue he gave of his sense of desperation and frustration was a slow half-shrug of his shoulders at the end of the interview fol-lowed by a long pause. It had a fatalistic 'this is it and nothing can be done about it' quality.

'Now my life is a battle,' he told us.

> *Like that of all Angolans, struggling from day to day, try-ing to make ends meet. You see the way I am living. My conditions are terrible. I am unemployed. We hardly ever have breakfast. For a person to have three meals a day he has to be in a better position.*

When asked about Angola's oil wealth, we are greeted by an-other half-shrug of the shoulders.

> *We know that Angola has great potential in relation to oil. Now where it goes, who are our customers, I don't know.*

Mateus is but one of five million people living in squalor in Luanda, a city designed for one million, but it's not just the urban abandoned of Lunada's population who feel they have been cast aside. Felipe Mbongo and the fishermen of Damba Maria had the same story. He was only twelve years of age when he joined the ultimate losers, UNITA. Now he simply does not understand why he joined. When we met Felipe and other former members of UNITA in the fishing village, just outside Benguela, they were dragging their empty nets ashore after a night's fishing. There was little to show for their ten hours of labour apart from four puny, life-draining fish.

As they returned, what seemed like the whole village looked on in silence. The fishermen mechanically dragged their nets ashore while the onlookers drifted away. Another day without fish or food awaited them. That day would be no different to most other days.

Some women hovered at the water's edge, then hunkered down, backside to the ocean, in search of clams. All in a line, they scraped the sea-bed as the tide ebbed and flowed around their ankles. We watched from a distance and filmed as discreetly as possible, but these were canny women and they were not deceived by the reach of the long lens. One or two reacted angrily, so we moved on. That's what most Westerners do when confronted by the wrath of the poor in Africa. Quietly but determinedly we avert our eyes and move on. We like the poor to be passive, we even expect it, caught in the pleading stills of our highly pixilated cameras or in atmospheric slow-motion high-definition video.

On the beach in Damba Maria, there was no escaping the faces of despair. We walked from the beach, chided by the women clam-pickers, past the village, past the living, the barely living and the dying. Their poverty was truly shocking, shocking and distressing. You know the images: the distended stomachs, balding, prematurely ageing children with discoloured hair, emaciated adults, people dying on their feet. Many of the children we saw that day were not long for this world. Looking back at the film we made I often wonder who survived and who didn't. There were no fish that day, nor was there the previous day – the following day, who knows? Instead of fish, death stalked this African village.

All the while, the great wealth of Angola is by-passing the seventy per cent of the population who continue to live in abject poverty. The people who need it most. And Angola has enormous wealth, even rivalling Nigeria. Between 1997 and 2008, gross domestic product (read oil) grew more than tenfold from $7.8 billion in 1997 to some $83.4 billion only 11 years later.[51] Income from oil may be spiraling up but there is no trickle down. Unlike in 1975 when Ryszard Kapuściński stood on Luanda's docks and witnessed Angola's very visible wealth sail away, today's wealth disappears off-shore into a fraudulent fog. Neither the oil nor the enormous revenue that flows from it touches Angolan soil. Both are secretively spirited away to distant lands, the oil to China, the United States and Europe.

And the revenue? Who knows? That paper chase is beyond our capacity to follow except that we certainly know that it is not to the country of origin. To every cow its calf, it is not. The irony is that Angola has to import petrol and queues at petrol stations are a regular feature of life in Luanda. One of the biggest oil producers in the world and there is a shortage at home.

While Europe and the United States were the traditional beneficiaries of Angola's wealth, towards the end of the last century China became a major player, not only in Angola but throughout Africa. By early 2006, Angola overtook Saudi Arabia to become China's biggest source of imported oil (p. 3).[52] Linked to this deal was aid and Chinese investment in Angola. Like the deal that was struck with the Chinese government, the Chinese people working in Angola like to keep a low profile. They live in self-contained enclaves in big construction sites cut off from the rest of Angolan society. In fact, all of China's trade, not just with Angola but with Africa in general, has been conducted in a hush-hush atmosphere.

It is not surprising then that huge sums of money have gone unaccounted. According to a Human Rights Watch report, an estimated $4 billion went missing between 1997 and 2002.[53] An act passed in 2002 classified all financial, monetary, economic and commercial interests as state secrets. When the International Monetary Fund queried the missing money, the government replied that they couldn't provide any information because of confidentiality agreements with the oil companies. A 2003 Economic Intelligence Unit[54] report estimated that thirty-nine individuals in Angola were worth at least $50 million, and another twenty were worth at least $100 million.

Despite the destitution that all too visibly characterises Luanda, the city holds within it a mini-city of enormous wealth. Today Luanda stands amidst all the squalor as the most expensive city in the world. Hotel rates of $500 a night are commonplace, and that's for a single room. Nicholas Shaxson was aghast at the astronomical prices.

> The cost of living staggered me: one hotel offered me scrambled eggs for $32 (p. 42). A rented two-bedroomed flat at $7,000 a month is considered fairly cheap. A take-away hamburger cost $13, a glass of fruit juice $5, a pair of rubber flip-flops $34. Car-rental at $500 a day. Annual fees for a day pupil at the international school in Talatona, a brand-new suburb 20 km (12 miles) south of Luanda's city centre, are $23,000 for a founding expatriate parent – and $38,000 for late-comers.[55]

We simply could not afford to stay in any of the city's hotels – the only city in the world we have visited where that was the case. Instead, we were happy to avail of the facilities of a convent for what we thought was in itself a pricey rate of $70. The room had a single iron bed – similar to the ones that featured in those black and white films of institutional homes in Ireland in the fifties. The cold shower was a pipe in the wall. We were not complaining, but such is the cost of living in the city that the Sisters are forced to charge such rates if they are to have any hope of surviving.

To live on two dollars a day in a low-cost economy may be doable at a very minimal level; asking people to live on two dollars a day in Luanda is beyond imagining. Meanwhile, the Mercedes and BMW-driving elite fight for space on the city's pulsating streets.

While its wealth is siphoned off, the people are reduced to a nation of beggars. Even those who are not reduced to begging still go hungry, but here the poor have to cope not just with the very real pangs of hunger but also with the dreadful knowledge that, in the short-term at least, things will not improve. Those who believe that oil can rescue Africa from grinding poverty can find no solace in Angola's experience. Far from it. It has proved itself to be poisonous not only of the physical environment but of the politics and morality of a continent as well.

Human rights campaigner Carlos Figuereido summed it all up for us.

> The war was rooted in international interests because we had oil. We destroyed the country and we are in the shape we are in because we have oil. These are the complexities of the situation.

From discussion of oil, Figueredo moves seamlessly to a discussion of power.

> People who have great power have lots of power. People who have political power also have economic power. They have a very strong capacity to buy other people.
>
> Everywhere in the world it is like that. People with wealth and power rarely take the initiative to share that power.

And then Figuereido's counter-intuitive final comment.

> It's a curse to have the amount of oil and diamonds we have.

As we gather up our gear, Figuereido tells us somewhat enigmatically of an old Angolan saying:

> When elephants collide, it is the grass that suffers.

As we left Angola in December 2008 it was party time in the departure area of Luanda's bleak airport. There were hordes of men knocking back beer, straight from the bottle and all in a haze of blue smoke. We edged our way through them to the bar with a sense of nostalgia. We were heading home and once upon a time this too was what bars were like in Ireland: noisy and smoke-filled.

There were only two flights out of Angola on the night of 15 December 2007. One to London Heathrow, the other to Houston Texas. It was as if only white males could apply to leave the country such was our dominance on the flight. Ten days before Christmas and the plane was packed with men leaving the country, oil men for the most part, plus us five. This is the only visible expression of the draining of Angola. One man got so drunk that he hardly made it to the airplane. His friends cajoled him on, assuring the anxious flight attendants that he would be fine. To wake up in Luanda airport with a hangover instead of home would leave him looking anxiously for an altogether different kind of cure. We were all hoping that we wouldn't be sitting beside him on the way to London Heathrow.

Home for Christmas with . . .

Christmas was coming and Heathrow Airport was decked out as well as Heathrow Airport ever is as we inched our way through the interminable security checks. We took the long walk to the Irish departure area, which was packed with returning Irish reading the *Sunday Independent*, anxious for home news even in this digital age. The flight was delayed and like many others we bought copies of the *Indo* and settled down to coffee and croissants. Even the Business page might while away the time spent waiting. Senator Shane Ross was then Business Editor of the *Sunday Independent*. It was that time of the year when plaudits are being given out. A simple task really, who are the winners and who are the losers, there is no grey area. This was Senator Ross' citation for Ireland's top chief executive.[56]

> *Ireland's oil baron Aidan Heavey snapped up most of this year's analyst votes for top chief executive. The 54-year-old Lamborghini-driving Heavey founded Tullow Oil in*

1985, reportedly after a tip from a banker prompted him to acquire a license to develop gas fields in Senegal. [Heavey] also struck lucky in Ghana when its drilling operations uncovered a major oil find. This was followed by another gusher in Ghana . . . the stock market reacted positively . . .

All the while we were in Angola we had been hearing that oil was a curse. Now we read from one of Ireland's most prominent business journalists that it is in fact a blessing, but a blessing for European explorers and the shareholders, beneficiaries of a resource that has impoverished a continent. No questions asked. No investigation as to the appropriateness/impact of the extraction of this oil from Africa's coast might have on the people of that continent. No need to because local boy does well. That's our story. Ross's implied and mistaken assumption, common amongst international financial commentators, was that what serves the West's interests serves Africa's interests. A neat confluence of interests. That a senior Irish parliamentarian lauds the expropriation of African resources without reference to the impact of such expropriation on African people is profoundly depressing.

The truth that Senator (now Deputy) Ross did not allude to was that Angolan oil seeps from the country at a rate of $10 billion dollars a year leaving in its wake a country mired in poverty. Nearly half the population survive on less than a dollar a day, and seventy per cent of the population live in abject poverty with a life expectancy of forty-six years of age. Further up the West African coast in Nigeria the story is the same. According to Ross, oil is gushing out of Ghana, there for the taking. Gushing no less. As the eminent Cameroonian scholar Achille Mbembe has stated, 'the act of violence often begins with language . . . a language that excuses all and refuses to expose . . .'[57]

We desperately need to resist the local boy does good story, as we need to resist the suave spin that conglomerates like the oil companies pump out on a daily basis. It's a story that has little resonance for the people of Damba Maria village. Whether in fact they even know of the riches that lie just beyond their desperate poverty is a moot point. There is nothing on the horizon that would indicate a world of unimaginable wealth. Nor do the metallic, crab-like structures that suck the sludge from the depths of the ocean come within the radar of their small fishing pirogues. But we know, and we cannot remain silent in that knowledge. If business editors are reluctant or incapable of asking critical questions about the oil industry and how it operates in the global world, then who will? Who is going to act as a conduit for the voices of Africa's poor? Otherwise, the prospect of angry despair receding from villages like Damba Maria remains even more remote. And we will be left with even more shocking and distressing images of the increasing numbers of the world's poor with their wrath ringing in our ears.

Postscript

Just days before we went to print, Bill Corcoran reported in *The Irish Times* that Isabel dos Santos, the forty-year-old daughter of President dos Santos, had become Africa's first billionaire. A spokesperson for Ms dos Santos in Portugal said that any suggestion that her fortune originated from illegitimate sources were 'speculative, unreasonable and without academic merit'.[58]

Endnotes

[1] Hume, D. (1996). 'Of National Character' [1748], in *The Philosophical Works of David Hume*, Volume III, Bristol: Thoemmes Press, p. 228.

[2] Dowden. R. (2009) *Africa: Altered States, Ordinary Miracles.* Portobello Books London.

[3] Burke, J. 'Mission accomplished'. *Sunday Business Post,* 19 October 2008.

[4] White, A. (1996), 'Conrad and Imperialism' in Stape (ed.) *The Cambridge Companion to Joseph Conrad*. Cambridge University Press. p. 180.

[5] Conrad, J. (2007). *Heart of Darkness*. Vintage Books. London.

[6] Dinesen, I. (1952) *Out of Africa.* Penguin. London.

[7] Butcher, T. (2008) *Blood River: A Journey to Africa's Broken Heart.* Vintage Books. London.

[8] Achebe, C. (1988) 'An Image of Africa: Racism in Conrad's *Heart of Darkness*' in *Hopes and Impendiemts: Selected Essays*. 1965-1987. London. Heinemann, pp. 1-13.

[9] This was part of a longer interview with the author and reproduced in full in *Exploring Masculinities*. Department of Education. Dublin 2000.

[10] Reservation of Separate Amenities Act, Act No 49 of 1953: Forced segregation in all public amenities, public buildings, and public transport with the aim of eliminating contact between whites and other races. 'Europeans Only' and 'Non-Europeans Only' signs were put up. The act stated that facilities provided for different races need not be equal.

[11] The 1913 Land Act set aside 7.5 per cent of the land in South Africa for black people. The Natives (Urban Areas) Act of 1923 restricted black occupancy to less than eight per cent of South Africa's land.

[12] Group Areas Act, Act No 41 of 1950.

[13] Population Registration Act, Act No 30 of 1950 led to the creation of a national register in which every person's race was recorded. A Race Classification Board took the final decision on what a person's race was in disputed cases.

[14] Bantu Education Act, Act No 47 of 1953 established a Black Education Department in the Department of Native Affairs which would compile a curriculum that suited the 'nature and requirements of the black people'. The author of the legislation, Dr Hendrik Verwoerd (then Minister of Native Affairs, later Prime Minister), stated that its aim was to prevent Africans receiving an education that would lead them to aspire to positions they wouldn't be allowed to hold in society.

[15] Patton, A. (1988) *Cry, The Beloved Country*. Penguin Books. London.

[16] The full interview is available at http://www.pbs.org/wgbh/pages/frontline/shows/mandela/interviews/coetsee.html.

[17] The full charter is available at http://scnc.ukzn.ac.za/doc/HIST/freedomchart/freedomch.html.

[18] Mandela, N. (1995) *Long Walk to Freedom*. Abacus. London.

[19] See International Apartheid Debt and Reparations Campaign http://kosa.org/documents/ADRflyereng.pdf.

[20] Klein, N. (2008). *The Shock Doctrine*. Penguin Books. London. (p. 202).

[21] Sparks, A.(2003). *Beyond the Miracle: Inside the New South Africa*. University of Chicago Press. Chicago.

[22] Sparks, A. (1994). *Tomorrow is Another Country: The Inside Story of South Africa's Negotiated Revolution*. Struik Book Distributors. Sandton.

[23] *Irish Examiner.* 'Health minister who advocated beetroot to treat HIV dies' Thursday, 17 December 2009.

[24] Leibbrandt, M., Woolard, I., Finn, A. and Argent, J. (2010), 'Trends in South African Income Distribution and Poverty since the Fall of Apartheid', OECD Social, Employment and Migration Working Papers, No. 101, OECD Publishing, OECD. doi:10.1787/5kmmsot7pims-en

[25] Ó Máille, P. *Living Dangerously: A Memoir of Political Change in Malawi.* Dudu Nsomba. Glasgow.

[26] Chabal, P. (1988). *Africa: The Politics of Suffering and Smiling.* Zed Books.

[27] Meredith, M. (2005). *The State of Africa: A History of Fifty Years of Independence.* Free Press. London.

[28] http://newint.org/features/1999/01/01/5

[29] Meredith, M. (2005). *The State of Africa: A History of Fifty Years of Independence.* Free Press. London. p. 384.

[30] le Carré, J. (2007). *The Constant Gardener.* Penguin/Viking. Toronto.

[31] Hawley, S. (2003). Turning a Blind Eye: Corruption and the UK Export Credits Guarantee Department. The Corner House. London.

[32] McCully, P, (1996) *Silenced Rivers: The Ecology and Politics of Large Dams,* Zed Books, London and New York, 1996, p. 261

[33] British House of Commons Select Committee on International Development. 2001. Recent Cases of Corruption Involving UK Companies and UK-Backed International Financial Institutions. http://www.parliament.the-stationery office.co.uk/pa/cm200001/cmselect/cmintdev/39/39ap06.htm

[34] Miller, C. *The Lunaatic Express* (1972) Macdonald & Co. London.

[35] Jeyifo, B. (2004). *Wole Soyinka: Politics, Poets and Post-Colonialism.* Cambridge University Press. Cambridge.

[36] See Article 51 of the United Nations Convention on the law of the Sea http://www.un.org/Depts/los/convention_agreements/texts/unclos/unclos_e.pdf

[37] See http://hdrstats.undp.org/en/countries/profiles/SEN.html

[38] Kingsolver, B. (1998). The *Poisonwood Bible.* HarperFlamingo. New York.

[39] Micklethwait, J. and Wooldridge, A. (2009). *God is Back: How the Global Rise of Faith is Changing the World.* Penguin Books. London.

[40] O'Kane, M. 'The story of Zenibou'. *The Irish Times* Saturday 20 March 1999.

[41] Clarke, R. and King, J. (2006) *The Atlas of Water.* Earthscan. London.

42 http://www.luachra.com/dambe/

43 Creedon, C. (1995) *Passion Play*. Poolbeg Press. Dublin.

44 Winchester, S. (1986). *Outposts Journeys to the surviving relics of the British Empire*. Sceptre. Great Britain.

45 'Law Lords Quash Chagos exiles hopes for return' *The Independent* Wednesday 22 October 2008. http://www.independent.co.uk/news/uk/home-news/law-lords-quash-chagos-exiles-hopes-for-return-968937.html

46 Blair, T. (2010) *Tony Blair: A Journey*. Hutchinson. London.

47 BBC. News. 'Blair promises to stand by Africa' Tuesday, 2 October, 2001 http://news.bbc.co.uk/2/hi/africa/1575428.stm

48 Fanon, F. (2001). *The Wretched of the Earth*. Penguin Books. London

49 Kapuściński, R. (1987) *Another Day of Life*. Penguin Books. London.

50 Paul Nugent, (2004) *Africa since independence: A comparative history* Basingstoke cited in the film treatment prepared by Kevin O'Sullivan.

51 Human Rights Watch. (2010) Transparency and Accountability in Angola. Human Rights Watch. New York. http://www.hrw.org/en/node/89454/section/2

52 Shaxson, N. (2007). *Poisoned Wells: The Dirty Politics of African Oil*. Palgrave Macmillan. New York.

53 Human Rights Watch (2004). 'Some transparency, no accountability: the use of oil revenue in Angola and its impact on human rights', *Human Rights Watch,* Vol. 16, No. 1 (A) (January 2004), p. 1. http://www.hrw.org/reports/2004/angola0104/angola0104.pdf .

54 Figures quoted in Martin Meredith (2005), *The State of Africa: A History of Fifty Years of Independence,* The Free Press, London, p. 616.

55 Russell, A. 'Rents rocket in Angola's oil boom', *The Financial Times*, 8 October 2007.

56 Ross. S. 'The best and the worst of 2007' *Sunday Independent*, 16 December 2007, Dublin.

57 Mbembe, A 'A Critique of Nicolas Sarkozy' in Africa Resource. 18 August 2007. http://www.africaresource.com/index.php?option=com_content&view=article&id=376:a-critique-of-nicolas-sarkozy&catid=36:essays-a-discussions&Itemid=346.

58 Corcoran. B. 'Angolan president's daughter first female African billionaire' *The Irish Times*, 26 January 2013, p. 178.

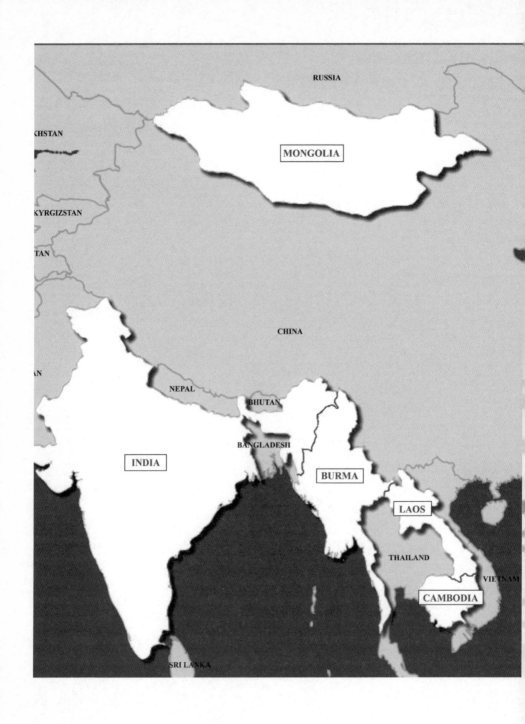

Section Three

ASIA

Asia is not going to be civilized after the methods of
the West. There is too much Asia and she is too old.
– Rudyard Kipling[1]

Mongolia

Under the Mongolian Sky

*My teacher often tells me that the mind should be like the
sea, not a river: deep and still. It should be as clear and
bright as the sky in Mongolia where everything sparkles
in the light . . . the mind should hover very high over the
world like an eagle that only occasionally flaps its wings.*

So wrote Michael Harding[2] in his occasionally wistful, fre-
quently thoughtful and always enjoyable column in *The Irish
Times*. Good teachers are indeed a great blessing and Liam Ashe
was one. His seamless and seemingly endless historical anec-
dotes and his story-telling ability became a matter of some folk-
lore amongst those like me who passed through his classroom.

I heard that Liam had retired and, under pressure to source a
researcher for the Mongolian shoot, I made contact. A 'you may

not remember me' email was met with 'I certainly do and I certainly will' response which resulted in Liam joining Bob O'Brien, Mick O'Rourke and Mick Cassidy under Mongolia's 'clear bright sky where everything sparkles in the light', and it certainly did, but not at first acquaintance. We arrived in Ulaanbaatar, a harsh, unforgiving city which is a less than edifying monument to the social engineering of Stalinist architecture. Towering blocks shadowed one another, echoing John Betjeman's poem, 'The Planster's Vision'.[3]

> *I have a Vision of the Future, chum,*
> *The worker's flats in fields of soya beans*
> *Tower up like silver pencils, score on score.*

Mongolia's sparking light was shut out by a dense cloud of pollutants hemmed in by a necklace of mountains. The twenty, thirty-floored tower blocks were testimony to a misguided and doomed attempt at modernisation. People were forced to live cheek by jowl in one of the lowest-density countries in the world, long after the social engineers had moved on to practice their engineering elsewhere. Into this soup-bowl of smog, thirty-seven per cent of the people of Mongolia were crushed. Ulaanbaatar, like other large capital cities around the world, offers no model to compressed living. It was quite literally a concrete example of the abject failure of humans to construct humanised, large-scale living quarters.

We did not stay long.

We drove north on a ruler-straight black asphalt road that cut like a dark wound through the exquisite whiteness of the blanket-covered snow. Mick O'Rourke, Mick Cassidy and Bob O'Brien were in one jeep, while Liam, I and our wonderful fixer/translator Ulziisuren Altangerel followed in the other. (With her permission we shortened Ulziisuren's name to Ulzii.) Five glorious hours later, we arrived close to the Russian border about two hours from Altanbulag. It was the start of the White Moon festival, probably not the best of times to arrive – something like arriving on a stranger's doorstep on Christmas Eve in Ireland – yet we received a most gracious welcome.

It truly was a breathtaking, snow-capped journey, the beauty, the stillness, the sheer vastness. At times we were lost in the silence, at times in the beauty and I was at times in and the apposite music of the heavily orchestrated 'One Day Like This' from Elbow's not long released album *The Seldom Seen Kid*.[4]

The journey had the scale and expansiveness, but clearly not the drama, danger or indeed the pace of Boris Pasternak's epic novel *Doctor Zhivago*[5] and of David Lean's masterful cinematic interpretation. His snow journey from Moscow to the Urals, like ours on the cusp of spring, captured all its beauty.

> *The snow smoothed and rounded all contours . . . tucked up . . . like a child in its cot with its head under the eiderdown (p. 207) . . . all that thick, deep layer of snow which had settled as far as the eye could see over the immense distances of hills and plains (p. 211).*

> *At first the snow melted quietly and secretly from inside. But by the time half the gigantic work of melting it was done, it could not be hidden any longer and the miracle became visible. Waters came rushing out from below, singing loudly. The forest stirred in its impenetrable depth, and everything in it awoke (p. 211)*

We travelled on.

Half-way there, we saw another reminder of Mongolia's recent history, towering smoke stacks from the provincial town of Darhan. As elsewhere, Mongolia's authoritarian experiment masquerading as a socialist workers' republic ended in disaster. The country had its own little Stalin, a mass murderer named Choybalsan, its own secret service, its own purges. In 1921, Mongolian freedom fighters captured the capital, which was renamed Ulan Bator ('Red Hero') and declared itself a communist state, the second country in the world to do so. Very quickly, Mongolia became a Soviet client, marching in step with the USSR, and in keeping with the socialist fondness for establishing People's Republics, it did just that three years later. The Mongolian People's Republic was born.

As communism began to implode in Eastern Europe and in the Soviet Union itself, so too it imploded in Mongolia. By 1992, Mongolia, abandoned by its self-appointed benefactor, was unable to feed itself or employ its workers. That was the Soviet legacy. That and the *de rigueur* realist art. As we passed Darhan, the strutting wired sculpture of the proletariat male worker was still on his plinth.

As in Ulaanbaatar, we did not delay in Darhan. Very soon we were back on ice-land. Now the only occasional break on the smoothed and rounded contours of the land were the occasional *gers* or yurts, and the herds of cattle, horses, camels and goats that managed to graze under the eiderdown. *Gers* are quite extraordinary constructions. They appear as if they have been dropped like helium balloons on the surface of the snowed earth, perfectly round and each a mirror image of the other. Sporadic conversation in our jeep veered from early seventies school recollections between Liam and myself to the threat to the nomadic way of life. Ulzii may have been a product of Soviet indoctrination and been force-fed on a diet of collectivisation, but she had a real feel for the way of life of the herders of Northern Mongolia, notwithstanding her urban roots.

It was that drive to modernise that led to one of the many conversational *cul de sacs* that Liam, Ulzii and I ended up on during that journey. Coincidently, both Liam and I came from rural West Clare, and while both my parents were farmers, his father was the local teacher and his mother the farmer. Both of us had grown up in what was essentially a peasant society, but one under siege. The dominant political narrative in the Ireland of the 1960s and 1970 was one of modernisation. In short, that meant urbanisation and industrialisation. This was the era of the Mansholt Plan, dreamt up by the then European Commissioner for Agriculture, which sought the removal of five million small farmers from the land. Having cleared the land of its people, intensive factory style farming could begin. The expectation was that we would shake the mud off our boots and fall meekly into the conveyor belt line of industrial production. Instead of having control of our own working day, we were to become compliant, automated units of production. We would be workers no more, just units of production.

The rush to embrace modernisation and industrial production was underpinned by a disparaging anti-rural, pro-urban narrative. Even the very word urbane remains synonymous with sophistication, modernity, progression. In the narrative that was underpinning the new Mongolia, that was clearly evident there as well. It was that kind of conversation that Liam, Ulzii and I drifted in and out on the road to Altanbulag.

The Mongolians too had been pressurised to give up their independent lifestyle. Clearly, the right to roam did not feature as a priority within the Politburo. By the time we arrived to meet with Enkhchimeg, her family and other herders, the Communists had long since departed and the mirror-image capitalists had arrived. In Mongolia, backed by the International Monetary Fund, politicians and economists were working on what they call 'a new development model' for the country. In reality, it was a re-run of the old failed model. Former Prime Minister and later president Nambaryn Enkhbayar had predicted the inevitable demise of nomadism, and declared that Mongolia's nomads had to adapt to new realities if the country was to survive in the modern world.[6] Even the social displacement and claustrophobia of Ulaanbaatar has not dented official enthusiasm.

There is a much more sinister rationale lurking beneath the desire to reign in Mongolia's herders, however, and it is not one that has just become recently apparent. 'Still more pregnant with future possibilities is our great Far Eastern Neighbour Mongolia,' remarked Victor Ippolitovich Komarovsky, Yuri Andreyevich Zhivago's arch-nemesis.

> Mongolia has nearly a million square miles of untold mineral wealth; it is a virgin land which tempts the greed of China and Japan and the United States. They are all ready to snatch at it. (p. 380).

Over a half a century later, that prophesy has come to pass. The largest mining boom on earth is about to take off. The Canadian company Ivanhoe, along with the Chilean company Rio

Tinto and the Mongolian government, are investing $5 billion in the Oyu Tolgoi or Turquoise Hill mine – a mine that is bigger than the state of Florida – making this the largest foreign investment in Mongolian history.[7] While horses, camels, cattle and goats roam under Mongolia's eternal sky, along with the untamed wolf, bear, squirrel and the endangered snow leopard, from under Mongolia's earth copious amounts of copper, gold, coal, silver, tin and uranium are soon to be extracted. What effect the latter has on the former, quite apart from the nomadic herders, remains to be seen. Writing in *The Guardian* on 11 January 2011,[8] Brian Awehali, a member of the Cherokee Nation of Oklahoma, who knows a thing or two about the displacement wrought by modernisation, is despondent in the extreme. Awehali bemoans Mongolia's:

> ... *deteriorating environmental situation (that) is exacerbated by irresponsible vested interests, poor coordination among ministries and agencies, inadequate monitoring of natural resource conditions and weak enforcement of environmental regulation.*

By the time we arrived in 2008, the transformation of Mongolian society was well underway with over half of the 2.6 million population living in urban areas. Thirty per cent of public land had been leased to Canadian, Chinese, Russian and Japanese mining companies for exploration, land that had become closed off to its herder citizens. Mongolia's clear, bright sky might very well have remained a constant, but storm clouds of a very different kind were gathering. For our part, we had reached the end of our journey. It was time to meet with the people we had come all this way to see. It was their story we wanted to tell.

A Film Crew Comes Calling

Eventually, we had to get out of the car. The minus twenty-seven Celsius temperature assaulted us to the core, despite the layers. The cold seemed to swirl around us as if it were looking for any opening into which it could lodge itself against our still warm bodies. Ice crystals seemed to have taken up permanent residence in our nostrils, and risking a pee in the open steppes – even for an all-male crew – posed a number of challenges quite apart from the usual required decorum.

John of Plano Carpini, an Italian friar who visited Mongolia in 1245, didn't comment on whether or not he encountered that particular difficulty, but he did regard the weather as 'astonishingly irregular.'[9] He experienced 'fierce thunder and lightning' that 'caused the death of many men, and at the same time . . . heavy falls of snow'. Carpini described a fierce hailstorm, which was followed by such warm weather that the resultant flash flood killed 160 people. He thought the country 'more wretched than I could possibly say'.

On the weather he was right, on the country and its people he was wrong. We arrived into Enkhchimeg's family home on the eve of the White Moon festival. Unfailingly courteous, the herders made allowances for our unseasonal arrival. We were warmly welcomed, fêted with generous hospitality and more early morning vodka and butter-flavoured, salted hot milk than we could cope. Both the vodka and the hot milk provided desperately needed sustenance. I was doubly insulated. Liam did not drink vodka and Mick O'Rourke did not drink hot milk so we surreptitiously swopped glasses and bowls. By ten o'clock in the morning I was fuzzily warm.

After exchanged seasonal greetings, it was time to leave the intimacy and warmth of Enkhchimeg's yurt, or in her own language *ger*. She was awarded best herder in the country in 2007 and was anxious that we film her among her enormous herd of cattle and goats. 'Our family lives close to the Russian border,' she began.

> We make our living minding 1,000 animals. We call our animals 'live objects of great value'. Our whole family lives off them. We raise most of our cattle by meat type but 20 cows are bred for milk. With our 1,000 animals, we pay over 300,000 MNT (€170) in tax. We supply our country with meat, milk, dairy products and all kind of raw materials from the animals.

A mother and grandmother, and well into her sixties, she mounts her horse and imperiously rides with a lightness of touch that would be impressive in someone forty years her junior. Two of her sons ride beside her commandeering presence. Both have that deep cheek-red complexion, which is no doubt a product of exposure to the elements, as does the youngest of her grandchildren, an eighteen-month-old boy dressed for the festival in his ornate neck-to-toe coat and that distinctive Mongolian hat. In his case, it was bright green with black felt and a golden point standing about three inches from the centre. He will be President of Mongolia yet, Enkhchimeg indulgently tells us.

We walked among the herd, amazed at the way in which they could find spring grass between the iced tufts, their hot, clouded breath rising noisily from the snow. Enkhchimeg exudes pride and knowledge. She has this deep sense of continuity with previous generations and is anxious that the nomadic tradition be maintained, that her extended clan of children, in-laws and now grandchildren will be able to continue the tradition. She is also a realist, and fearful too.

> *Yet in the last few years, the government has paid no attention to the herders. The government's policy is to stop nomadic farming and to have intensive farming instead. Mongolia will face so much difficulty without pasture animal husbandry. Privatization of the land does not suit us and I take it to heart. The main problem is that people who own land can sell it to foreigners. Even if Mongolians buy land, there is often a foreigner behind them. We worry about that a lot. I think our Mongolian land is being sold to foreigners. I worry our children and grandchildren might not have places to live.*

Not wanting to overstay our welcome during their festive season, each day we dropped into different herder families. A rhythm quickly developed. Each night we returned to Altanbulag and each morning the chain-smoking Ganbat and Gansukh Batmunkh had a warmed bus waiting for us, and each morning Ganbat and I had the same exchange. Just prior to arriving in

Mongolia I had watched *The Blues Brothers* for the umpteenth time. Ganbat hadn't seen the film but was greatly taken by some of the lines in it including:

> *We got a full tank of gas, a half a pack of cigarettes, it's dark and we're wearing sunglasses . . . hit it.*

Each morning before starting the engine Ganbat gave us Elwood's lines in Mongolian. For the record it translates as:

> *Bidend bank duuren shatakhuun baina. Khagas hairtsag tamkhi baina. Gadaa harankhui bolson baina. Tegeed bid narnii shilee zuusen baina.*

Dressed from neck-to-toe in a heavily-padded, fur-trimmed, bottle-green coat, with a large orange belt with a silver buckle around his waist, Tumen-Ulzii, who was stacking timber when we arrived at his *ger*, exuded gravitas. A former engineer, he abandoned life in Ulaanbaatar for what he regarded as the freedom of rural living. His passion for the nomadic way of life was palpable, as was his unswerving pride in Mongolia's great heroic figure, Chinggis Khaan, better known in the west as Genghis Khan. Unbridled nationalism might be a fair assessment of his views, ones in which everyone might not agree.

> *In my opinion, he has established the first state country in the world and he united all nations that were weak and divided against each other. So Central Asian countries and some eastern European countries should be grateful to Chinggis Khaan for establishing their states. He had an honesty of character and a generosity of spirit.*

Having established Chinggis Khaan's bone fides, Tumen-Ulzii went on to describe the Mongolian people.

> *We have the most merciful country because even if a six-teen year-old girl carries a full bag of gold on the horse-back, she would be safe. Mongolians keep their valuable things with them in their heart. Gold silver and other valu-able things are considered outside things not part of Mon-*

*golia. Mongolians are the most good-hearted humanistic
and merciful nation.*

*Mongolian people don't like so much for something of luxury. We like to have pleasant life standard. Even he/she is
very rich, he/she doesn't sleep on three beds. He/she sleeps
on one bed. She/he has three meals in a day not ten meals
even he/she is very rich.*

But it was the relationship that Mongolians have with the soil
and their animals that Tumen-Ulzii wanted to talk about most.

*The methods we use to care for our animals date back
5,000 to 6,000 years. Every animal has its own baby animals. And they love each other. Because the temperatures
are so extreme and the soil so brittle, so sensitive and the
plants so fragile, we coax nature and our animals. So we
have a history of connectedness with nature and animals.*

Tumen-Ulzii believes the technological changes are in harmony with traditional nomadic life, and rather than undermining it he argues that it will add to the longevity of nomadism.

*Today herders are talking on the cell phones. We can make
calls to every corner of the world and get information.
Thanks to the solar power we have electricity and watch
TV. And we have cars and trucks.*

While there might have been an element of mythologising
the past and nomadic life as it is currently experienced, Tumen-Ulzii was a realist about the threat posed by the mining companies.

*The last few years the mining companies have started
digging and destroying our land, so we, especially elderly
people, are very regrettable for that. Natural resources are
limited. But life is endless. So we will raise objections if the
mining starts here.*

Equally committed to the nomadic tradition, though much
younger, was the father of two toddler boys.

My family name is Chinsetgeltiinhen. My father's name is Hujin. I am 35 years of age. For over three generations, we have been minding animals: my grandparents, my parents. So we love animals so much. I have 500-600 animals, around 20 cows, over 10 horses, 300 goats and 200 sheep.

Our visit to his *ger* also started with vodka and hot milk. The routine was now well-established. We peeled off layer after layer and gathered round the heat of their wood burner and chatted, the women filling and re-filling our bowls of milk and, even after protestations to the contrary, our glasses of vodka. Then each layer had to be painstakingly put back on before we left the comfort of the *ger*. Outside, Chinsetgeltiinhen explained how the *ger* is constructed and how easily it is to transport from one place to the next.

We move every four seasons. So the Mongolian ger is easy to erect and transport. The frame is made of wood. The outsider is called a canvass we call 'burees'. Generally we use three belts around the ger made from wool from animals. Under the burees there is a 3-4 cm thick hand-made felt, which is made of sheep's wool and we cover the frame with it to keep us warm. The walls and poles of the ger are made of willow grove. Ger is compact/handy, warm, easy to move transport and erect. We spend 20-25 minutes to erect and also 20-25 minutes to take down a ger. This our dwelling is very comfortable to move and transport.

Securing water in these frozen conditions is a major undertaking. We follow Chinsetgeltiinhen, pick in hand, to a frozen river where he dug deep to allow the water to seep out. Later the cattle drank hungrily from it. I shivered from the thought of any warm-blooded animal drinking such cold water in minus twenty-five degrees.

We returned to the plains as Chinsetgeltiinhen drove his considerable herd of 500-600 cattle and goats to new grazing ground. Then, as if he was unaware of our presence, he broke into song, that deep-throated Mongolian singing. Set against the expansive landscape, Chinsetgeltiinhen singing while he

rode his horse with a mixed herd of goats and cattle had a mesmerising effect on us all. Later, back in Batkhishig's *ger,* we were
served with more hot milk, this time mixed with meat dumpling
and thankfully no vodka. In the end of the day warmth, Chinsetgeltiinhen talks to us of his love of wrestling and horses. Mod-
estly, he tells us that he is not a famous wrestler, but boastfully
he claims that Mongolia has the best wrestlers in the world. As
for the horses:

> *We say a Mongolian without a horse is like a bird with-
> out wings. Thousands of years ago, the great Mongolian
> leader Genghis Kahn conquered the world on horseback.
> Thanks to our horses, we can do our work. We are so
> proud of our horses.*

They are proud of their horses and of their traditions, but
the herders of Mongolia are not caught in a time wrap, are not
frozen in time. They have adapted new technologies including
satellite television, solar power panels and mobile phones. They
have a degree of comfort with the natural elements at which our
westernised, urbanised selves could only marvel. That, and of
course their extraordinary horse-handling skills while herding
hundreds of sheep, goats, camels and cattle on what seemed to
us the majestic endless open spaces of the Central Asian steppes.

India

Against the Clock

Ruth Meehan was already at the Delhi departure gate of Schiphol airport when I arrived, still somewhat aghast at having almost missed my early morning flight from Cork. It takes weeks if not months of preparation to set up and coordinate these trips. There are all kinds of variables to take account of, from crew and participant availability to local weather and various hard-to-anticipate eventualities. And I had nearly blown it. Ruth was her usual composed and reassuring self. 'It was meant to be,' she said, displaying what was to become a trademark feature of her unyielding belief in the powers outside of ourselves.

This was our first time working together and we would have two days in India to put a plan into effect before Mick O'Rourke and Mick Cassidy were to join us. While we had a plan, Ruth was nervous. It was a very ambitious schedule. Filming children at work in what at the very least would be inhospitable and more than likely illegal workplaces just might not be without its challenges. Ruth wondered what our Plan B was. The reality was that there was no Plan B, but I had been working on this schedule for months now with the MV Foundation based in Hyderabad in the southern province of Andhra Pradesh, and I had every confidence in their ability to get us the kind of access we required.

Neither Ruth nor I had ever been to India before and when we arrived in Delhi at midnight we were somewhat overwhelmed, as many people are, by the intensity of the place. We had six hours to kill before we caught our internal flight to Hyderabad. Rather than hang around the international airport, we decided to head for the domestic airport only to find that by the time we arrived it was closed. The taxi driver said that he knew a good hotel that a friend of his had and before we could express an opinion he was carrying our bags up the well-trodden stairs. One look inside the hotel and we decided we were sleeping together, more out of expediency than desire.

Hyderabad is a pulsating, crowded city with a rhythm that was as foreign to us as were the sounds and smells. Our travels though are different from most others. The reality is that we are chaperoned from the moment of arrival by our local fixers. Once she or he is at the gate to greet us, I always sigh with relief. Padmanabhan Gura-Rao was there and for the next ten days he was at our side constantly. He was not only our physical but our cultural guide as well. The first stop was the offices of the MV Foundation and a meeting with its founder and director, Shantha Sinha.

The MV Foundation operates on the principle that 'every child should be in school and enjoy childhood'. For them any child out of school is a child labourer. We spent the first day being briefed by Shantha Sinha's colleagues on the scale of child labour in India, the legal environment in which it operates and the efforts being made by the Foundation to counteract it. This is how we work and it has been like this on every trip, learning on the hoof. We are the beneficiaries of people who have spent years working in the field and are always impressed by their often dogged pursuit of justice. While we parachute in and piggy-back on their work for a short intense period, they are in it for the long haul. But here, as elsewhere, people are welcoming of Western television crews who can carry their struggles to new audiences, even if the results in terms of advancing systemic change are intangible and elusive at best.

The plan was that we would film children in three work settings: a quarry, a cotton-field and in a small cottage industry. It was also agreed – the rationale for which I have long since forgotten – that we would film in a Muslim part of the city as well as in more mainstream Hindu communities. Child labour is of course non-sectarian; it is an equally religious-unfair employer. We also agreed that we would film in an urban and rural setting. We were told that we had to be discrete, move quickly, reduce our presence in the urban area as much as possible, and that while they had negotiated access for us, there were real obstacles and certain people would be very hostile to our presence. Of course, it is hard to disguise a film crew at the best of times and four white people in rural India are hard to mask.

Having been thus warned, we set out the following day for the cotton fields outside Hyderabad. After hours of incessant driving on cratered roads and seemingly interminable negotiations between our fixers and a range of people to whom Ruth and I were never introduced, no plan for the shoot was emerging. Our sense of foreboding was growing. The journeys resumed. Eight hours later and we still had nothing to show. Nobody was willing to talk to us. No interviews. We couldn't stop to film anywhere. If ever a Plan B was called for it was now, but no such plan was in sight.

As darkness began to fall, we were promised that the next farm would yield results, that we would definitely see children working in the cotton fields. They were right. We did (briefly) see children working in the cotton fields, but when they saw four land rovers pull up, they fled. It was an amazing sight in itself – a whole group of colourfully dressed girls and boys running away from us as fast as they could and then dive-bombing into the ground. It was only at that stage that we learned that four children had died the previous week from pesticide poisoning and the farm owners had warned all children not to talk to television crews under pain of being sacked.

For Ruth and me that was doubly sobering. Child labour had deadly consequences for children and we were seeing that at first hand. Of lesser importance in the great scheme of things, but of pressing concern to me at that moment, was the growing sense that our prospects of being able to film child labourers at work were swiftly diminishing. The pressure was enormous. This was our first series and I still had to establish my credibility to a doubtful broadcaster. We were now floundering, careering around rural India with a whole retinue of people we had just met and making no progress. If I could not deliver here, I was in serious trouble. I had a full crew arriving in two days and nothing to film. Ruth must have also doubted the whole enterprise, although if that were the case she kept her counsel to herself.

So, silently, we moved off and started the merry-go-round again. Another journey, more discussions, another cotton farm. To say that our expectations were low would be an under-statement, but sometimes things happen when one least expects it. I still don't know who okayed it, but permission was granted – the owner relented, the children agreed and their parents would be contacted and all would be cleared. It was seven o'clock in the evening – eleven hours after we first started out and the staff of the MV Foundation had delivered. We had one story. We needed three more but that was for another day. For now, we could breathe a sigh of relief. Normal conversation could resume.

Sovereignty for Whom?

India's thousand million people constitute the world's largest democracy, and amidst much hoopla and high rhetoric, as is often the case in such celebrations, the sixtieth anniversary of that sovereignty was celebrated in 2007. While it seems churlish to rain on the parade of nationalistic celebrations, the stark truth is that in India, as elsewhere, such celebrations are the sole preserve of the few and the harsh reality of grinding poverty makes a mockery of the grandiose claims about sovereignty that are almost mandatory on such occasions. What sovereignty means to the approximately one-third of the world's poor who live in India remains a moot point.

According to Sabina Alkire and Maria Emma Santos in *The Multi Dimensional Poverty Index* published by the Oxford Poverty and Human Development Initiative in collaboration with the United Nations Development Programme, there are more poor people in eight states of India than in the twenty-six countries of sub-Saharan Africa.[10] Alkire and Santos estimate that India is the thirtieth poorest country on the planet, just behind earthquake hit Haiti and war-ravaged Democratic Republic of the Congo. Almost forty per cent of the country's one billion plus population survives on less than €6.00 a month in rural areas and €9.00 a month in urban ones. Nearly half of the children of this teeming country are malnourished. The 'intensity' of the poverty in parts of India is equal to, if not worse than, that in Africa. Meanwhile, the country's capacity to churn out billionaires continues apace. The 2010 Forbes India Rich List puts the combined net worth of the country's 100 richest people at $300 billion, up from $276 billion the previous year. In 2010 there were sixty-nine billionaires on the India Rich List, seventeen more than in 2009.[11]

Contrast that wealth with the wretched poverty that is such a dominant feature of Indian life. As in most cases in the Third World, children are at the receiving end of the gaping disparity in wealth, a disparity that is fed by a culture that discriminates in particular against what were formerly called 'the untouchables', now known as 'Dalits'. India currently has the unenviable reputation of having the largest child labour force in the world, the bulk of whom come from the Dalit class.

Traditional Indian society organised itself on the basis of a caste system, which is about 3,000 years old, and the relationship between the heavily stratified groups of people was unequal and hierarchical. At the top of the five-tiered hierarchy were priests, holy men and judges. At the bottom of the pile were 'the untouchables', and the only expectation of them was that they behaved in a servile and submissive way while unquestioningly accepting their lot as if it were in some way inevitable. They were not allowed to either eat or drink in the company of others, or enter any public places or temples. Currently, Dalits constitute sixteen per cent of India's population, around 139 million people.

During the colonial struggle, both B.R. Ambedkar and Mahatma Gandhi brought the issue of 'untouchability' to the centre stage of India's freedom agenda and fought relentlessly for their dignity. Gradually, a consensus emerged that independent India must not tolerate untouchability in any of its forms. Consequently, the Indian constitution rendered untouchability illegal and those who violated the code were to be punished. Furthermore, there were provisions for affirmative action. Positive discrimination in favour of the Dalits was legalised. In theory, the 'untouchable community' was given preferential treatment in education, employment and in the offices of the parliament and State assemblies. As a result, many of them could go to school,

travel as equals on buses, move into cities, seek jobs and participate in public life on a par with others. As was found during the
Civil Rights movement in the United States in the 1960s, however, society often moves not just slowly behind legislative change
but in downright opposition to it.

Dalit Child Labour

According to Shantha Sinha, Professor of Political Science at the
University of Hyderabad and one of India's best-known campaigners for the eradication of child labour, most of whom come
from the Dalit class, the legal changes have meant very little.

> *The majority population continued to heap insults and
> humiliations on the Dalits. The social stigma with which
> they have to live with on a daily basis is deeply entrenched.*

Influenced by Mahatma Gandhi's ideals of social transformation, Professor Sinha established the MV Foundation in 1981, an
organisation that has become synonymous with the campaign
to end child labour and the right of each child to attend school.
Now chairperson of the National Commission for the Protection
of Child Rights, Shantha Sinha confronted us with the simple assertion that 'child labour exists because people find it acceptable',
plus the fact that we often fail to make the connection.

Take, for example, fashion writer Deirdre McQuillan's piece
'Penneys from Heaven' in *The Irish Times* in November 2009.[12]
McQuillan declared that:

> *. . . fashion has never shone so much and cost so little as
> evidenced by Penneys' latest razzle-dazzle, rock'n'roll col-
> lection.*

Concluding her interview, Shantha Sinha left us with a sobering assessment.

> *When it comes to children's rights in India (and the rest of
> the Third World), the West simply does not care.*

It remains a chilling indictment.

As McQuillan continued:

> ... *with a silver dress for €21, a jacket for €31 and an off-the-shoulder top for €19 ... prices that can make a trendy outfit for the most cash-strapped followers of fashion fun.*

The question is though, fun for whom?

It's not that the media spotlight has not been on Penneys, or on Primark, as its international brand is known. In 2006, War on Want produced a ground-breaking report, *Fashion Victims*,[13] which showed employees in Primark factories in the Bangladeshi capital Dhaka working for up to eighty hours a week in direct violation of Bangladeshi law, which has a ceiling of sixty hours a week. In these factories, working conditions were described as appalling and the wages significantly below what could be reasonably described as a living wage. In response, Primark said that it was working 'tirelessly' to ensure workers are treated better, but when War on Want returned, they found that instead of conditions having improving they had in fact worsened.

In 2008, BBC's *Panorama* put the Primark claim to the test.[14] Posing as industry suppliers, the *Panorama* team reported that some of India's poorest people worked long, gruelling hours in slum sweatshops and refugee camps. Children as young as eleven years of age were found working there. The result of the exposé? Primark sacked the suppliers and announced it was setting up a children's foundation. When I contacted Penneys in Dublin to establish how much funding had been committed to this Foundation, or to provide any details on it, they refused to comment.

Penneys/Primark are not alone. Major companies source their products in India for the very simple reason that labour laws can be circumvented, goods can be produced at the lowest cost possible and shareholder profits can increase. Child labour exists because the global market wants cheap labour and refuses to look closely at the reality of child workers' lives. The drive for maximising profits results in skilled workers being replaced by less skilled workers, women replacing men, children replacing adults – all in the name of keeping costs down. Child labourers drive down wages and that is why the demand for child labour is growing.

Not only do these child labourers support our growing avariciousness, they also fuel shareholder greed. The desire for greater profits and banner headlines that announce record returns do not take account of the circumstances in which this profit is based. The 'externalities' or human dimension to financial or business transactions, as Noam Chomsky has consistently pointed out, rarely enter the Western economic equation.[15] While child labour has been part of the human story, the evidence indicates that it is a growing phenomenon, and that globalised capitalism is driving more and more children into exploitative, life-threatening labour. The future looks bleak for many of the children of the world. The International Labour Organisation (ILO) predicts a surge in the number of children at work in the next ten years unless something is done to turn the tide.

While Article 24 of the Indian constitution prohibits children under the age of fourteen years of age from working in any factory or mine,[16] the constitutional guarantee fails to meet ILO standards as it does not prohibit all child labour. Child labour is still allowed in small-scale industries and in agriculture. While child labourers form a visible army of labour in the streets and the countryside of the world's poorest countries, equipped as they often are with mops, hoes, shoe-shine brushes and a dazzling array of consumer items, child labourers in India are often less visible, hidden away in back rooms of factories, workshops and restaurant kitchens, or sitting as distant solitary figures in fields minding cattle.

In an oft-quoted sound-byte long before sound-bytes were invented, Martin Luther King once remarked that:

> . . . *we come into contact with the Third World every day at the breakfast table.*

The tea, coffee and fruit juice we consume come to us compliments of the over-stretched hands of the young. The nimble fingers of the young make the incense sticks from which we create a warm, sweet-smelling glow in our homes. They also tie the knots in the carpet weave that adorn and add comfort to our houses. They handpick cotton and do so with diligence, dexterity and speed for the branded t-shirts that we buy cheaply and discard quickly. They chisel stone for the lavish adornment of a world they cannot comprehend. They stitch footballs that form such an integral part of our recreational lives.

Millions of children across the world are born into bonded labour and this is particularly so in India. Many of these children were born to parents who were or still are bonded labourers. These families are in perpetual debt and can never make their re-payments except through their labour and that of their children. Children who are bonded labourers are vulnerable to all kinds of abuse and violence. When asked why this continues to happen, Shanta Shina says it is simply that we don't care.

> We (the Indian government and people) don't care that our children are being exploited, that they are suffering.

While we consumers in the Western World are beneficiaries of that exploitative labour, the Indian government and Indian society must also take some of the responsibility for what is happening in their country. Unscrupulous employers are content to have a steady stream of workers who have no bargaining power and no rights, as are unscrupulous entrepreneurs in the West who have no qualms about self-enrichment at the expense of these Dalit children. Finally, we met some of these children.

Childhood Stories

Jayaramudu Vudagachetla's Story

From a distance, the picture of children herding goats or cows has an epic, Biblical quality. With its compelling imagery of re-storative rural tranquility, 'The Lord is my Shepherd', may be one of the most beautiful pastoral psalms in the Old Testament, yet for many children around the world, this picture of soft-focused rural tranquility belies the harsh world of children in the fields. From dawn to dusk, often under the oppressive heat of the sun, children live out a world that is far removed from the comforting certainty of the Old Testament psalm. Jayaramudu Vudagachetla described life as a cow-herd for us.

> *My father kept saying that I did not learn much at this school and no point in sending me to higher school in other big village and I was removed from school to look after our cows.*

> *It was very hard in summer at this job . . . we had to take the cows to the hills. They are very far from here. There used to be thirty cows. The stones and thorns pierce into my legs and give me hard time. I used to wear chappals (flip-flops) . . . those thorns used to break under my chappals . . . and they used to pierce into m legs . . . my legs used to get cracks like this . . . sometimes I used to get bruises and scratches on my knees when I fall while running after cows.*

> *My legs used to pain when I ran after the cows. Sometimes the cows would escape somewhere. In the evening I used to cut the fire wood or get the water. Then I used to tie all the cows and get the fodder from backyard and feed them. I used to do this every day . . .*

> *One day, our elder cow got lost . . . all other cows were there but they were scattered . . . so, I was running here and there to get them at one place . . . the cow was near the water and later went somewhere and vanished . . . I didn't tell this to my father after coming back home in the evening . . . the next morning, I woke up very early and went alone to look for the cow . . . I didn't find it even after searching in all those hills . . . then it rained on that day . . . it was very wet . . . then my father noticed that the elder cow is missing and asked me about it . . . then I told him that it got missing and I couldn't find it after searching everywhere in the hills . . . then he scolded me a lot on that day . . .*

Thanks to the MV Foundation, Jayaramudu got a second chance at education and attended one the bridge schools they have established for older children who need to start again.

> *I was like a fool without any knowledge when I used to go for grazing the cow but I am gaining knowledge at school*

. . . friendship with other kids . . . we can play and sing
along nicely . . . I like to play cricket . . . the food at home
is not great . . . it's always rice and daal . . . but here, they
make lot of varieties . . . it's very good food here . . . here in
hostel, they give nice rice, colour rice, upma, rasam, chut-
ney buttermilk, daal, curd . . . and everything else . . .

Vadde Balanjaneyulu's and Vadde Rama Devi's Stories

Stonetown is where Bala and Rama (inevitably we shortened their names) worked, twelve rutted kilometres off the main road. As we came over the crest of a hill it was as if a whole world opened up before our eyes. Suddenly as we looked down stone quarries the size of five football fields opened up before us. The sheer greyness of the stone, the slag heaps and the trucks that seemed to move silently below us was only broken by the tiny, multicoloured figures that were bent over slabs of stone, eyes to the ground, hammer and chisel in hand. It was a most amazing sight, the scale of it, and from what I remember the silence. It was a Sunday and most of the trucks were stationery, and we could not hear the sounds of breaking stones through the windows of the bus. With half-muttered invocations of Jesus, we stopped and looked. Below us nobody took any notice.

When we eventually got down to quarry level, two children, a boy of about thirteen and what we presumed was his four year-old sister, were stretched out asleep on the stone impervious to our arrival. Her left hand stretched out across the stone and seemed strangely disembodied in the haze of the yellowing sun. Both children were covered with a thin layer of slate-grey dust. Incongruously, it seemed to us, the little girl had a fresh flower in her hair. Eventually, our arrival must have disturbed them because they woke up, she sleepily squinting against the light breeze that carried dust particles in its wake. The older sibling gathered up his yawning sister and headed away from us in the direction of the other children who were at this stage deeply engrossed in their world of stone.

Then Bala and Rama told us their stories.

I get forty rupees (€0.66) every day for work. If we can't come to work, we don't get paid. If we stay back home because of fever, headache, stomach-ache, they will cut 40 rupees per day from our payment for the days we were absent . . .

If we break the corners of stone in an awkward way, then the boss scolds us and cuts some money from our payment for that day's work but when we work nice, then he appreciates us.

I feel very sad when the hammer falls on my fingers and squeezes them. I get hurt when the hammer slips from my hand and falls on my fingers . . . sometimes my little finger hurts a lot while moving the chisel on stone grabbing it tight in my fist . . .

While breaking the stone, small pieces will be flying and they fall in my eye then they become sore and become red . . . if I get an eye ointment and apply while going to bed, the piece will come out by next morning . . . and then we go back to work

The difficult part is to lift the stone after breaking them . . . then it's also difficult to carry them. While breaking the stones, my arms and shoulders become sore . . . we have to bear the pain and they keep aching like that . . . and we have to keep going with work . . . after work, we walk home and my legs and hands start giving pain again . . .

While breaking stones . . . after coming back home, my hands and legs start paining . . . then my back and waist take the toll . . . my mother suggest us to pour lukewarm water on the aching parts . . . the pain doesn't go off even after pouring warm water on them . . . we have to work just like that again every day.

It hurts a lot. It hurts a lot and I feel not doing it, but there is no other way since my parents are depending on us . . . and I can't stop working . . . It would be great not to come for work . . . it should have been not so painful if I at least be at home . . . That's how I feel.

Chakali Pullamma's Story

Twelve-year-old Chakali Pullamma is one of an estimated 400,000 children working in the cotton fields in Andhra Pradesh in India. Hybrid cotton-seed production was introduced into India in the 1970s and produces more and better quality cotton. It involves mating or cross-pollinating two very different plants that in normal circumstances would not produce any cotton. Because nature does not provide for this type of cross-pollination, it has to be done manually and can only produce one crop so the process must be repeated every year. It is highly labour-intensive, and because of the level of dexterity required girls are perceived to be better at this kind of work than are boys.

The industry requires a constant supply of child labour so many of the girls are bought at the start of the season and are bonded for the year. Very often one year extends into two, and two into three. Currently there are about 200 seed companies involved in production and marketing of hybrid cotton-seeds in India. These companies do not directly employ child labourers, but through a complex structure of subsidiary companies they are clearly beneficiaries of the work of children. All of these companies claim that they are committed to the highest standard of social responsibility; their actions would suggest otherwise.

Chakali Pullamma described life in India's cotton fields. Without the visuals it is not always easy to follow what Pullamma is saying, but the care that is required and the repetitive nature of the work is clearly evident.

> *Look you should keep this cover on this bud like this . . . then you should turn it like this . . . then you should remove it from the shell like this . . . you should take it out without breaking the whole thing . . . I have to rub this with the flower in my hand like this . . . after that take out the white flower, the male flower and rub it on it like this . . . you should insert this in the grove and move it like this sir . . . then catch it on the tip and turn it like this . . . it will grow a little bit big by tomorrow . . . see I need to rub it like this . . . that's all.*

I have been working from my young age. I stopped going to school at 4th standard. My father is dead and also my sister is dead too . . . then I was sent to work in fields like this . . . first I used to go for paddy field work . . . I used to go to remove weeds in fields and cotton fields . . .

The master came to my house and explained everything to my new father and gave that money to him to take me here for work . . . if I don't go to work any day, then they will come to my home and fight with my father . . . some or other way they will convince my father for sending me to his field and I have to come back to work here . . .

First I came here to learn for three days . . . the fourth day they put me on duty . . . I did 100 buds on three days . . . then he offered me thirty rupees (€0.50) per day as my pay . . . and he asked me to come for work the next day.

The master told me that, he is going to cut my pay if I leave any bud . . . it's thirty rupees if you miss a bud . . . then I have to plead them saying it's the first time and won't repeat this mistake again . . . if they get more angry on us . . . they will beat us, sir . . .

We go at 8.00 a.m. to work, sir and come back home at 6.00 p.m. . . . after working from morning to afternoon, we take a break for our meals . . . after some time we start our work again while bending till evening . . . we should not take rest while working . . . they will scold us if we take some rest . . . if we leave any bud, they will scold us and say, no need to come from tomorrow . . . then we have to beg/plead them saying that . . . it happened without my knowledge, this is the only time and I won't repeat it again, I am sorry sir . . . then they will pardon you and say that they are going to cut from my pay if I do it again . . .

If we are seen by someone while taking rest, it will be a problem . . . they will scold us . . . they scold us like anything and we have to bear that and keep quiet . . . that's why we don't take rest and it hurts us too . . . my back is

aching . . . I don't know why . . . I am feeling thirsty now . .
. I have a stomach ache from my childhood . . .

I worked like this correctly for four months . . . after four
months of work, correctly, I took my money to repay my
father's debt . . . my father has good amount of debt . . . we
were not able to pay interest on that . . . even my sister got
bitten by a dog and her health was very bad . . . so, lot of
my savings went for her treatment . . . all of our savings
was enough to clear the problems of my father, sister and
mother . . .

I like to watch TV . . . we have TV at home . . . but you know,
we don't get time to watch it . . . after waking up in the morn-
ing, I have to broom the house, clean the utensils, cook food
and do our own work then go to work . . . it's the same work
of brooming the house, clean the utensils after coming back
from work too . . . we won't get time to watch TV as we have
to sleep early to wake up early in the morning . . .

In the Muslim quarter of Hyderabad, we met with ten-year-
old Nusrat Sultana. She is one of about 120 million Muslims in
India, large by any standards but a vulnerable minority within
India's teeming millions, and almost all are very poor. Their
sense of fear and persecution was further heightened when in
2002 anti-Muslim riots raged in India culminating in the death
of 2,000 people in response to the death of fifty-nine Hindus
who were burned alive in a train torched by a mob. But when
we met with Nusrath, she knew little about the outside world,
confined as she was between her twin worlds of domestic chores
and the daily grind of incense making.

I have two sisters and two brothers . . . my father drives auto
rickshaw . . . my mother makes incense sticks . . . I get up at
7 am . . . and I clean the utensils and I broom the house . . .

I first started to work . . . because my mother got sick and
she asked me to go . . . we make incense sticks here . . . my
cousins and sister also work with me . . .

I go in the morning to get the plain sticks . . . then we roll the sticks in shining powder . . . then I bring them down to the factory . . . I make one kilo per day . . . every day, I get 12 rupees (€0.20).

I get home by 6 pm . . . yes, back home by 6 pm . . . after getting home, I get groceries from the shop . . . then I make dinner and eat dinner and go to sleep.

Other kids go to school, but I don't have anything. I want to become a nice child and help my parents. I want to go to school . . . It's my ambition . . . to go to school . . . if you go to school . . . you can do a job . . .

The Indian government has proved itself highly sensitive to international criticism about its abject neglect of children's rights. Following our production of the film on child labour, the Indian embassy in Dublin refused to grant us a visa to return to the country, despite the fact that we had intended in 2006 to make a film on the extraordinary life of environmentalist and social activist Baba Amte, who sadly died on 9 February 2008 at the age of ninety-three. Technically, the application is still live. Four years on we are still waiting for them to respond. More tellingly, the children of India are also waiting for their government to respond.

It is not that India is an improvished country. Its economy is flourishing with very high growth rates in the industrial, science and technological sectors. The last five years have consistently yielded high growth rates and it promotes itself overseas as the rising star of the information age. Its economic confidence is matched by its growing assertiveness in foreign policy. Here, too, economic self-interest of the few is prioritised. India has given tacit recognition to the reviled Burmese dictatorship in a weapons-for-natural-resources deal. While its sixty-six-year old sovereignty allows it to decide on such issues, the extent to which that sovereignty serves the interests of its own poor, or is merely the preserve or its elite, is open to question.

Laos

Game off: Game On

How's the travellin' going'? Bernie O'Connell, Don O'Sullivan and Fergus O'Brien wanted to know as we stood on the sideline of the Lee Field in Cork City watching Wilton United under-16 Girls play Lakewood in December 2007. 'There's a strike in Bangkok airport,' I absentmindedly said, lost in the high intensity of the game. 'We may not be able to travel.' 'Well, you're probably the only one here that's worried about that,' Don somewhat dryly replied.

Bob O'Brien, Mick Cassidy, Ken O'Mahony and I were to travel to Laos in December 2007 and the only way in was through Bangkok airport. But Bangkok airport was blockaded by red-shirted supporters of telecommunications billionaire and ousted Premier Thaksin Shinawatra, one of the most influential and polarising figures in Thai politics. Reviled by Bangkok's elite but lionised by the rural poor, he was overthrown by the army in 2006. In exile, he turned his attention to football. He purchased the blue-shirted Manchester City FC in June 2007 for $81.6 million and installed the controversial former English manager Sven-Göran Eriksson into the managerial chair. Neither was to last long. Thaksin sold it just over a year later for a reputed $200 million. Sports and politics, parallel universes that are not supposed to cross but keep crashing into each other.

On the sidelines of the Lee Field the only politics that mattered was the draw, the timing of the games and the right to a cancelation. Controversial matters all. The politics of getting through Bangkok would have to wait. Maybe it would blow over in a day or two, I thought. Maybe we might be lucky and make it through, but even if we did get through, nobody was quite sure if we could get out again, and I guessed none of us wanted to spend Christmas in Bangkok. Before the game was over the decision was made. Trip deferred.

So on 2 January 2008 we belatedly flew to landlocked Laos, via a still troubled but now somewhat more stable Bangkok. From Bangkok we flew to Phonsovan where we stayed in the Plain of Jars Hotel. First, though, a lesson in how to pronounce the name of the country. With or without the 's' sound? With, we quickly learned.

Laos – The Belgium of Asia

Ever since Germany invaded neutral Belgium in 1914, neutrality has failed to protect small nations from the marauding presence of imperial powers. In the lead-in to the Second World War, neutrality did not protect Abyssinia, likewise the Baltic and Benelux countries, Norway, Greece, Yugoslavia or Denmark. Given the conflagration that erupted in Southeast Asia in the 1960s and 1970s, and given the intensity with which the Cold War was being fought, it was always unlikely that Laos's neutrality would be protected. And, as it transpired, it was not.

Humiliated by the Vietnamese at Dien Bien Phu in 1954, France withdrew from Southeast Asia, its dream of carving out a Francophile world in the region in tatters. But with its large and strategic landmass, Laos remained a critical player in the hotly contested battleground between Communism and Western-style democracy in the region. However, the country's future seemed secure when in July 1962 the international neutrality of Laos was guaranteed at a conference in Geneva under the joint chairmanship of the Soviet Union and Great Britain, and attended by, among others France, China, Vietnam and the USA. Belgian neutrality might have lasted eighty-three years but neutrality for Laos lasted a mere two.

As part of his anti-communist drive in Southeast Asia, US President Lyndon B. Johnson lost no time in disregarding Laos's neutrality. On 19 May 1964, he authorised the first reconnaissance flights over Laos and less than three weeks later, after the

Pathet Lao, the Vietnamese-backed Laotian communists, shot down two American aircraft, US fighter-planes bombed the communists' positions for the first time.

For the next nine years, the US-Vietnam war was vicariously played out on neutral Laotian soil. Determined to cut off what it perceived as the North Vietnamese supply line, along what became known as the Ho Chi Minh trail which criss-crossed the Laotian-Vietnamese border, the United States government unleashed a sustained bombing campaign the likes of which no country had ever previously experienced. The consequences for Laos were catastrophic. In October 1968, in an effort to placate the increasingly vociferous opposition to the war at home and in an attempt to de-escalate the conflict in Vietnam, Johnson paradoxically intensified the campaign in Laos, increasing bombing sorties from 4,700 in that month to 12,800 the following month, with a concurrent jump in B-52 bombing strikes from 273 to 600.

Richard Nixon and his advisor Henry Kissinger took up where Johnson left off. In February 1971, they launched the invasion of Laos, Codenamed Lam Son 719, which proved to be a spectacular failure from the US perspective. The South Vietnamese were decimated and driven out of Laos. That defeat was a prelude to the ultimate defeat of the United States and signalled the victory of the North Vietnamese communists, leading to the eventual withdrawal of United States forces from Vietnam.

The Johnson-Nixon-Kissinger violation of Laotian neutrality failed to stem the communist surge. In *Nixon and Kissinger: Partners in Power,*[17] Robert Dallek describes their Southeast Asian policy as follows:

> *The entire policy was a disaster . . . costing more than twenty thousand American lives . . . a misjudgement . . . a failure deserving of condemnation. Their determination to stay the course . . . was a product of political cynicism (concerned more) with Nixon's return to the White House in 1972 (p. 619).*

Yet Kissinger never acknowledged his culpability in breaching international law. He has never apologised to the US Congress for hiding his actions in Laos. Time and again, he has railed against his critics who have sought to have him prosecuted for war crimes. In an interview with Pat Kenny on RTÉ Radio One, in February 2002, Kissinger characterised US foreign policy as always informed by 'selflessness' and 'moral purpose'. That more benign retrospective view of his actions sharply contradicts his earlier moral compass. In an interview quoted in Dallek's book Kissinger declared:

> *If I had to choose between justice and disorder on the one hand, and injustice and order on the other hand I would always chose the latter (p. 46).*

Laos paid an enormous price. For nine long years from 1964 until 1973, the people of Laos suffered terribly from a violation that left a hidden and deadly legacy for future generations. In *A History of Laos*,[18] Martin Stuart-Fox described what unfolded as 'the most savage warfare in the nation's history' (p. 136) in which both the United States and the Democratic Republic of (North) Vietnam demonstrated a 'callous disregard for the (Laotian) people caught up in the war' (p. 135) and of whom Stuart-Fox says both 'consistently lied over what each was doing' (p. 153).

Every day, the United States ran 100 bombing missions over Laos – one every eight minutes, for twenty-four hours a day, seven days a week, fifty-two weeks a year for nine years. Between 1964 and 1973, 260 million bomblets poured down on the people of Laos. Seventy-eight million bombs were dropped in all. Of these, 30 per cent failed to explode leaving a hidden and deadly legacy.

> *By the time a cease-fire was declared early in 1973, over two million tonnes of bombs had been dropped on the Pathet Lao zone, or more than two tonnes for every in-habitant. The destruction was horrific. Almost 3,500 vil-lages had been partly or wholly destroyed. An estimated 200,000 died and twice that number of wounded would be a conservative estimate. At one time or another as many as three-quarters of a million people, a quarter of the en-tire population had been driven out of their homes to be-*

Peadar King and Enkhchimeg (Mongolia, 2009)

Enkhchimeg's son (Mongolia, 2009)

Tumen-Ulzii outside his ger (Mongolia, 2009)

Mongolian herder Tumurkhuyag Enkhtsetseg (2009)

Mongolian landscape (2009)

Professor Shantha Sinha (India, 2004)

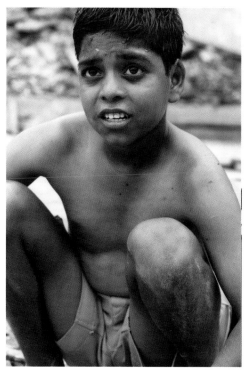

Child labourer Vadde Balanjaneyulu (2004)

Child labourers in India sleep in the midday sun (2004)

Nusrat Sultana (centre) earned twenty cents a day rolling incense sticks (India, 2004)

Children with bomb shells in Laos (2009)

A victim of cluster bombs in the hospital where Dr Vouna Van works (Laos, 2009)

*Kham Kom and Por Vandee who lost two children and whose son was
injured by a cluster bomb (Laos, 2009)*

KNLA General Jonny (Burma, 2008)

Mu Ko Lay with her husband Mauang Mya (Burma, 2008)

Vann Nath as he revisits Tuol Sleng prison (Cambodia, 2006)

Him Huoy telling Peadar King how he killed people in Cambodia's Killing Fields (2006)

*Ronan Fox filming the controversial monument outside Phnom Penh
to those who died in Cambodia's Killing Fields (2006)*

Peadar King with Chum Mey on his return to the notorious Tuol Sleng prison (Cambodia, 2006

come refugees in their own country. The impact was also deeply damaging in less tangible ways, in the terror and trauma that scarred individual lives, in families uprooted and torn apart, in social disintegration (p. 144).

And all of this in a neutral country.

We travelled to Laos to talk to some of the people whose lives have been torn apart by the legacy of that war – lives blighted long after the guns have been silenced, long after the main protagonists have left their theatres of politics and war, long after the politicians and diplomats have drifted away from the inevitable compromises of the conference table to record for posterity their exculpatory memoirs. The aftereffects of their handiwork live on.

The Legacy of War

The war on Laos was the first to witness the extensive use of cluster munitions. Cluster bombs are large cases that carry within them hundreds of small bombs or 'bomblets' the size of tennis balls. These are released from aeroplanes as they fly over an area. Their impact is wholly indiscriminate, and when they hit the effect is devastating. Those 'bomblets' that do not kill or injure immediately just lie there on the ground with a capacity to kill or injure that can last for decades. Those that did not explode are referred to as Unexploded Ordinances or UXOs. In Laos these small bombs are known as 'bombies'.

Dr. Voua Van was only a child when the war started. Now working as the only woman surgeon in the country, and still binding the broken bodies of the war wounded, her story graphically illustrates the long-term consequences of sustained warfare and aerial bombardment, a story we seldom if ever hear. In the hospital where she worked, we met people who had single and double prosthesis, painfully re-learning how to walk. These were adults reduced to the status of young children, dependent, incapable of looking after themselves. Some were mute from shock.

Born in 1959, Dr. Voua Van talked to us as she cared for a young man wounded in an age-old war. Both her grandparents were killed during the war. As she told us her story, her professional poise gradually gave way to barely concealed raw emotion as she remembered her terrified childhood.

> *The village was burning and the planes kept bombing – all day long. We had to hide in the bunker under the ground to avoid the bombing. There was all night bombing. I didn't know then who was doing the bombing. They just bombed all the time non-stop. All day I had to stay in the bunker. Even now, sometimes I still think about it and imagine what it was like. I was so afraid. All I remember hearing is the boom boom of the bombing. I can still hear the sound of the firing and the burning and people screaming and crying. All of those things are still in my memory, even now. Whenever I think about the past, it is like something breaks in my heart. The war has finished for forty years but I still feel afraid and when I think about it I feel goosebumps on my skin.*

It was some testimony. Later we watched as she bound the wounds of other men. Laotian males are the group most at risk from UXO, and boys between six and fifteen years of age are the most vulnerable of all. A 2007 Handicap International report, *Circle of Impact: The Fatal Footprint of Cluster Munitions on People and Communities*, reported that this age-group represents almost one-in-four of all UXO casualties.[19] Por Vandee told us how two of his sons met their death and how one son was left wounded and broken.

> *In 2001, my family and I were working here in our field, preparing it for planting rice. One of my sons hit a bombie and his body just collapsed. He died instantly. His body was covered in burns. My two other sons were both lying face down on the ground. They carried my son Poui to the hospital and left Aun there because he was already dead. By the time we got to the district hospital, it was too late for Poui. He was dead too. My wife was hit by fragments on her arms and on her neck. I was hit here (pointing to the side of his head). We all fell down unconscious. And my son was hit by fragments here. They hit his eye and*

there are ball bearings still inside. This eye was blinded. Fragments ripped through his leg. He lost his penis and his testicles.

Other people we met told us similar stories.

My five year-old son was playing. I heard the explosion, heard him crying and then he died.

While fewer girls are killed, they are not immune from their insidious impact, as one woman told us.

I lost my daughter when she was thirteen years old from a war that ended thirty years ago.

These are just some of the casualties that have afflicted the country since the official end of the war. The International Red Cross claims that the full civilian casualty list exceeds 10,000. While the human cost is enormous, the socioeconomic cost has also left the country reeling. Linkage between UXO and poverty is undisputed. Subsistence agriculture, dominated by rice production in the lowlands, accounts for about 30 per cent of GDP and 75 per cent of total employment. A 2004 study of Kaleum district in the Sekong province noted the extent of the problem.[20]

[A]part from causing fear, injury, and death, [UXO have] also stunted socioeconomic development. Digging, clearing undergrowth or making a fire all became potentially lethal activities. For an essentially agricultural economy, having more than half [the] land mass contaminated by UXO is a crippling development handicap preventing farmers from using arable land and limiting expansion into new agricultural areas.

Loss of the primary earner in the household amplifies the problems of these rural communities. The majority of the families surveyed in a 2004 Handicap International report[21] related being:

> *... poorer as a result of the accident in terms of lower lev-*
> *els of food security, lower earning ability and fewer mate-*
> *rial possessions including cattle and land.*

Xoualor, a single mother with four young children, took us to see unexploded ordnance on her land. On our way we watched where we walked in a way we never did before. 'The land here is still contaminated with UXO bombies,' she told us.

> *We cannot be very productive. Other villages have the*
> *same problem as well. I found a UXO when cutting the*
> *grass. I had no idea whether it was a bombie or a piece*
> *of steel. I kept digging and left it there. Then I warned my*
> *children and my parents not to touch it. It might explode.*
> *I can now only plant a small piece of land because there*
> *are too may UXOs.*

Por Vandee told us the same story.

> *Before I looked after my family very well. Since I had the*
> *accident with the bombie, life has changed.*

We were witness to that change. No longer able to till his fields in the way he once did, his family had very little rice when we arrived, ten sacks in all and no prospect of any more in the immediate future. We saw Por and his wife ration out the rice with their remaining children. Added to the rice was a cooked rat. That was their evening meal and with a bit of luck they would have the same the following day. Our luck held: they did not offer us any. Perhaps they sensed our unease. Had they offered, it would have been difficult not to accept. It would have been even more difficult to accept.

The Cluster Munitions Convention

Laos is not the only country to have suffered from the indiscriminate use of cluster bombs. In a US Congressional Research Service Report published in January 2011, Andrew Feickert and Paul K. Kerr detailed the extensive and sustained use of cluster bombs. Both Soviet and US forces have used cluster bombs in

Afghanistan. NATO forces have used them in Kosovo and in the former Yugoslavia. Both the US and Britain have used them in Iraq. Israeli forces have used cluster munitions against Hezbollah forces in Lebanon. Israel's use of cluster munitions supposedly affected twenty-six per cent of southern Lebanon's arable land and contaminated about thirteen square miles with unexploded submunitions having an estimated failure rate of upwards of seventy per cent.

The Irish government has been to the fore in seeking to ban the production of cluster bombs. A diplomatic conference held in Dublin in May 2008 resulted in the adoption of a Convention on Cluster bombs signed by 107 countries. Steve Goose, spokesperson for the Cluster Munitions coalition, described the Convention as a 'gift to the world'.[22] That gift included a commitment not to:

> ... use cluster munitions (or) develop, produce, otherwise acquire, stockpile, retain or transfer to anyone, directly or indirectly cluster munitions (or) assist, encourage or induce anyone to engage in any activity prohibited to a State Party under this Convention.[23]

Not every country in the world came bearing gifts, the United States included. The acting Assistant Secretary for Political-Military Affairs, Stephen Mull, is reported in Feickert and Kerr's report[24] as saying that the United States relies on cluster munitions as an important part of its defense strategy and therefore would not be signing.

> Cluster munitions are available for use by every combat aircraft in the U.S. inventory, they are integral to every Army or Marine maneuver element and in some cases constitute up to fifty percent of tactical indirect fire support. U.S. forces simply can not fight by design or by doctrine without holding out at least the possibility of using cluster munitions (p. 4).

The United States was not the only country not to participate in the Convention: Russia, China, Israel, Egypt, India and Pakistan also did not sign the agreement in Oslo in 2008.

The convention entered into force on 1 August 2010. As of 10 January 2011, 108 states had signed the convention and 49 had ratified it. The Lao People's Democratic Republic ratified the treaty in March 2009.

But for many of the people we met on our journey that was eventually made possible by the ending of the red-shirted protests in Bangkok airport, that ratification has come too late. The determination of the US and some other nations to retain cluster bombs as a weapon of war remains an affront to the suffering of these and other people. That and the failure of the US government to make any reparations for the extraordinary trauma they inflicted on the neutral country of Laos.

Burma

Meeting the Karen

It was cold, cold like I had never experienced before. Not even in Mongolia had we experienced this kind of cold. A deep, bone-chilling cold that seeped up between the floorboards on the stilted house of our Karen hosts on the Burmese highlands close to the Thai border. The soldiers who slept with us were curled up against each other like babies in a cot, but we man-and-womanfully kept our distance. Then, just before dawn, the crackling of firewood drew me from my floor-bed. Respite at last. Already our hosts had silently hunkered down, backs to the fire, hands clasped behind them as the flames licked the emerging dawn.

Slowly, some of the thirty Karen soldiers, members of the Karen National Liberation Army (KNLA), who had thrown a mountain-side security cordon for our protection around the house in which we half-slept, began to emerge from the dawn-mist with their distinctive root cigarettes glowing in the morning greyness. They cradled their home-made weapons with gloved hands against their slim bodies, their well-worn uniforms offering little protection from the insidious cold. No words were spoken even though many Karen speak perfect English, a hangover from the very pro-British stance they adopted during the Second World War, and for which they were subsequently betrayed. For now, though, heat was all that mattered.

We shared pre-breakfast cheroots, something I hadn't done since my college days, and while the anti-smoking lobby might disagree, there appeared to be no adverse effects. As the fire-circle widened, we were soon joined by Mick Cassidy, Ken O'Mahony and Liz Gill. While this was Liz's first shoot with us, and this was the first time we had entered any country illegally, we were all in strange territory. Had they known, the despotic military junta that ruled Burma, or Myanmar as the junta has renamed the country even though few outside official circles are prepared to use the name, would not have welcomed our presence.

That was our second night in Burma. Under the protection of the KNLA, the previous day we had crossed the Moi River from Thailand into Burma, a country of fifty-five million people. The first night we stayed in a KNLA camp. These Karen were yet another generation of men caught up in the world's longest running civil war. Forced by circumstances they did not create, these young men were compelled into violent conflict against one of the most reviled regimes on the planet.

The following day we filmed as they drilled, repaired their makeshift weaponry and prepared to move upstream to meet with some Karen refugees whose lives had been traumatised by the Than Shwe-led dictatorship that has scarred and wounded the country and its people since it took control from Burma's other despotic dictator, Ne Win. Heading up the narrow river corridor between the splendor of the towering forests of Burma to our left and Thailand to our right, it was difficult to imagine the horror stories we were to hear. It was also difficult to imagine that behind such beauty lurked such brutality. It was a memorable journey, not least because of the uncertainty and, despite reassurances to the contrary, the prospects of ambush. The fact that the KNLA had guns to the ready added to rather than eased our concerns. We were sitting ducks in our heavily laden boat.

As we moved upstream, I was reminded of the journey of the fugitive Henri Charrière in the famous story *Papillion*,[25] first published in France in 1969, which had captured my childhood imagination. He had no option but to put his trust in the most unlikely of sources as he made his way through the jungle. In a very limited sense we too were fugitives as we travelled with the KLA, who were regarded as a terrorist army by the official Burmese government.

Karen and Aung San

It might have been all very different had not Aung San, father of Aung San Suu Kyi, one of the world's most famous prisoners of recent times, not been assassinated on Saturday, 19 July 1947. In his highly accessible *Perfect Hostage: A Life of Aung San Suu Kyi,*[26] an hour by hour account of that day and the events leading up to it, Justin Wintle paints a portrait of Burma's iconic leader that is a mirror image of Irish Republican leader Michael Collins. 'On that day "in a blink of an eye", Wintle recalls, 'it all went grotesquely wrong' (p. 137).

The parallels between Collins and Aung Sang are uncanny. Both were the last born children of large families. Aung San was the youngest of nine children, five boys and four girls, Collins was the youngest of eight children, five girls and three boys. While Aung Sang came from a privileged background with strong roots in the countryside, Collins came from a comfortable small-farmer background in rural West Cork. Both were regarded as the hard men in their respective struggles for independence. Both held the rank of 'General' in their respective armies. Both were regarded by the British as reviled traitors to the empire. Both had negotiated their independence in Whitehall from Britain. Both had people in their ranks who refused to sign the deal, including in Aung Sang's case U Saw. Both had high profile and highly ambitious rivals for their country's leadership. Both were just thirty-two when they were assassinated. Both of their rivals were early suspects. While Eamon de Valera was in the vicinity of Collins' ambush on 22 August 1922, it is now widely accepted that he had no prior knowledge of, nor did he in any way approve of, Collins's murder. Not so Aung San's main political rival U Saw. On 30 December 1947, six days before Burma's formal declaration of independence, he was found guilty of Aung San's murder. Five months later, along with five other accomplices, he was hanged. Fortune smiled more favourably on de Valera who died in his sleep at the age of ninety-two.

There were also points of divergence. Wintle describes Aung San 'as a handsome slightly feminine looking male', a description that is the apotheosis of the swaggering Collins.

There is one other uncanny connection, but this time not between Collins and Aung San but between Collins and the Karen people. Michael Collins was assassinated at Beal na Bláth, which some modern writers transcribe as the 'Mouth of the Flowers'. The Karen's land is known as *Kawthoolei* and one of the translations for that is the 'Land of the Black Flower or Garden of Flowers'. When researching the commonalities between the two nationalist heroes, given that there were so many, I wondered if they were born or died on the same day. They were not. Points of convergence across decades and continents can only stretch so far.

Like Collins, the *what if* historians have had a field day trying to unpack what might have happened in Burma if Aung San had survived. Two questions have absorbed historians and others interested in Burma's development. Would he have grabbed power himself and become yet another Asian strongman in the way that Mao Zedong did in China, Bung Sukarno did in Indonesia and Ferdinand Marcos was to do later in the Philippines, though as Whittle rightly points out, Ho Chi Minh never did in Vietnam? Clearly his supporters in Burma, and there are many, think not. The second question that has bothered historians is whether or not he could have held together within a unitary state Burma's disparate ethnic groups, of which the Karen were one of the strongest and most vocal for their own independent state. One tell-tale sign suggests he would not. No Karen representative was included in his negotiating team.

While Aung San was negotiating independence for Burma in London, Karen representatives were vying for an independent state. They felt the British owed them one. The Karen had backed the British against the Japanese during the Second World War. On good grounds, they expected independence as a reward. In the heat of battle, rash British promises had been made. They were not to be. When Burma gained independence from Britain in 1948, the Karen were abandoned by the British to their age-old enemies.

Even Winston Churchill, who coincidentally was on the British negotiating team opposite Michael Collins, felt that the Karen were badly treated. In a debate in the British House of Commons in 1947 Churchill gave a warning.[27]

> *Burma is likely to reproduce, though, of course, on a far smaller scale, the horrors and disasters which have overspread her great neighbour (India) and which should ever haunt the consciences of the principal actors in this tragedy. All loyalties have been discarded and rebuffed; all faithful service has been forgotten and brushed aside . . . We stand on the threshold of another scene of misery and ruin . . . the abandonment by Great Britain of her responsibilities. I say this to the Government: You shall bear that burden.*

How right he proved to be.

Prior to making the film on the Karen, I was told that I really should talk to what might appear to be an unlikely source, Conservative politician Benedict Rogers, author of *A Land without Evil: Stopping the Genocide of Burma's Karen People.*[28] I flew to London not knowing what to expect from a young Tory Turk. We met in a West End upmarket hotel for a light lunch of perfectly cut goats' cheese, crisp lettuce and onion marmalade sandwiches with sparkling water. So far so predictable. But as often is the case, face-to-face meetings upend easy stereotypes. His knowledge of, commitment to, and passion for the struggle of the Karen people was beyond question, as was his generosity in sharing what he knew and the contacts that would help us make the documentary. We had a common interest and he did graciousness and intelligence very well indeed. More importantly, he has doggedly pursued the cause of Burma while I have moved on.

Amongst the stories Ben, a devout Christian, told me that day was of the Karen's conversion to Christianity. Apparently Karen mythology held that they once possessed a Golden Book that was lost to them. They believed that a white man would one day return with it. Not only that, they too had a creationist story that mirrored Genesis in the Old Testament. According to Karen belief, the god T'wa made the world and as a test for his creation he appointed a 'fruit of trial'. He demanded that this not be eaten, but in the age-old manner of wanting what we cannot have, the people obeyed not. For their sins, they were subject to sickness, ageing and death. Compared to what other Christian missionaries had to contend with, this was easy street. Not all, but a substantial number of Karen took to the Baptist missionaries' conversion like ducks to water. Whatever about the eschatological benefits, from a purely secular point of view, this was not a good move. Now another layer was added to the age-old rivalry between the smaller Karen and the more numerous Burmese.

First There Was Ne Win

With the possible unifying forces and moral authority of Aung San gone, the power vacuum that followed was filled by the first of two despotic dictatorships under which Burma has suffered greatly. In 1962, Ne Win led a coup of which the only surprise was that it didn't come much sooner. With aching predictability, his 'Burmese Way to Socialism' was marked by a narcissistic, paranoid yet tenacious grip on the country.

That grip almost evaded him in 1988 in what is now known as the revolution of 08 08 88. A tea-room fracas in August 1988 between three young students and a group of older regime loyalists over what music should be played on a jukebox seems like the most improbable start of a revolution, but it was the military's over-reaction to this storm in a teacup that galvanised Burma's students onto the streets in open defiance of the dictatorial government. Six hours later, under the cover of darkness, the killing started. Defenseless protestors were slaughtered and the killings went on all week. People were butchered, bayoneted, disappeared, incinerated and many of those unlucky enough to survive were tortured, one by one, as their comrades looked on helplessly. An estimated 3,000 were killed in the week. A Buddhist monk, U Ong Batha, told us that the uprising was a result of years of human rights abuses and poverty.

The military were committing human rights abuses against the people well before 1988. But the situation got worse in '88 because the people were getting poorer and hungrier. This desperate situation led to the popular uprising against the military that saw thousands of students, monks and civilians killed. Our people are slaves in their own country. Nobody like the military rule but dare not say so. Those who dare face torture death and long sentences in prison.

U Ong Batha was in Rangoon on 26 September of that year. When we met with him, he was keeping a low profile in Thailand.

I went to Rangoon to join the other monks. The soldiers started shooting at us and beating us on the 27th. I was struck on the head that day and injured. The shooting started as the secondary school children were coming home from school. I saw ten people fall near where I was. Among these were four young students who seemed to be about thirteen-to sixteen years. The situation was chaotic because some people were trying to retrieve the dead, while some were trying to help the wounded. A lot of people were killed trying to retrieve their loved ones. Many monks were among them. After the crowds were dispersed, the soldiers began their search in the monasteries. They arrested all the monks who they thought were the leaders. They also confiscated their possessions that belonged to the monasteries. A few monks were tortured to death in some interrogation centres. I was on the run from the military police so it was no longer safe for me to live in Rangoon. The only safe place is to come to the Thai-Burmese border. That is why I am here.

The state violence that was unleashed and the mass protests that followed forced Ne Win out of office the following July, but not out of power. A puppet regime, prepared to do his even more brutal bidding, took control and in the process became even more out of control.

By a strange coincidence, two months earlier, Aung San Suu Kyi, the daughter of Aung San, who had been living in Oxford with her husband and two sons, had returned to Burma to visit her ailing mother. Little did she know when she arrived in Rangoon that she would be subjected to various forms of detention until her release from house arrest of in November 2010.

And Then There Was Than Shwe

Consistently featuring in the world's top five worst dictators, along with Robert Mugabe of Zimbabwe, Omar Al-Bashir of Sudan, Kim Jong 11 of North Korea and King Abdullah of Saudi Arabia, Than Shwe, now in his eighties, retired as Burma's head of state in 2011. His particular mix of megalomaniac military mis-rule was marked by ostentation, self-enrichment, rampant avariciousness and an opulent lifestyle.

In his heavily censored world, and much to the chagrin of Than Shwe, that ostentatious avariciousness came to light shortly after our visit to the country in 2006. Than Shwe's daughter Thandar married in a ceremony that observers estimate cost, including presents received, well in excess of $50 million. This in a country where two out of every five children are severely malnourished. Burma is also the only country in the world where beriberi, caused by vitamin deficiency, still kills children. Much to the enragement of the father of the bride, the wedding ended up on YouTube. Few outside that tiny, outlandishly corrupt elite got to see these images of decadence as internet use inside this wholly repressive country is restricted.

Arrival in Burma

Mick, Ken, Liz and I arrived in Burma before the physical storms struck, but we were all well aware of the political storms that had been raging inside the country since independence in 1948. We should have anticipated the quiet horror that people would recount. While in Thailand, we heard of the petty but painful torture experienced by Lae Lae New during her incarceration in Insein prison. But in an age when we have almost become immune to the loss of life from war, poverty and the callousness of other human beings, Mu Ko Lay's story of the death and rushed burial of her two young sons in the jungle as she and her village were being pursued by the Burmese military was as stark and emotionally wrenching an account as we heard in all our travels. Not that there is a competition in grief, each person tells their own story in their own way, but this took us to a different level.

> *In our current situation we have to run all the time. Our two sons when I was on the run. We had no food, they got sick and died. I had to leave my two sons in the jungle. We buried them quickly in the jungle as if they were animals. It's a horrible way to leave your children behind. I don't know how it all happened. It happened so fast.*

Then came the uncontrollable outburst. In a way that we had not experienced before, we were suddenly awash in her bitter tears. Quite apart from the suddenness, it was the intensity that caught us off guard. Her sobbing was relentless. It was as if she had become engulfed in a wave of grief that she simply could not hold back, a grief that seemed to emanate from the depths of her very being; this was her own personal tsunami. And all the while her husband sat stoically by her side looking into the middle distance.

Like many other Karen, Mu Ko Lay had fled to the very edge of the country close to the Thai border beside the Moi River where she and her family eke out a precarious existence in temporary shelters. Fearful of the night-time attacks by the Burmese army, many cross the river Moi into Thailand where they sleep in temporary huts and hammocks. Fearful of being detained by Thai authorities during the day, they cross the same river every morning back into the Karen state. Interminable movement, day in day out, lives framed by fear. For the briefest of periods surrounded by Karen National Liberation Army soldiers, we experienced the entrapment that is a daily reality for millions of people. Physically cold it might have been but that was only a temporary inconvenience. As always we could move on. However, a year after our return, I heard from friends there that another of Mu Ko Lay's sons had lost both his arms in a landmine explosion. Her personal odyssey of horror continues, as it does for the whole of the country. Not until full democracy is secured and those who were responsible for the atrocities that occurred are tried in a court of law that is not bound by the current constitution, will some semblance of peace come to these deeply traumatised people.

Cambodia

Introduction

It had all the allure of the ultimate revolution, at least as seen through the eyes of a teenager about to sit his Leaving Certificate on the other side of the world. For the briefest of periods, hours rather than days, the people of Cambodia once again held their collective breath in the belief that this time the nightmare that had gripped their country for the previous five years and beyond might come to an end, that this time peace and prosperity might come to Cambodia. The awful reality was that the real nightmare was just about to begin.

However when the Pol Pot-led Khmer Rouge (KR) entered Phnom Penh on 17 April 1975, for very many people, particularly on the political left, this was perceived as peasant power at its very best. A repeatedly crushed rural populace taking power from the Imperial Yankee forces was something to celebrate. Black-clad teenagers brandishing small weapons wrestling power from a nuclear force country had all the seductive power of a world about to correct itself. The US army, beaten in Vietnam and now beaten by the peasants of Cambodia – the world was looking like a very different place. It appeared to be a revolution fired by youth, idealism and no little courage, free from the constraints of western ideology, religion, and capitalist-inspired modernisation.

For a semi-incarcerated rural youth in a Catholic boarding school full of youthful idealism, this was the stuff of dreams. The images might have been grainy and the reports stuffed with unrestrained outrage, but that only added to the audacity of the Khmer Rouge achievement. But like all international stories, interest soon waned. Little or nothing was heard again of what I had presumed was a triumphant revolution. Typical. The West could not admit that they got it so spectacularly wrong. Quite obviously the revolution was bedding down, the peasants organising in spontaneous solidarity with the cause of a classless society and with each other. The fact that nothing was being reported seemed a reflection of western indifference to socialism's star performer. Or so I thought.

Even as stories began to leak out that all might not be well in the newly born Democratic Kampuchea, well, that was yet another indication that the West could not bring itself to admit that there was another way. If only. Little did any distant cheerleaders realise that rather than this being the field of dreams, this was actually the stuff of nightmares. The Killing Fields of Cambodia were being drenched with the blood of its own people. The Khmer Rouge, an ultra nationalist group of communists, were attempting to carry out one of the most radical programmes of social change ever undertaken. And the result? A genocide in full flow, the annihilation of its people on a scale unparalleled since the Nazi genocide in Germany. By the end of this grotesque experiment over two million people – between twenty-nine and thirty-one per cent of the population – had perished.

A chance meeting with Craig Etcheson, then teaching at John Hopkins University near Washington DC, re-connected me but in a very different way to the events of April 1975. A considerable part of Etcheson's life work has been spent chronicling the genocide of the Khmer Rouge years. He subsequently became an investigator at the Extraordinary Chambers of the Courts of Cambodia that was established to try seven of the main genocidal perpetrators who had survived into old age.

Craig encouraged me to make a documentary on the story and briefed me on some of the key people with whom I should talk. As a result, I spent weeks immersing myself in the horror that subsequently unfolded. He provided me with a book list of readings of which Dublin-born Samantha Power's master class on genocide, '*A Problem from Hell*': America in the Age of Genocide,[29] for which she won the Pulitzer Prize for Non-Fiction in 2003, was my starting off point. Her book remains a *tour de force*. That journey back in time to the days of the Khmer Rouge was undertaken with Stephen O'Connell, Mick Cassidy and Ronan Fox. This was the epic story we set out to tell.

The Rise of the Khmer Rouge

Cambodia gained its independence from France in 1953, but the Cambodia that developed became little more than a plaything in a regional power struggle that involved China, the Soviet Union, the United States and Vietnam. A failed state, the Cambodian people were eager to believe that the utopia promised by the Khmer Rouge could become a reality.

In 1970, General Lon Nol overthrew the Prime Minister, the former King Norodom Sihanouk, in a US-backed coup in what became known as the Khmer Republic. Sihanouk turned to his old adversaries within the Khmer Rouge who had been opposed to his growing tendency to autocratic rule and were successfully gnawing away at his regime from the jungles of Cambodia. A merciless five-year civil war ensued in which half a million people were killed.

Having defeated the US-backed Lon Nol government, the Khmer Rouge, backed by the Chinese and influenced by Maoist ideology, triumphantly took control of Phnom Penh, under the leadership of Saloth Sar, better known as Pol Pot. Despite the Khmer's Rouge's burgeoning reputation for cruelty, by the time they reached Phnom Penh in 1975, war-weary Cambodians were ready to believe anything in the hope that they could get some respite from conflict. Vann Nath, who chronicled the shocking excesses of the Khmer Rouge regime in his memoir, *A Cambodian Prison Portrait: One Year in the Khmer Rouge's S-21*,[30] described in one of his final interviews that brief sense of relief the day after the Khmer Rouge took control of the capital. War, he and others thought, was finally over.

The morning of April 18th arrived but I did not go to work. We (my wife and I) passed through the centre of town: the doors of all the shops were shut although food, cakes and drink were set in front of each house to welcome the new army. People said that our army friends had fixed the price

> *of goods for people to sell. Yesterday the price of pork was 5,000 riel per kilo, but today it was lowered to only 100. Everyone was very happy. (p. 7)*

That brief sense of optimism was shared by Theary Seng, whose whole family was wiped out by the Khmer Rouge. 'Cambodians were like ostriches with their heads stuck in the sand,' she told us.

> *There were warning signs but we were so shell-shocked and numbed that when they walked in my family along with the rest of the city came to greet them with jubilation because we thought peace was at hand.*

'We believed them,' Vann Nath told us when we met him in 2007, 'because those in power had oppressed us for thousands of years.' It was to prove the shortest and last period of happiness that the people of Phnom Penh were to experience for a long time. Unhappily for them, the worst was yet to come. A genocidal bloodbath was about to be unleashed, the figurehead of which was an inscrutable figure called Pol Pot, otherwise known as Brother Number One.

Saloth Sar aka Pol Pot aka Brother Number One

Pol Pot biographer David P. Chandler describes him as the most unlikely source and inspiration of that bloodbath.[31] Son of a prosperous father and pious mother renowned for her good works, he was the eighth of nine children, many of whom lived through the genocide he inspired. His family had connections, albeit somewhat tenuous ones, to the royal palace in Phnom Penh. His whole persona challenges the easily assigned caricature of a coldly cruel individual unaffected by human suffering. Known for his genteel charm, his childhood was by all accounts happy and content. No clue there of what was to come. While his early life is well documented, his later life, particularly in the years leading up to the revolution, is much less clear. He remains for many to this day the ultimate enigma. Even his birth date is shrouded in mystery. Chandler favours September 1928 over the officially recorded French colonial date of May 1925.

Reclusive and retiring, he eschewed the kind of personalised deification that other revolutionaries crave and hid behind his adopted name Pol Pot, and his pseudonym Brother Number One, for the bulk of the Khmer Rouge reign. His real identity did not become known until two years after the April 1975 revolution when he visited China in September 1977. It was only then that international observers realized that Pol Pot, Brother Number One, was in reality a fifty-two-year-old former schoolteacher named Saloth Sar.

What seems to have been a major turning point in his life was winning a scholarship in 1948 at the age of twenty to study in France. In Paris, Saloth cemented an earlier friendship with Ieng Sary, one of the chief architects of the Khmer Rouge tyranny and who is currently (2012) before the Extraordinary Chambers in Phnom Penh. Both he and Sary were to marry sisters, Khieu Ponnary and Khieu Thirith – Sisters Number One and Two respectively. Together, they are known as the Gang of Four.

In 1953, Saloth Sar returned to Cambodia and taught French history, geography and civics in a private school in Phnom Penh. According to Chandler, his students regarded him as:

> . . . *composed smooth-featured who was fond of his students, deep voice, calm gestures, eloquent but unpretentious, honest, humane, easy to befriend – up to a point – and easy to respect (p. 5).*

Hardly the stuff of a future genocidal maniac. This did however provide a veneer of respectability that allowed his clandestine organising and recruiting for the Communist movement, the Workers' Party of Kampuchea (WPK), to go unnoticed. That party was established in 1960 by twenty-one radicals including Saloth Sar. It was also during this period that he met Nuon Chea, who was to become Brother Number Two, and Khieu Samphan who was to become Brother Number Five, both of whom are also before the UN-backed Extraordinary Chambers.

A decade later, in 1963, that double life was increasingly difficult to maintain and Saloth Sar along with Ieng Sary slipped out of Phnom Penh for a Vietnamese military camp on the Vietnamese-Cambodian border. Along with his young Khmer Rouge cadres dressed in their trademark black uniforms, red-and-white chequered scarves and Ho Chi Minh sandals, he re-emerged triumphant in Phnom Penh in 1975, infused with a ruthless determination to utterly transform the country, and in the process write himself into the ignominious horrors of history – a history that students of the former young, respected and gentle teacher of civics and French history could never have imagined.

Cambodia's Wasteland

'April is the cruelest month,' declared T.S. Eliot in the opening line of 'The Wasteland'.[32] It is a line that knowingly or unknowingly has a particular prescience for Cambodians who lived through April 1975, because on that month and for most of the following four years, Cambodia or Democratic Kampuchea as it was then known became an utter wasteland of skull and bone.

In this brave new world, intellectuals, teachers, Buddhist monks and others were now enemies of the state and were to be ruthlessly exterminated. All private property was abolished. All vestiges of the old regime were to be swept away. It was to be a new beginning, the clock was re-set for Year Zero. But as Francois Ponchaud points out in his book *Year Zero*:[33]

> (I)n this new regime in which all possessions have been abolished and knowledge confers no privilege, the one thing that is not shared is power: it remains wholly concentrated in the hands of a very small number (p. 192).

Year Zero marked not a new dawn for the people of Cambodia but its darkest hour. On that fateful morning in April, something terrible was born.

The soldiers who took control of the capital were little more than children overawed by the sights and sounds of the city, but imbued with a deep sense of grievance against their urban counterparts. Theary Seng described for us the abrupt change that took place on the day that the Khmer Rouge took control of Phnom Penh.

> *Within a matter of a few hours the situation changed. These young boys, there was a grimness and a hardness about them. They viewed us as enemies. They viewed us as foreign, as the class that had oppressed them that had helped to destroy their villages that had made their life very difficult.*

Almost one-third of Cambodia's eight million people died as a result of their actions. In total, an estimated 2.2 million people died or were killed during this period. To date, about 20,000 mass graves have been uncovered strewn across 200 prisons and hundreds if not thousands of Killing Fields.

The interrogation, torture and death that had been the hallmark of their reign in areas the Khmer Rouge controlled between 1970 and 1975 now became commonplace all over Cambodia. Tuol Sleng prison, otherwise known as S-21, a former secondary school, became the most notorious of all the interrogation centres. Like the Nazi regime, the Khmer Rouge were meticulous in documenting their own barbarities, so many of the records of have survived.

Three Years, Eight Months and Twenty Days in Democratic Kampuchea

Seldom do we have a title for a documentary before we make it but this was the exception. We wanted to capture the horror of the Khmer Rouge regime which lasted for three years, eight months and twenty days, and this became the title of the film.

Dublin-born Rory Byrne, a freelance journalist in Southeast Asia, worked with us in putting the documentary together and he did an extraordinary job. We wanted to feature two of the five survivors of Tuol Sleng and he managed to secure both. Furthermore, he introduced us to Theary Seng whose extraordinary recall of her early childhood still gives me goosebumps when I hear her testimony in the film we made. All three were compelling and profoundly moving witnesses to the unimaginable horror of that era. This is an extract of Theary Seng's story as she related it to us.

> *They separated my three older brothers from the rest of the prison population. From my Mom and me and my youngest brother. So they went away having a premonition of something. And then two prison guards came into our room. I asked my mother what was happening and she just said 'go back to sleep'. The next morning I woke up with everyone gone in the room. I woke up crying with my youngest brother with my Mom gone. They tried to lie to us 'your Mom is working in another building'. That night they took my Mom and all the other prisoners and had them killed. How, I can only guess. That's how I lost my Mom with the other prisoners.*

Van Nath, who sadly passed away in September 2011 as I was writing this, and Chum Mey were but two of the survivors of the notorious Tuol Sleng prison, in which an estimated 17,000 people were killed. Most of those who were killed were taken to the now infamous Killing Fields whose infamy was brought to a wider public by the 1984 Roland Joffé film of the same name. A Vietnamese cameraman, Ho Van Tay, now (2013) aged eighty, was the first person to record the horror of S-21. In *Nine Lives*,[34] he describes how he came upon the prison.

> *As we were driving, my crew – an assistant and a driver – were confronted with a pungent order. In search of its source, we found an abandoned compound surrounded by barbed wire: S-21. Five children were inside, some crying and some asleep, children of Khmer Rouge cadres that Pol Pot had sent to prison. Hiding under a pile of discarded clothes, they were emaciated and on the verge of death. Among them were eight-year-old Norng Chan Phal and his brother and sister, Chanly and Rumduol aged five and three (p. 94).*

As we entered the courtyard on our first day of filming, the school resembled any other and indeed was not unlike parts of the Ennis Technical School where I first taught. Five nondescript school buildings.

Chum Mey took us to the room in the school in which he was held. Not surprisingly, he was deeply emotional about his return visit. We were about to hear an account of some of the most traumatic experiences to which any person could experience.

> *I get very emotional and even cry whenever I come here. This room brings back very painful memories for me. I really want to ask: why did Pol Pot kill my family? What did they do wrong?*

Chained to the floor, he had to ask permission to move or to reposition himself to the left or to the right. Otherwise he would have been severely beaten. If the guards even heard the sound of his shackles moving, he would be beaten badly. Despite the pain and torture he experienced, it was the loss of his family that still haunts Chum Mey to this day. His voice cracking with emotion, he told us what happened.

> *My four children died. I was with my wife the day before she was killed.*

Vann Nath described his arrest.

> *The day after I was arrested, they took me and electrocuted me. They made me sit in a chair and handcuffed my hands behind my back. Whatever they wanted to hear, I would tell them in order to reduce the pain. All I could hear was screaming ohh . . . arg . . . screaming as loud as they could, everywhere in here. When I would hear them like that my legs and hands would shake with fear and I would wonder when it was going to be my turn.*

Vann Nath survived because he kept on painting heroic images of the Revolution, including portraits of its leader Pol Pot. Later he was to paint the real story of the genocide. His paintings are now on show in the Tuol Sleng museum and many are also reproduced in his memoir. The images are extraordinarily disturbing. Images of waterboarding long before it became widely known as an instrument of torture. The dismemberment of babies. Fingernails pulled out. People strung up like animals. People who were whipped to within an inch of their lives and then had their throats slit.

But for Vann Nath, the regime was more barbarous than his paintings could ever show.

Vann Nath demonstrated extraordinary composure as he walked us through his paintings. Occasionally and with tremendous poignancy he would gently touch the surface of a figure in his work and his words would trail off. It was as if he wanted to heal the pain, to balm the wounds of the prisoner represented in his paintings. Witnessing it was one of the most moving sights I have ever encountered. It was as if he wished to reassure the tortured man that even in what must have been the darkest and most painful moments of that person's life that humanity prevails. It is often in the quietest and simplest of gestures that holds our common humanity.

It is also a tribute to Ronan Fox, Mick Cassidy and Stephen O'Connell that they could hold their composure while filming in these situations. And that was further tested when we went to the Killing Fields with Him Houy, one of the guards of Tuol Sleng and one of its many executioners.

It would be easy to caricature Him Houy as a merciless, bloodthirsty killer. In a tabloid world he could easily be stereotyped as a monster. In reality, he was none of those things. He was small in stature, quietly spoken, and lived in a poor rural community with his wife and young children. For whatever reason, perhaps as a gesture of recompense, he agreed to talk to us about his role in the Killing Fields.

There are thousands of Killing Fields in Cambodia but when the term is mentioned it inevitably refers to the one in which the prisoners of S-21 were killed. Fifteen kilometres from Tuol Sleng, the Killing Fields are no more than a couple of acres with a series of mounds, indentations and earthen pathways. Controversially, a monument containing the skulls and bones of some those killed there stands in the middle. Many believe that these bones ought to be interred and not used as a public spectacle. As we walked through the field, Him Houy pointed out the various pits where people were slaughtered and buried. This is his account of what happened.

> *Those who were imprisoned in Tuol Sleng were brought here and killed. Workers from Tuol Sleng and from other places, all were killed here. I was not sure how they decided who needed to be killed.*

> *These are the places where people were killed. Older people were killed here, but younger ones were killed in Tuol Sleng. At that time, Duch investigated me to be sure that prisoners were killed. He was sitting to see how the prisoners were killed. He tested me to see whether I was dedicated or not. If the answer was not 'yes' they will kill us. So, I had to answer 'yes'. Later on, I took a metal stick to beat prisoner to prove.*

> *When I brought people here from Tuol Sleng, I sent them into that house. They had a room underneath. They would park the truck near the house and put all the prisoners in that room. They took one prisoner out of the room at a time. I wrote down their name. Then they were killed here. They walked the prisoner one by one through this path to reach the grave and ordered them to kneel down, pulled back their handcuffed hands and started hitting them with a long big stick. Prisoners were beaten on the back of their necks. They were unconscious and fell down.*

> *Finally, they cut the neck of a prisoner with a knife. And then they unlocked the handcuffs. Guns were never used, as the sound would be heard.*

> *The most frightening thing I had to do was to bring prisoners to be killed. I didn't talk with any prisoners before killing them because my supervisors were watching.*

> *I have felt guilty about what happened under the Pol Pot regime. I tell them my actions were not voluntary. I had no choice at all. I always pray for the people I killed.*

*I didn't mean to harm anybody. May all souls stay in peace
and reincarnate as humans.*

Even in a language that we did not understand but instinctively could comprehend, it is extraordinary to hear someone
very matter-of-factly describe the way in which they systematically and repeatedly killed people, and then to look around and
think that this happened night after night, year after year. It is
impossible to conjure up the fear that those who were about to be
killed must have felt, and it is equally impossible to conjure up the
fear that drove people like Him Houy to kill. It was also extraordinarily difficult to emotionally connect with what happened.
Seventeen thousand people died here having endured the most
horrific of persecutions. Seventeen thousand people crushed
into the ground on which we were walking, Stephen O'Connell,
Mick Cassidy, Ronan Fox and myself and a victim/perpetrator of
genocide. This was beyond feeling, beyond imagination.

Him Huoy took his leave of us and we sat on a bench seat
in the quiet of the evening looking over the rise and hollows of
Cambodia's Killing Fields. Him Huoy was prepared to acknowledge his guilt. Others were not, particularly those indicted by
the Extraordinary Chambers in the Courts of Cambodia for the
Prosecution of Crimes Committed during the Period of Democratic Kampuchea (ECCC), which was established in 2001.

In his self-exculpatory account, *Cambodia's Recent History
and the Reasons Behind the Decisions I Made*, Khieu Samphan
(Brother No. 5)[35] insists that he too was at best a helpless by-
stander and at worst acting under duress, despite holding the office of President of Democratic Kampuchea. He claimed to have
been appalled by the emptying of Phnom Penh in April 1975.

*Powerless, I had to keep my regrets and despair to myself.
Once during those first weeks, I spoke privately with Pol
Pot and conveyed my misgivings to him (p. 57).*

That distancing from the Khmer Rouge leadership is the
dominant theme in his autobiography.

> *How erroneous are the accusations made against me that
> I was one of the architects of the genocidal regime of Dem-
> ocratic Kampuchea. I cannot be judged to have been com-
> plicit in the crimes and massacres that followed, because I
> was unaware of them. It is common knowledge that apart
> from vague general presumptions, there is no significant
> evidence that implicates me in the arrest or massacres
> committed under the Democratic Kampuchea regime (pp.
> 117-119).*

Khieu Samphan is not the only unrepentant leader of the
Khmer Rouge. In an article in the *New York Times* on 16 September 2010, Nuon Chea (Brother No. 2) is reported as saying that 'the
killings of "enemies"' were a necessary part of the revolution.[36]

> *If we kept these people they would kill the nation. I have
> feelings for both the nation and the individual, but I clear-
> ly distinguish between them. If we must choose one or the
> other, I choose the nation. The individual I cast aside.*

We had more questions than we had answers, questions we
did not outwardly share but instinctively must have felt. Just
how did it all happen? How did what would appear to have been
a kindly schoolteacher induce such carnage, create such havoc,
destroy so many lives, cause such pain? How did he succeed in
getting so many people to go along with his grotesque experiment? This was after all what Chaim Herzog referred to as auto-
genocide, a phrase he probably borrowed from the French author Jean Lacouture. This was, as Theary Seng reminded us, the
story of Cambodians killing Cambodians.

To these questions there are no answers, only this one terrible truth: That we are all capable, given certain conditions, of
killing each other. Cruelly. Mercilessly. Unapologetically.

Meanwhile, the four of us sat there silently, exhaling cigarette
smoke while in the middle distance a group of children came
running into our line of vision. Incongruously, as it seemed to us
then, they began a version of ring-a-ring-a-rosie around a tree
against which young Cambodian men had just three decades
earlier used to smash babies' heads. Babies who were battered

by seventeen year-old boys, boys who in a very different setting may have been preparing to sit for their Leaving Certificate while dreaming of revolutions in far away places.

We left Cambodia's Killing Fields with the strange but delightful sound of children laughing uproariously ringing in our ears.

Postscript

On Monday, 26 July 2010, history was made as the former chief of Tuol Sleng, Kaing Guek Eav, otherwise known as Duch, became the first major Khmer Rouge figure to be tried and convicted for war crimes and crimes against humanity (murder, extermination, imprisonment, persecution and other inhumane acts) and grave breaches of the Geneva Conventions (willful killing, willfully causing great suffering, unlawful deportation or transfer or unlawful confinement of a civilian). He was sentenced to life in prison in February 2012.

Others awaiting the outcome of their trial are the increasingly frail Ieng Sary (Brother No. 3), Prime Minister and Minister for Foreign Affairs 1975-1978, Nuon Chea, alias Brother Number Two, and Deputy Secretary of the Communist Party of Kampuchea, Khieu Samphan, Head of State of Democratic Kampuchea.

Proceedings against Ieng Thirith, Minister for Social Affairs (and Ieng Sary's wife) were suspended and she was conditionally released on 16 September 2012. Expert testimony indicated that she suffers from dementia, and is not competent to stand trial.

Endnotes

[1] Kipling, R. (1987). *Life's Handicap*. Oxford University Press. Oxford.

[2] Harding, M. 'November's empty skies and a house full of leaves'. *Irish Times,* Friday, 5 November 2010.

[3] Betjeman. J. (2006). *Collected Poems*. John Murray. London.

[4] Elbow. (2008) 'Seldon Seen Kid' Polydoor Ltd. UK.

[5] Pasternak, B. (2002) *Doctor Zhivago*. Vintage Books. London.

[6] Scharf, K. M., Fernández-giménez, M. E., Batbuyan, B. and Enkhbold, S. (2009) 'Herders and Hunters in a Transitional Economy: The Challenge of Wildlife and Rangeland Management in Post-socialist

Mongolia', in *Wild Rangelands: Conserving Wildlife While Maintaining Livestock in Semi-Arid Ecosystems* (eds, J. T. du Toit, R. Kock and J. C. Deutsch), John Wiley & Sons, Ltd, Chichester, UK.

7   Awehali, B. 'Mongolia's wilderness threatened by mining boom' *The Guardian* Tuesday 11 January 2011 http://www.guardian.co.uk/environment/2011/jan/11/mongolia-wilderness-mining-boom.

8   Ibid, p. 7.

9   Tim Cahill, 'A Good Hair Week in Mongolia' http://outside.away.com/magazine/0496/9604fmon.html.

10 PA 8 Indian states have more poor than 26 poorest African nations *The Indian Times.* 12 July 2010 http://articles.timesofindia.indiatimes.com/2010-07-12/india/28276383_1_measure-ophi-multidimensional-poverty-index.

11 'India has 69 billionaires, Mukesh Ambani richest' ibnlive.com 30 Sep 2010 http://ibnlive.in.com/news/mukesh-ambani-tops-forbes-indias-rich-list/132017-7.html.

12 McQuillan, D. 'Penneys from Heaven', *Irish Times* November 2009.

13 War on Want (2006) *Fashion Victims: The True Face of Cheap Clothes at Primark, Asdo and Tesco.* http://www.waronwant.org/attachments/Fashion per cent20Victims.pdf.

14 http://news.bbc.co.uk/2/hi/programmes/panorama/7461496.stm.

15 Chomsky, N. (1990) 'The Victors' *Z Magazine*, November, January, 1991; and April, 1991, p. 8.

16 http://www.indiankanoon.org/doc/237570/.

17 Dallek, R. (2007) *Nixon and Kissinger: Partners in Power*, Harper Perennial, London.

18 Stuart-Fox. M. (1997). *A History of Laos.* Cambridge University Press. Cambridge.

19 Handicap International (2007) 'The Fatal Footprint of Cluster Munitions on People and Communities.' http://www.stopclustermunitions.org/wp/wp-content/uploads/2009/02/circle-of-impact-may-07.pdf

20 Water Environment Partnership in Asia, 'Case study on UXO vulnerability and poverty in selected villages of Kaleum District, Sekong Province', WEPA (http://www.wepa-db.net/policies/cases/laos.htm#case01) (23 October 2008).

21 Handicap International, *Life after the bomb: A psychosocial study of child survivors of UXO accidents in Lao PDR* (Vientiane: Handicap International & Lao Youth Union, 2004), p. 25.

²² Goose, S. Opening Remarks in the Closing press Conference of the Dublin Diplomatic Conference on Cluster Munitions. 30 May 2008. Dublin http://www.hrw.org/en/news/2008/05/30/opening-remarks-closing-press-conference-dublin-diplomatic-conference-cluster-muniti

²³ http://www.clustermunitionsdublin.ie/pdf/ENGLISHfinaltext.pdf

²⁴ Feickert, A. and Kerr, P.K. Cluster Munitions: Background and Issues for Congress. 11 January 2011. Congressional Research centre. Washington.

²⁵ Charrière, H. (1970) *Papillion,* Harts-Davis Macgibbon.

²⁶ Wintle, J. (2007). *Perfect Hostage: The Life of Aung San Suu Kyi.* Hutchinson. London.

²⁷ HC Deb 05 November 1947 vol 443 cc1836-961, and the debate can be found online at http://hansard.millbanksystems.com/commons/1947/nov/05/burma-independence-bill#S5CV0443P0_19471105_HOC_256.

²⁸ Rogers, B. (2004). *A Land without Evil: Stopping the Genocide of Burma's Karen People.* Monarch Books. Oxford.

²⁹ Power, S. (2002) *'A Problem from Hell': America and the Age of Genocide.* Perennial. New York.

³⁰ Nath, V. (1998) *A Cambodian Prison Portrait: One Year in the Khmer Rouge's S-21.* White Lotus. Bangkok.

³¹ Chandler, D.P. (1999) *Brother Number One: A Political Biography of Pol Pot.* Silkworm Books. Chiang Mai.

³² Eliot, T.S. (1963) *Collected Poems 1909-196.* Faber and Faber. London.

³³ Ponchaud F. (1977) *Cambodia: Year Zero.* Holt, Rinehart and Winston. New York.

³⁴ Braaksma, P. (2009) *Nine Lives Making the Impossible Possible.* New Internationalist. Oxford.

³⁵ Samphan, K. (2004). *Cambodia's Recent History and the Reasons Behind the Decisions I Made* Published by Mr. Puy Kea. Khmer Printing and Publishing House.

³⁶ Mydans, S. 'Khmer Rouge Leaders indicted'. *New York Times,* 16 September 2010.

Hope, Beauty, and Redemption

It just grows ever more apparent that there
are two classes in society that their interests
are irreconcilable, and that one survives at the
expense of the other – *Ken Loach*[1]

Introduction

In the helter-skelter world of filming across three continents
and countless cultures, there was very little time to reflect on
the totality of the experience. In the hard-pressed journalistic
world of tight deadlines and even tighter budgets, we are, as
Mick O'Rourke has often remarked, just 'hit and run merchants'.
Six or seven day shoots. Five days in one instance. Criss-crossing
countries. A couple of hours here and there and then off again.
Conversations grabbed under pressure of the stop-watch. Cal-
culations on the number of tapes shot, the number of interviews covered and the ever-present pre-occupation with GVs,
the shorthand for general views of the people and the landscape.
That is the nature of it all.

But while my colleagues and I operated under what were at
times daunting and difficult circumstances, we were determined
at the outset to avoid the pitfall of what Lilie Chouliaraki characterises as the spectators of suffering.[2] Conscious that we were
endeavouring to tell other people's stories and not our own, stories of people separated by culture and tradition but with whom

we shared a common humanity, we invested time in securing the consent and collaboration of individuals and communities. That consent was made possible by the many Irish and other people working in all parts of the globe – missionaries, development workers, activists, teachers, journalists and diplomats. It was also made possible by local fixers, activists and community leaders who put their trust in us, without whose consent none of this would have been possible. The people whom we filmed also put their trust in us in the belief that the 'outside' world should hear their stories and that the trauma they encountered would not go unnoticed.

What follows is an attempt to disentangle the many contesting emotions and understandings that I have experienced while making these documentary films. That reflection is tempered by two conversations I had in the course of writing this book. The first of these was with President Michael D. Higgins. Recognising the great sense of despair, which he acknowledged he too often shares, he nonetheless struck an optimistic note.

> *None of us have earned the right to have perfect resolutions to that which we look at. Change isn't linear. It is something that comes and goes. It has setbacks and so forth. And that is really what I think is happening in many cases in South America. When I went there first is incomparable with what is there now. There is an unstoppable transition, a transformation taking place all over South America. There are people talking about land, about rights, women are more participating. It differs from place to place but the one thing I am certain of is that the process of change is moving in the right direction.*

Much less optimistic was author and activist Susan George who told me in 2011 while filming the *What in the World?* series on the UN's Millennium Development Goals, a series that does not feature in this book, that she is angry with the world. It is a statement that also prefaces her most recent book, *Whose Crisis, Whose Future?*[3]

I am angry, perplexed and frightened: angry because so many people are suffering needlessly on account of the economic, social and ecological crisis and because the world's leaders show no sign of bringing about genuine change; perplexed because they don't seem to understand or care much about the public mood, the widespread resentment and the urgency of action; frightened because, if we don't act soon, it may well be too late, particularly where climate change is concerned (p. 1).

Incomprehension, Sadness and Admiration

There were certainly moments when I could identify with the anger that George expressed, but for the most part what I felt was incomprehension. Incomprehension at our utter failure as human beings to share the bountiful resources of this planet with each other in an equitable and fair manner, and in a way that does not irrevocably damage the planet.

Incomprehension that the people we met on this journey have been so abandoned by the rest of us who share the planet with them.

Incomprehension at the British Labour Party's collusion and active participation in the eviction of the Chagos Island people between 1966 and 1973, and their subsequent and steadfast determination to deny them their right of return. Had it been a Conservative government, perhaps it would not have seemed as hard to understand, as they were more likely to defend past imperialist policies, but that former British Secretary of State, David Miliband, whose father was the well-regarded Marxist historian Ralph Miliband, should be such an apologist for their eviction was hard to take. How is it possible to grow up in a household like that and and then pursue an imperialist cause?

Incomprehension at the resilience of the 3,000 year-old Dalit culture in India. How can they be regarded as lesser human beings on whom, as Shanta Sinha told us, the majority of the population continued to heap insults and humiliations. How is it possible to disregard the needs and rights of 139 million people in your own country? Meeting these people in the knowledge of how they are regarded by the rest of society just left me with a sense of disbelief that this is still possible in a country that sees itself as a modern functioning democracy.

Incomprehension that Luciano Benetton, an Italian of relatively humble origins, would feel the need to purchase 900,000 hectares in far-off Patagonia and in the process throw off many of the indigenous people who have lived in this area for thousands of years. Why would anyone want that amount of land?

Incomprehension that the oil-produced wealth of Angola could so easily leak out of the country, leaving millions of people destitute in its wake, and that all of this wealth could be controlled by close to one hundred families acting in cahoots with international oil companies. There is a saying in Angola, that 'when elephants collide, it is the grass that suffers'. A parallel saying might very well be, 'when oil conglomerates and the African countries collide, it is the poor who get trampled'.

Incomprehension that one man, Pol Pot, and a few of his henchmen and women, could cause such carnage, such mayhem in their own country, and that China, knowing what was going on, could stand idly by and latterly seek to thwart any international investigation of the genocide that was perpetrated on the people. Incomprehension too that it was possible to empty the capital city of Phnom Penh in a matter of hours and upend a whole country in a matter of weeks, resulting in the death of over two million people, between twenty-nine and thirty-one per cent of the population in a matter of three-and-a-half years.

There were other emotions, too, among them a profound sadness.

Sadness for Mu Ko Lay and her stoical husband Maung Mya in Burma, her bitter tears, her relentless sobbing as she described the death of her two small boys whose bodies she did not have time to burry as she fled from the marauding Burmese army through the jungle of the Karen state. Subsequently we were to hear of another son, whose life was destroyed by a landmine explosion in which he lost both of his arms.

Sadness for Por Vandee's son in Laos whose maiming seemed to take on a particular significance. We could not be sure but we hoped for his sake that he could not fully comprehend the significance and extent of his injuries, and for the whole family, disabled and destitute as a result of ordnance left over by a war now fading into the midst of time.

Sadness for Francis Kamwenda in Malawi who seemed overwhelmed with his problems but who despite that was determined to ensure that his family received an education that would propel them out of the poverty bind in which he found himself. There are days, he told us, when he doesn't eat, just to save a few pence, just to save a few pence.

Sadness for Mbaye Sene, forced from his native Senegal because of the way in which factory ships from Europe and Asia have undermined the West African fishing industry, and at his decision to join the throngs of illegal refugees in Europe where further exploitation inevitably awaited him, his natural flair for the sea lost in the metropolis of an inland European capital city.

Sadness for Chacho Liempes who was profoundly perturbed by the changes in the barbed-wire landscape that resulted from the purchase of huge swathes of Patagonia by super wealthy entrepreneurs from the United States and Europe. His guitar playing and singing in the home of one of the Mapuche people will remain an abiding memory.

Sadness for Sanda Abdou and Rakia Ousman, who described for us in detail the excruciating death of their two-year-old grandson Sani Yahaya from the wholly preventable disease of Noma, while sitting disconsolately outside their hut in the searing heat of Niger.

There was admiration too.

Admiration for the late Kader Asmal who educated generations of Irish people about the nefarious apartheid regime in South Africa, and who subsequently went on to become one of the most effective ministers in post-apartheid South Africa. Admiration too for his refusal to countenance the self-aggrandisement that very often becomes a feature of the newly elected, and for the joy and enthusiasm for life that he exuded.

Admiration for the commanding strength and presence of Enkhchimeg, Mongolia's 2007 herder of the year, as she rode magisterially along with her sons among her 1,000 cattle-herd, and for her unrestrained delight in her extended family and in particular for her youngest grandson. Admiration also for her steely determination to maintain the herder lifestyle despite state-sponsored attempts to rein in their centuries-old right to roam.

Admiration for the sheer eloquence and charm of Bryan Stevenson whose ability to speak in perfect sentences, nay perfect paragraphs, never ceased to amaze. Not just that but also for his determined pursuit of justice for those wrongfully accused of murder and other heinous crimes, and who have been sentenced to die in the ever-expanding prisons of the United States.

Admiration for Evo Morales, who turned 470 years of history on its head when he became the first indigenous president of Bolivia, and not just for his political achievements, significant as they are, but for his humour and for his refusal to kowtow to the global financial institutions.

Admiration for the power and passion of Peruvian parliamentarian Nancy Obregón and for her dogged determination to protect the cultural and economic rights of indigenous people, including their right to grow and consume the highly contested coca leaf.

Illuminating moments all.

Analysis, Action and Reaction

Writing over one hundred years ago, Irish republican and socialist James Connolly passionately argued that capitalism has failed and must go. In the intervening century the evidence of its failure has become more and more incontrovertible. There were signs of hope that capitalism could reform itself, particularly in the United States, from Franklin D. Roosevelt's New Deal to Lyndon Johnson's Great Society, whose achievements were significant. In what might surprise many commentators, African-American lawyer Cathleen Price, whom we met in Alabama, described Lyndon Johnson, notwithstanding his disastrous involvement in Vietnam, as one of the great reforming Presidents of the USA whose anti-poverty and civil rights legislation transformed the lives of African-American people. Much of that work was subsequently undone with the emergence of what became known as the neo-conservatives, people who wanted lower taxes for the rich, fewer services for the poor, more spending on defence and the higher levels of incarceration – policies which disproportionately impact on the poor, African American and Hispanic peoples, as well as people with physical and mental disabilities.

In Britain, the emergence of the Labour Party that grew out of the trade union movement and the socialist parties of the nineteenth century briefly offered the possibility of a softer, more caring capitalist model. Under subsequent Labour party governments that model was swept away by the Thatcher-light policies pursued by the Tony Blair and Gordon Brown and their New Labour governments. In Europe, the emergence of Social Democratic governments, particularly in Scandinavia, has had some success in promoting policies that favoured workers, the unemployed and those who could not work, but even there many of the long-established practices are under threat.

Other changes were made that were supposed to significantly rebalance the capitalist system. Post-World War II reconstruction saw the emergence of a plethora of institutions, including the United Nations, that were intended to reflect a more egalitarian, collegiate world. The 1944 Bretton Woods Agreement that birthed the World Bank and the International Monetary Fund was to mark yet another attempt at creating a more integrated and responsible global economic order. Naomi Klein, in her internationally acclaimed book *The Shock Doctrine*, which gives an account of the new economic order that has evolved in the last forty years or so, describes the original mandate of each of these institutions.[4]

> *The World Bank would make long-term investment in development to pull countries out of poverty, while the IMF would act as a kind of global shock absorber, promoting economic policies that reduced financial speculation and market volatility. When a country looked as though it was*

falling into crisis, the IMF would leap in with stabilising grants and loans thereby preventing crisis before they occurred. The two institutions, located across the street from each other in Washington, would coordinate their response (p. 162).

If only, if only.

There were solemn declarations that this time things would be different, including the 2000 UN Millennium Development Goals (MDGs). These goals were intended to signify the collective responsibility of the global community to uphold the principles of human dignity, equality and equity. The Assembly committed itself to 'spare no effort to free people from abject and dehumanising conditions of extreme poverty and to free the entire human race from want'.[5] This was the historic pledge, and this is what then Secretary General Kofi Annan had to say.[6]

The century just ended was disfigured, time and again by ruthless conflict. Grinding poverty and striking inequality persists within and among countries even amidst unprecedented wealth. Extreme poverty is an affront to our common humanity.

The gross disparities of wealth in today's world, the miserable conditions in which well over a billion people live, the prevalence of endemic conflict in some regions, and the rapid degradation of the natural environment: all these combine to make the present model of development unsustainable, unless remedial measures are taken by common agreement.

The central challenge we face today is to ensure that globalization becomes a positive force for all the world's people instead of leaving billions of them behind in squalor.

Yet despite all the talk, despite all the polemics, despite all the rhetoric, life for the poor remains precarious, a precariousness that is underscored by climate change. For the poor, and particularly the ultra poor of the world, very little has changed. The stark reality is that inequality is on the increase.

Countless millions of people, even billions, live life on the edge. People who have been betrayed by the very institutions that claim to have their interests at heart. People who have been betrayed by politicians and public institutions.

The truth is we live in a grotesquely and shockingly unequal world, a world where needless suffering is the norm, a world that is incrementally cannibalising itself. While filming the *What in the World?* series we were witnesses to that world.

Class, Authority and Fatalism

The political class have ceded power and authority to the financial institutions who now control the lives of the world's population in a way that has never happened before. These new breeds of financers are, as Susan George calls them, the masters of mankind.

> *The masters of mankind . . . determined, powerful, well-mannered but truly dangerous people whose narrow class interests profit mightily from the status quo and who know each other, who stick together and who don't want anything fundamentally changed and whose motto is taken from Adam Smith's the wealth of Nations: All for ourselves and nothing for other people (pp. 6-7).*

It is the kind of analysis with which Connolly, I would imagine, would be in broad agreement.

Writing this book and reading some of the literature in this area has been a constant reminder of the scale of that failure. Despite it being so well documented in academic journals and by many activists and civil society organisations, it still fails to make the cut in mainstream media in which, as Michael Seib[7] reminds us, 'parochialism flourishes', and where major news outlets are content with 'a self-perpetuating cycle of close-to-home scandal and the foibles of the celebrities of the moment' (p. 2). The virtual invisibility of the poor, the oppressed and the disfavoured of the world from mainstream media is a real challenge for key decision-makers in the media.

Ultimately, though, it is the failure of elected politicians to represent all of the people that is the most disquieting, that is the greater indictment. This is the legacy of that failure. Over one billion children, more than half the children in the Third World, suffer from at least one form of deprivation, and 700 million suffer from two or more forms of deprivation. More than one in three children does not have adequate shelter, one in five does not have access to safe water and one in seven does not have access to health services. Every five seconds, a child dies of hunger. Over 23,000 children die needlessly every day in the Third World. And that's just the children. Their parents fare little better.

A landmark study published in 2006 based on data from six years earlier concluded that the richest one per cent of adults own 40 per cent of global wealth, and that the richest 10 per cent of adults accounted for 85 per cent of the world's wealth.[8] In contrast, the bottom half of the world's population owned barely one per cent of global wealth.

In her searing indictment of current and recent US economic policy, Frances Fox Piven trawled through the US Census Bureau data and reports the following.

> . . . *14.3 per cent of the population, or 47m people – one in six Americans – were living below the official poverty threshold, currently set at $22,400 annually for a family of four. Some 19m people are living in what is called extreme poverty, which means that their household income falls in the bottom half of those considered to be below the poverty line. More than a third of those extremely poor people are children. Indeed, more than half of all children younger than six living with a single mother are poor. Extrapolating from this data, Emily Monea and Isabel Sawhill of the Brookings Institution estimate that further sharp increases in both poverty and child poverty rates lie in our American future.[9]*

'The willful ignorance and cruelty of it all can leave you gasping,' concludes Fox Piven. Calling for a new kind of moral economy, one based on goodness, fairness and justice, Fox Piven sees hope in the Occupy Wall Street and similar movements throughout the Western World as a sign that change may yet happen, but that change will be strongly resisted by the political class.

Clinton, Bush, Blair or Cameron, Cowen or Kenny, the difference is negligible. What Obama will yet deliver, the jury is still out. The documentary film *Inside Job* directed by Charles Ferguson tells a very dispiriting story.[10] The reality is that Obama is extraordinarily constrained. Even those who wish to make changes are unable to do so. The well-intentioned are simply swept aside. Former US President Jimmy Carter is testimony to that. The US military juggernaut powers ahead as does its corporate counterpart, irrespective of the democratic wishes of individual nations.

Even that most wily of campaigners, Archbishop Desmond Tutu, who has seen more party politicians up close and personal than almost any other non-party political operator, despairs of the ability of mainstream global political figures to affect change.[11]

> *Our governments must shoulder a lot of the blame. Their policies and practices are propping up a broken system that benefits a few powerful companies and interests groups at the expense of the many . . . they have neglected the 500 million small-scale farmers that together feed one-third of humanity. They have spent more than a decade debating climate change but pledged emissions reductions that put us on course for catastrophic warming.*

All of this is part of what French intellectual Pierre Bourdieu calls 'neo-conservative reconstruction'.[12]

> *It erects into defining standards . . . the law of the market, the law of the strongest. It ratifies and glorifies the rule of what we call the financial markets, a return to a sort of radical capitalism answering to no law except that of maximum profit: an undisguised unrestrained capitalism but one that has been rationalised, tuned to the limit of its economic efficiency, through the introduction of modern forms of domination ('management') and manipulative techniques like market research, marketing and commercial advertising (p. 125).*

In a speech given to mark his acceptance of the Ernst-Bloch Prize in Germany in 1997, Bourdieu claimed that politicians are confronted with economic fatalism. In this world, Bordieu argues the agents of high finance and the people who run large multinationals are rarefied by politicians and journalists alike.

> *[They] know and recognise no purpose but the ever increasing creation of wealth and, more secretly, its concentration in the hands of a small privileged minority: and it therefore leads to a combat by every means, including the destruction of the environment and human sacrifice, against any obstacle to the maximation of profit (p. 126).*

Bourdieu states that the bankers of the world and their political acolytes want us to believe that the world cannot be any different from the way it is. And if they cannot believe it is possible, then they have ceased to work towards making it possible. Political change has never and will never come from the top, and certainly not from the mainstream parties who are so deeply embedded into the existing capitalist order. For Bordieu, change will come not from the professional class of economists and politicians but from:

> *. . . institutions of this or that: truckers, publishers, teachers and so forth but also defenders of trees, fish, mushrooms, pure air, children and all of the rest (p. 128).*

It is a hugely refreshing and liberating thought, and one that tallies with our experience, particularly in Latin America but in Africa and Asia too. Despite it all, there are grounds for hope, and redemption.

Hope, Beauty and Redemption

While there may be hope, there are no miracles in this globalised world – there is only hard-fought change. Even then, given the tenacity with which, as outlined, a tiny elite have grabbed the earth's resources, it will not be easy to prize their fingers away. But better try than not. From the evidence garnered while filming the *What in the World?* series, there are many people who are not just pushing the counter-narrative that the resources of the planet do not just belong to the few but to the many, but who are active agents for change – people convinced that we do not have to settle for the failure of politics, that we do not have to cede political engagement and agitation to the few.

We met with extraordinary people who are not just content to articulate a counter-narrative, but who agitate and organise for an equitable share of the world's resources in the belief that re-distributive justice is possible, that in this global inn, there is room for all. Many of the people we met have paid a heavy price for their resistance: personal injury, death of family members and friends, imprisonment, penury and more.

If nothing else, the stories in this book are a testimony to the sheer bravery of people and a testimony to human resolve, determination, resilience, defiance, solidarity, love and, above all, generosity, beauty, hope and the occasional victory.

And there have been some victories.

Victory to the thousands of indigenous people of Ecuador who have successfully challenged one of the biggest corporations in the world. Victory to the people of Cambodia who have succeeded, however late, in bringing some of the leaders of the Khmer Rouge to trial at the Extraordinary Chambers of the Courts of Cambodia. And victory too of sorts for the *cocaleros* of the Andean region – at least for those living in Bolivia.

And of beauty, there was an abundance.

The stunning colours of Senegal. The undulating whiteness of Mongolia. Timbuktu with its achingly beautiful desert. The intricate beadwork of the women of Turkana and their Pokot sisters. South Africa's stunning sunsets. Breathless Potosí, the highest city in the world. A ropey bridge in Argentina defying us to cross it. Alabama's deep red clay. The azure blue sea that washes the coast of Mauritius. Early morning mist shrouding the mountains of Burma. First glimpse of the ancient Inca city of Machu Picchu. Shafts of sunlight through the Ecuadorian rainforest. The lethargic flow of the Mekong River. The colourful kaleidoscope of Hyderabad in India. The beach in Damba Maria in

Angola – despite it all. The solitude of a guesthouse in Zinder in Niger.

Generosity too.

A world of generosity bestowed on strangers. The greeting we received in Mali from a Bozo fisherman, who was moved that we came so far to hear his story. Lunch on a leaf from the Achuar deep in the Amazonian jungle. Elsa Amador's freshly-baked tortillas in Posoltega, Nicaragua. Tea in the afternoon in a convent in Lilongwe in Malawi. Tea from the coca leaf everywhere we went in Peru. And more.

Hope and compassion as well.

Compassion for human frailty but not for systemic neglect and oppression. Bryan Stevenson told us:

> *. . . all human beings are more than the worst thing they have ever done.*

Words of consolation, words of redemption. For Bryan redemption was not just possible at an individual level but in a broader, more collective sense too.

In this remarkable journey through Africa, Asia and the Americas, we encountered compassion but not denial or easy forgiveness. We discovered another world. One beyond greed, beyond hubris, beyond petty small-mindedness and paranoia.

Finally there is that last memory of the great campaigner Cristina Rodriguez, sitting on one of those distinctive Nicaraguan rocking chairs silhouetted against the doorway of her house that lead to a dusty backyard where chickens picked over morsels of food. Cristina urged us to keep going, as she did all her life, but offered no easy way out.

> *The truth is we always suffer. Those at the bottom always suffer. Everything falls harder on us. But we always have to be strong to resist the next blow life deals us.*

Michael D. Higgins also urged us to keep going.

> *You keep on going, you keep on going because you are envisaging the unrealised humanity. And that's enough.*

Endnotes

[1] Hayward, A. (2004). *Which Side Are You On? Ken Loach and his Films*. Bloomsbury. London.

[2] Chouliaraki, L. (2006). *The Spectatorship of Suffering*. Sage. London.

[3] George, S. (2010). *Whose Crisis, Whose Future?* Polity Press. Cambridge.

[4] Klein, N. (2008). *The Shock Doctrine*. Penguin Books. London.

[5] See Resolution adopted by the General Assembly[*without reference to a Main Committee (A/55/L.2)*] 55/2. United Nations Millennium Declaration http://www.un.org/millennium/declaration/ares552e.htm

[6] Annan, K. (2000) 'We the Peoples: The Role of the United Nations in the 21st Century'. United Nations Department of Pubic Information New York.

[7] Seib, P. (2004). *Beyond the Front Lines: How the News Media Cover the World Shaped by War*. Palgrave. New York.

[8] Davis, J., Sandström, S., Shorrocks, A. and Wolff, E.N. (2010), *The World Distribution of Household Wealth* World Institute for Development Economics Research of the United Nations University (UNU-WIDER) Helsinki.

[9] Fox Piven, F. 'The war against the poor in America Rampant poverty and further welfare cuts have created a need to move towards a moral economy of the many, not few'. 14 Nov 2011 http://www.aljazeera.com/indepth/opinion/2011/11/2011117132329620899.html.

[10] www.sonyclassics.com/insidejob/

[11] Tutu, D. 'Governments must lead to solve hunger problems'. *Irish Examiner*, 21 June 2011.

[12] Bourdieu, P. 'A Reasoned Utopia and Economic Fatalism'. *New Left Review* 1-127 Jan-Feb 1998.

INDEX

List of Documentaries

Breaking the Chains *(Nicaragua, 1999)*

What in the World? Series 1 *(2004)*

- Child labour in India (India)
- Coffee matters (Guatemala)
- Give us this day our daily bread (Malawi)
- Chasing the rainbow (South Africa)
- Muddying the waters (Ecuador)
- No Macho (Nicaragua)

What in the World? Series 2 *(2006)*

- Black death in Dixie (USA)
- Coca – A leaf of life? (Peru)
- Dam corruption (Kenya)
- Fish and ships (Senegal)
- Not so sweet (Philippines)
- Three years, eight months and twenty days in Kampuchea (Cambodia)

What in the World? Series 3 *(2008)*

- Keeping your head above water (Tuvalu)
- Partners not masters (Bolivia)
- The Chagos Islands are closed (Mauritius)
- The curse of oil (Angola)
- The generals' genocide (Burma)
- The united colours of the Mapuche (Argentina)

What in the World? Series 4 *(2009)*

- Flowers for the Gringo (Colombia)
- Message from the river (Mali)
- Noma in Niger (Niger)
- So you think the war is over … (Laos)
- Soya – Silvino's story (Paraguay)
- Wrestling with change (Mongolia)

What in the World? Series 5 *(2011)*

- Millennium Development Goals (Bangladesh)
- Millennium Development Goals (Malawi)
- Millennium Development Goals (Vietnam)
- Millennium Development Goals (Zambia)

What in the World? Series 6 *(2012)*

- Beyond the lens of famine (Ethiopia)
- Leaving the conflict behind? (Democratic Republic of the Congo)
- Log on (Honduras)
- Timor's traumas (Timor-Leste)